The Grove of the Eumenides

Also by Frederick Glaysher

Into the Ruins: Poems

The Bower of Nil: A Narrative Poem

Edited

Robert Hayden, *Collected Prose, Collected Poems*

The Grove of the Eumenides

Essays

on

Literature, Criticism, and Culture

Frederick Glaysher

Earthrise Press

I thank the editors of the following publications in which several of these essays first appeared: *Continental Drifter, Modern Age, The Hillsdale Review, Studies in Browning and His Circle, Saul Bellow and the Struggle at the Center.*

I wish to thank the Fulbright Commission for a grant in 1994 that enabled me to study in Hong Kong, Taiwan, and China, including at Beijing University and the Buddhist Mogao caves of Dunhuang; and the National Endowment for the Humanities for a 1995 Summer Seminar on Hindu and Muslim culture and literature at the University of North Carolina–Chapel Hill.

www.fglaysher.com

Publisher's Cataloging-in-Publication
(Provided by Quality Books, Inc.)

Glaysher, Frederick, 1954-
    The grove of the Eumenides : essays on literature, criticism, and culture / Frederick Glaysher.
        p. cm.
        LCCN: 2007928394
        ISBN-13: 978-0-9670421-8-3
        ISBN-10: 0-9670421-8-6

    I. Title.

PS3557.L37G76 2007   814'.54
                                QBI07-600116

Earthrise Press
P. O. Box 81842, Rochester, MI 48308-1842

For Elliot and Ethan

Contents

Whence it is manifest that universal peace is the best of all those things which are ordained for our blessedness.

Dante, *De Monarchia*

The Function of Criticism

I

This new swarm
Of sophists has got empire in our schools.
Matthew Arnold

During the twentieth century literature and criticism increasingly withdrew from their immemorial humanistic role into a repudiation of humankind's more noble capacities. The very possibility of such attributes received only dogmatic derision and scathing skepticism. Although valid reasons exist for scorning naive forms of optimism, since many of the events of the twentieth century negate much of what Western, as well as Eastern, civilization once revered, I take as axiomatic the observation that the intellectual climate of our age has become one of nihilism, nominalism, relativity, and every degrading interpretation of human nature of which man is capable of conceiving. These impulses have found vent in all the arts, proclaiming the death of humanism and the consequent loss of narrative action and intelligible human purpose. Precisely the same nihilistic interpretation of life found expression in the philosophy of Jacques Derrida and in the criticism influenced by him. As early as 1966 in "Structure, Sign, and Play in the Discourse of the Human Sciences," Derrida starkly highlighted the radical difference between past interpretations of the act of interpretation and the presently dominant one:

There are thus two interpretations of interpretation, of structure, of sign, of freeplay. The one seeks to decipher, dreams of deciphering, a truth or an origin which is free from freeplay and from the order of the sign. . . . The other, which is no longer turned toward the origin, affirms freeplay and tries to pass beyond man and humanism, the name man being the name of that being who . . . has dreamed of full presence, the reassuring foundation, the origin and the end of the game. The second interpretation of interpretation, to which Nietzsche showed us the way, does not seek . . . the "inspiration of a new humanism."

The skepticism seething in the phrase "dreams of deciphering" is characteristic of the alienated position of contemporary philosophy and criticism, which assume that degradation is the only realm of being and that to try "to pass beyond man and humanism" is commendable. I suggest the foremost poet-critics of English literature unabashedly sought, unlike so many critics today, the inspiration of humanism and held the highest task of criticism to be the creation of a current of ideas within which human capacities could develop in life, not merely in art. Such a conception ennobled the role of the critic and gave intelligibility to his social function that joined him to the human family. The Derridean criticasters signify the severity of both the alienation of criticism and the impasse at which intellectual and mass culture have arrived. For contemporary criticism merely reflects the tendencies of the time, the nihilism that pervades every level of modern, Western, indeed global, society. Despite themselves, the Derrideans have brought the turn away from "the origin" out into the open and have done so with a proclivity for sophistry and fatuous distinctions that puts Polonius to shame. Few perceptive readers would fail to say with Hamlet, "O Jephthah, judge of Israel, what a treasure hadst thou!"

It has always seemed to me that many of these academic critics fail to understand that criticism is indeed inferior to creative work. Often contemporary criticism affects a creative function that is beyond its ability to fulfill. Such affectation is a sign of confusion and, one cannot avoid the implication, a sign of their resentment and envy of the creative faculty. Such an observation seeks neither to denigrate criticism nor to overestimate the work of writers. It is to assert a time-honored principle, which, like so many invaluable principles, has largely been lost. Although this is an age of criticism that seeks to affect its brilliance, its ability to reduce literature to something else, it must be acknowledged that much work has been accomplished, that much has been done to form a current of ideas within which new modes of creative endeavor can flourish. The incomparable role of criticism in the development of the mind can never be gainsaid, and much of the polemical work against deconstruction attests to its vigor. I believe few thoughtful minds can deny that criticism has been vitiated by its isolation within the academy, has often led to the perversion of contemporary literature, has often prostituted itself to the expedient, and has often drifted with the flow of prevailing academic opinion. Often I have recalled the words of Saul Bellow on the deconstructionists—a real writer would bury them.

If the state of affairs in academic criticism cloys with pretension and expediency, the repulsive stench of scholasticism, I submit that the criticism by poets during the last fifty years hardly fares much better. Rather, the dominant impression made by many poet-critics is one of unmitigated mediocrity, while what comes out of the so-called creative writing programs leaves even more to be desired. Almost without exception postmodern poets have tended to accept the reasoning and conclusions voiced by Wallace Stevens in his essays of 1951, *The Necessary Angel*:

> In an age in which disbelief is so profoundly prevalent or, if not disbelief, indifference to questions of belief, poetry and painting, and the arts in general, are, in their measure, a compensation for what has been lost. Men feel that the imagination is the next greatest power to faith: the reigning prince. Consequently their interest in the imagination and its work is to be regarded not as a phase of humanism but as a vital self-assertion in a world in which nothing but the self remains, if that remains.

This "indifference" is the same assumption that undergirds the work of Jacques Derrida and his criticasters. The postmodern breakthrough, whether in academic criticism or that of poets, bases itself on the assumption that man has at last passed beyond humanism and the dream of "full presence" to embrace the absurdity and nihilism that constitute the true ground of being. This excerpt also evinces the common belief that art is "a compensation for what has been lost." Like the romantics, this interpretation deifies the artist and the imagination beyond all reasonable bounds and perpetuates hubris in its misguided attempt at "self-assertion in a world in which nothing but the self remains"—though even the self is called into question.

More recent poets have taken the self as the sole standard of their work. Elizabeth Bishop manifests in *The Collected Prose*, as in her poems, little awareness of anything outside her own small world. For a poet who makes so much of geography, who traveled widely, who lived in Paris, Mexico, San Francisco, Ouro Preto, London, Key West, Cape Cod, Boston, Worcester, Poughkeepsie, Petrpolis, North Haven, Seattle, Greenwich Village, and Rio de Janeiro, she nevertheless fails to perceive the dominant emerging tendency of the age. I would think that a poet who was as endowed with sensibility as Bishop would have recognized the undeniable Dynamo that churned at the center of her century. For Robert Hass, in his essays *Twentieth Century Pleasures*, the self appears to be the only pleasure of which he can conceive. The title itself reduces literature and criticism to a strictly modern libidinous world lacking principles and dominated by impulse and sensation, as in his free-associating tone exhibited throughout the book. Basically the same rambling irrationalism and loss of value pervade the prose of Robert Bly, Philip Larkin, Theodore Roethke, and others among the postmodernists. Virtually all the prose of poets during the past fifty years advocates, to one degree or another, "self-assertion" as an ersatz for a coherent understanding and interpretation of life. Often these poets are rabidly anti-intellectual and alienated, contend the rational mind has no role to play in creativity, and relegate literary criticism to the nether world of journalism. Such a failure to appreciate the role the critical faculty has in the creative endeavor underscores the extremity of their position, as does their frequently unqualified rejection of science and technology. Among postmodern poets, English or American, I look in vain for a single useful work of prose.

II

*'Tis one thing to copy, and
another thing to imitate from nature.*
John Dryden

To the state of utter decadence of contemporary criticism, I need
only to compare the work of such poet-critics as Sir Philip Sidney,
Samuel Johnson, Matthew Arnold, and T. S. Eliot. They all
demonstrate the function of criticism is the evaluation of literature
in its cultural and historical context in order to serve the reader in
understanding its moral and philosophical tendencies and in
discriminating between the genuine work of art and the fraudulent.
In 1580 Sidney summed up the entire humanistic tradition of poetry
and criticism in one pithy passage of his *Defence of Poesy*:

> Poesy, therefore, is an art of imitation, for so Aristotle termeth
> it in his word Mimesis, that is to say, a representing,
> counterfeiting, or figuring forth; to speak metaphorically, a
> speaking picture, with this end, to teach and delight.

In contrast to the "self-assertion" of postmodern criticism, Sidney's
and Aristotle's mimesis presupposes a given objective world that the
poet confronts in his work. Far from reveling in the subjectivism of
modern literature, Sidney holds the purpose or end of poetry to be
"to teach and delight." It is the "feigning" of "notable images of
virtues, vices, or what else" that enables the poet to move his reader
to strive after virtue and that bestows on poetry and criticism an
ennobling function. For Sidney, as for Homer, Virgil, and Dante, art
is not separated from life. Rather, in echoing Aristotle, Sidney
conceives of the poet as contemplating "what may be and should be"
in order to delight men and to move them "to take that goodness in
hand." Postmodern poets and critics, however, are alienated or
embarrassed by moral considerations and imagine poetry does not,
or should not, take cognizance of its responsibility to guide
humankind toward what "should be." They mistakenly equate any
vision of the moral duty of poetry with authoritarian regimes and

religions that repress the individual. Sidney's teleology, which reflects his age, is that the "final end," of poetry and learning, "is to lead and draw us to as high a perfection as our degenerate souls... can be capable of." Far from curtailing the development of the individual, Sidney views poetry in consonance with a divine order and in service to the individual within that order. I maintain this connects poetry with a coherent interpretation of life and gives the poet a public function of the highest importance. Conversely, postmodernists choose to ignore fundamental questions of human nature, to imagine they can escape the burden of moral influence upon their readers, and to drift with the anti-intellectual mass that Sidney believes it is the duty of the poet, within the limitations imposed upon him, to serve and guide.

Sidney asserts that the poet proffers guidance primarily through the "speaking picture." To emphasize only the lesson is to devolve into diatribes, while to emphasize only the delight is to degenerate into amusements that lead ultimately to the freeplay and linguistic games of deconstruction and of many postmodern poets. For Sidney the aesthetic is not the sole criterion of art and neither is the cognitive or the moral. Rather poetry embraces all these qualities and cannot be dissected into separate, artificial categories without wreaking violence on its essential nature. The beautiful, the true, and the good are one. And all systematic knowledge, science in the old and proper sense of the word, has the same end. This truth unites the writer with the public domain and gives intelligible, respectable purpose to his endeavors. Further, the poet "coupleth the general notion with the particular example," a "perfect picture" of the general or universal idea embodied in the particular or individual acts of men. Far from moralizing, the picture speaks for itself and moves the hearts of men in an intellectual realm beyond solipsism. Art becomes communal and serves the human family by embodying the highest vision of life that "should be" and by inspiring people to struggle toward it. As the ancient poet wrote, "Without vision the people perish."

In 1759 Samuel Johnson in *Rasselas* largely shares Sidney's conception of poetry as mimesis and his practice of criticism.

Johnson invokes the general or universal qualities of poetry as Sidney had two-hundred years earlier. He has Imlac say of the poet in *Rasselas* that

> He must be acquainted likewise with all the modes of life. His character requires that he estimate the happiness and misery of every condition; observe the power of all the passions in all their combinations, and trace the changes of the human mind as they are modified by various institutions and accidental influences of climate or custom. . . . He must divest himself of the prejudices of his age or country; he must consider right and wrong in their abstracted and invariable state; he must disregard present laws and opinions, and rise to general and transcendental truths, which will always be the same.

This excerpt presupposes that the poet takes his material from "all the modes of life." Far be it from Ashbery's statement that his own "poetry talks about itself." I cannot imagine Shakespeare or Johnson having had even a modicum of respect for such an assertion. Johnson holds that the very nature of the poet compels him to "estimate the happiness and misery of every condition," to create in his work that which is indicative of both the light and the fire. Such negative capability confronts the passions in all their horrifying manifestations and comprehends the "virtues" and the "vices" with which the embodiments of the point at which darkness meets light are so endowed. Johnson thrusts through the masks of the "accidental influences" of both "climate" and "custom" to "trace the changes of the human mind" from a critical perspective that unabashedly believes in a moral and religious meaning to life and that discloses itself in "general and transcendent truths." Such a capacious perspective permits him to penetrate the prejudices of his age and country and the state of right and wrong, of good and evil. All this is routinely regarded as preposterous by most postmodernists who shamelessly declare their work has no subject or is merely about their own petty self. Such pathetic decadence has become so common that many postmodern poets and critics fail to realize that their diminished state of affairs results from a dominant historical and accidental influence on the conception of the literary endeavor and not from the intrinsic nature of literature.

Often postmodern poets and critics deride mimesis as though it were a tawdry copy of reality. But as Johnson writes in his Preface to Shakespeare, "Imitations produce pain or pleasure not because they are mistaken for realities, but because they bring realities to mind." This conception is analogous to Sidney's understanding of the "speaking picture" that evinces the "general notion" through the "particular example." Both poet-critics believe in the existence of physical and ontological reality outside their own individual minds. To postmodernists, who dogmatically and irrationally deny any moral, religious, or humanistic interpretation of life, the word "reality" connotes fascist torture-chambers where those who waver from received ideologies are brought into conformity with the dictates of the ruling party. Such criticasters fail to realize the triviality and human treason of their own conceptions of reality that "pass beyond man and humanism" into an amoral cesspool of isolation and decadence. The sovereign power of mimesis lies precisely in its representation of universal principles in the particular example. Such a conception of literature maintains the poet and critic have a commonality of experience with the community of men in the real world.

In the middle to late nineteenth century Matthew Arnold registers the anomalous changes in the community of men throughout his criticism and poetry. The moral and religious function of criticism is no longer affirmed. His work stands a great distance from the certitude of Sidney and Johnson. In 1880 in "The Study of Poetry," Arnold states quite clearly his awareness of the intellectual tendencies of the modern period and the concomitant changes in the function of criticism and poetry:

There is not a creed which is not shaken, not an accredited dogma which is not shown to be questionable, not a received tradition which does not threaten to dissolve. . . . More and more mankind will discover that we have to turn to poetry to interpret life for us, to console us, to sustain us. Without poetry, our science will appear incomplete; and most of what now passes with us for religion and philosophy will be replaced by poetry.

Against the nineteenth century background of the discrediting of religion, Arnold turns to poetry for solace and intellectual sustenance, "to interpret life for us." Sidney and Johnson never conceived of poetry fulfilling such a role. Rather, with all humility, they both unabashedly held literature to be a handmaiden of religion. Conversely, Arnold stands in the full flood of the sweeping aside of the old order and declares poetry will replace religion and the philosophy of his day, the latter of which was still asking fundamental questions about human nature. His mention here of science appearing incomplete "without poetry" is actually nothing more than wishful thinking and a desperate stratagem to curtail the loss of the definition of science as the systematic knowledge of any discipline, which reduced its meaning to merely the natural sciences. He recognizes that all around him the old world is dissolving. His recognition of this background explains his oft-repeated definition of criticism as "a disinterested endeavor to learn and propagate the best that is thought and known in the world" since impartiality is always commendable but especially when the old certainties are "shown to be questionable." Hence he calls for criticism to stand off from politics and religion, the "burning matters," in hope of gaining a perspective that can ride the "turbid ebb and flow" of the tumultuous tide. Similarly he maintains criticism must be "independent of the practical spirit and its aims." This attempt to circumvent commitment leads him to a capitulation to the new tendencies by calling for a "growth toward perfection" that no longer is defined in any but the most nebulous and emotional terms. Without an external standard to determine both "the best that is known and thought" and "perfection," he can only rely, as Carlyle, Emerson, and Thoreau had, on the lingering values of Christianity, even as the latter two intensified the romantic turn to the East for sustenance.

Arnold vigorously asserts the utter inferiority of criticism to creative work and believes the poet must know life and the world in a sense still much closer to Sidney and Johnson than to the postmodernists. Further, he affirms, "the elements with which the creative power works are ideas." To such critics as the early T. S. Eliot, "ideas" are held in derision, are merely the matter that the "medium" has to express, the piece of meat one throws the dog to keep him content. Arnold could never have dallied with an autotelic conception of literature and criticism. His praise of the "high seriousness" of Homer, Sophocles, Virgil, and other classical poets presupposes poetry and criticism deal with concerns of the most universal importance. His Preface to his poems of 1853 evinces his awareness of the complexity of modern times, of the subjective sickliness of modern literature, of the malady that is still with us. In *Culture and Anarchy* Arnold writes of the malaise, "Everywhere we see the beginning of confusion. . . ." Still in the midst of the upheaval, he lacks the "clue to some sound order and authority." Yet he accurately perceives the turmoil of modern times, and, though he sought to replace religion with culture, salvaged, for a while, the humanistic, intellectual, social, and moral values that Western civilization had held in unity for centuries. Today, what could possibly be more evident than the failure of letters to replace religion and to relate, as Arnold writes in "Literature and Science," "knowledge to our sense of conduct"? For Sidney, all science is unified by its end of lifting "up the mind" to "virtuous actions." But for postmodern poets and critics both science and conduct are often held in contempt: Science for creating the industrial, technological civilization that they imagine is responsible for tainting, as Galway Kinnell puts it, "the life of the planet," and conduct or "virtuous action" for serving as a stratagem of repressive regimes and religions. In place of a unified conception of life, fragmentation and alienation now rule the day.

T. S. Eliot's vaunted tradition serves as an ersatz as much as Arnold's culture. His sense of a "simultaneous order" of "existing monuments" fails to acknowledge that "the changes of the human mind," the distinct and major intellectual tendencies of each age, are more important for the poet-critic than any synchronic and poorly defined order might be. For poetry is not an "organic whole." There are diverse and incongruous currents. It is the utter incompatibility of Homer and Pound, of Sophocles and Beckett, of Dante and Eliot himself, that merits contemplation. The "historical sense," what Lionel Trilling calls the "sense of the past," must fundamentally take into account the irreconcilable and aberrant, the anomalies in the mind of Europe, in one's own country, and in the rest of the world. Hence Eliot's attempt to salvage the function of criticism leads him to concoct a tradition that in one signification never existed and in another was widely recognized to be in decline. Following a pseudo-scientific program for poetry and criticism, Eliot dehumanizes the mind of the poet into a "receptacle" that performs a "fusion" for "combination" of inert feelings, ideas, images, and other bric-a-brac plugging up his brain. This leaves the poet with nothing to do but express his "medium" cut off from his own personality and the collective, diachronic history of humankind. Like Arnold, Eliot grasps that "the accumulated wisdom of time" is endangered in the modern world, but his mythical method merely capitulates to the general direction by discrediting what he seeks to preserve.

Eliot defines criticism as "the elucidation of works of art and the correction of taste." How one might determine the constituents of taste or the values by which correction might be made is left as amorphous as many of the pronouncements of Arnold. Eliot of course waves in the direction of the church and classicism, impugns romanticism or the "Inner Voice," lambasts "Whiggery," and makes a few pertinent suggestions regarding the "chief tools of the critic"—comparison and analysis—but none of this confronts the ontological dislocation at its root. It is the tinkering of one disconcerted and baffled by the general tendency. The firm values with which Sidney and Johnson elucidated works of art and corrected the vitiated taste of their countrymen are nowhere to be found, other than in a few vague flourishes. As laudable as much of Eliot's procedure may be, his own obnubilation runs throughout his early criticism if not most of his work.

New Criticism produced so much useless criticism because it failed to understand adequately the following statement by Eliot: "I have assumed as axiomatic that a creation, a work of art, is autotelic; and that criticism, by definition, is about something other than itself." The autotelic definition of art was increasingly applied by Eliot's epigones to the intrinsic nature of poetry, as if it had nothing to do with life whatsoever and as if to do so was to commit some reprehensible deed worthy of only the concerted censure of every practitioner of "pretentious critical journalism." Criticism also adopted autotelicism and has now come to be about nothing "other than itself" in a manner apparently mimicked by academic critics who delude themselves into believing there is no difference between creative work and criticism. Today I find it exhilarating to stumble onto an occasional piece of criticism that is about "something other than itself" or the extraction of tenure from the system of accreditation that is built squarely on the attenuated assumptions of modernity. Instead of confronting the major cultural tendencies of our time, most academic criticism is a virulent symptom of the nihilism advocated by Derrida, his followers, and much of our society. Eliot, for all his nostalgia, at least still believed in the "possibility of arriving at something outside ourselves which may provisionally be called truth." The adverb reflects both a sense of the endangered tradition and humility—a virtue few deconstructionists have, given their grandiose schemes of negation.

Later on in life Eliot often articulated more fully that the reasons for the decline of criticism were moral and philosophical. He suggests in "The Frontiers of Criticism" how very different Johnson is from the "lemon-squeezers." What could be more perceptive than Eliot's observation that criticism has "lost its aims" and mistakes "explanation for understanding"? Explanation has now been proffered in terms of not only the origin of a work, linguistics, biography, and psychology of every contemptible brand, but also sundry Marxist persuasions, radical interdisciplinary and "cultural" studies, structuralism, deconstruction, anti-intellectual reader-response, the "new" historicism, gender, and extreme forms of multiculturalism. Everything imaginable has been tried to reduce literature from its moral, religious, and philosophical reality into the image of some small expositor. In 1961 Eliot, almost for the first time and perhaps out of revulsion with the abominations to which he had helped give birth, states unambiguously the relation of criticism to life in "To Criticize the Critic":

> . . . it is impossible to fence off literary criticism on other grounds, and . . . moral, religious, and social judgments cannot be wholly excluded.

Since the time Arnold began to fence off criticism from life, criticism has increasingly corrupted poets and widened the gap between them and the human community. Critics and poets themselves, as much as science, are to blame for the utter trivialization of the literary endeavor. Literature must confront the eternal state of man wrapped in all his virtues and vices. Instead, it has become all too often content to remain a symptom of the crisis of modernity, the general malaise. Critical perspective depends not only on the diachronic sense of history but also on values that can be found only outside literature.

III

For I believe we do not wholly die.
Robert Browning

Sidney and Johnson unequivocally affirmed the locus of value in the transcendent, while the last two hundred years have witnessed the steady discrediting of any such locus. In "Mimesis and Allegory" W. H. Auden fully recognizes the relation between mimesis and the transcendent:

> Without an adequate and conscious metaphysics in the background, art's imitation of life inevitably becomes, either a photostatic copy of the accidental details of life without pattern or significance, or a personal allegory of the artist's individual dementia.

Since Auden wrote this excerpt in 1941, poetry and criticism have increasingly become "photostatic" copies of the "accidental details" of the self, bereft of any unifying vision of significance. I read everywhere chatty criticism, mildly vicious gossip, rambling interviews, anything but a unified perspective cognizant of the spiritual history of humankind as manifested in all the great religions of the peoples of the world. More often than not during the postmodern period we have had inflicted on us the "artist's individual dementia"—as in the work of Robert Lowell, Sylvia Plath, and Anne Sexton. Such a distortion of the literary endeavor is an accident of history, an acceptance of a certain narrow conception of the function of the poet or critic.

The values that make us most human are not the alienation and nihilism of the *poète maudit*, the detestation of the bourgeoisie, technology, and the pragmatic; nor are they any of the other clichés of modernism such as disdain for the family and democracy. Far from such fragmented conceptions, I hold the values that have been revered for millennia are the most humane to which an artist can aspire. To varying degrees such observers of literature and modern society as Max Weber, José Ortega y Gasset, Pitirim Sorokin, Alasdair MacIntyre, Robert Nisbet, Daniel Bell, Christopher Lasch, Gertrude Himmelfarb, Robert Bellah, Philip Rieff, Jacques Barzun, Allan Bloom, Alvin Kernan, and John M. Ellis have been especially sensitive to this truth, as were the best observers of civilization in the past, Ibn Khaldun and Giambattista Vico. These values and traditions are fundamentally spiritual in nature, transcend the individual and any particular era, connect the isolated consciousness with the community and with the past, and move the heart to sacrifice for higher ideals, as Achilles for honor and Aeneas for *pietas*. A healthy culture always reveres man's capacity for nobility, and so does a healthy literary period. Literature is the reflection of man's consciousness. Without virtue man is indeed a bedbug. Postmodernism has performed the mimetic duty of art by bringing us the news that mass society intuits but often continues to ignore: what we have lost.

The chief intellectual tendency of the modern age is the loss of belief in God—the transcendent One beyond the understanding of all religions. Whether in painting, literature, criticism, philosophy, architecture, or any other art since the Renaissance, the discrediting of the religious conception of life, whether in the East or in the West, has been progressing relentlessly and has had undeniably dire repercussions. I can only ask the reader to recall the appallingly barbarous acts of the many avowedly atheistic regimes to discern the perspicacity of Paul Johnson's observation that "the history of modern times" is largely the history of how the vacuum of the loss of belief has been filled. Influenced by the general background, many modernist and postmodernists have become so alienated from any religious conception of life that they uncritically adopt an attitude akin to Stevens' "indifference to questions of belief" or to Derrida's grandiose pass "beyond man and humanism."

Under the modern redefinition of science as only the natural and empirical sciences, many fail to realize that religious belief is based as much on conscious knowledge as is science. As T. S. Kuhn, Leon R. Kass, and others have shown, all science inescapably contains a subjective element. The objectivity of science has its limit since science requires the assuming of beliefs, theories, absolutes, unknowns, for experimentation to proceed, to say nothing of its faith that order inheres in nature and can be discovered and understood, while errors in analysis can be eradicated. In his *Personal Knowledge* Michael Polanyi delineates his "ontology of commitment" and his concept of the "personal," which is neither subjective nor objective:

It is the act of commitment in its full structure that saves personal knowledge from being merely subjective. Intellectual commitment is a responsible decision, in submission to the compelling claims of what in good conscience I conceive to be true. It is an act of hope, striving to fulfill an obligation within a personal situation for which I am not responsible and which therefore determines my calling. This hope and this obligation are expressed in the universal intent of personal knowledge.

As Polanyi says elsewhere, "the personal submits to requirements acknowledged by itself as independent of itself" and thereby is not subjective. Yet it is not wholly objective either since it constitutes what an individual conceives "to be true." The individual actively enters into commitment in an act of hope in a given situation "for which one is not responsible" and for which the "universal intent of personal knowledge" seeks to fulfill an obligation and calling, that is, a commitment. Such conscious commitment is "how a Christian is placed when worshipping God." Such a contemporary articulation of the understanding of the worshiping soul is just as true of all the great religions, whether Hinduism, Buddhism, or Islam, and can only highlight the tragedy of the pervasive loss of our era.

Sidney's affirmation of the traditional understanding of the unity of all knowledge highlights the triviality of the common misconception of the relation between science and the humanities today. There need be no fundamental disagreement since all knowledge serves to "lift up the mind" to the mystery which men have traditionally called God and to the enjoying of the individual's "own divine essence." Albert Einstein defined the mysterious as precisely the unifying realm of true art, science, and religion. The modern constriction of knowledge and meaning to science is actually indicative of the loss of the spiritual understanding of the mystery of being. Similarly the deterioration of literature indicates the same loss on the part of the artist as well as on the part of the mass of men. The narrow definition of knowledge is fallacious and now intolerantly denies half of what it means to be a human being since man is more than natural processes that are reducible to impersonal forces of determinism. By recognizing the fundamental agreement of all the sciences and humanities in their common creative urge to understand the principles of life and the universe, Sidney's era united human endeavor into an intelligible whole that gave meaning and purpose to the individual and to the community. For man is that being who seeks order, whether in science or art, by focusing his intuition and reason on the particular and moving to the universal. The postmodern abandonment of the search for a coherent understanding of life accepts the specious redefinition that relegates art and the transcendent realm of value to the nether world of the indifference of those who are content or eager to "pass beyond man" to what is less than human.

Another aspect of this redefinition of knowledge is the failure to appreciate that science is amoral or stands beyond good and evil. The discoveries of science merely present us with what is possible and not with an evaluation of how to use the new discovery or a judgment of what to do with it. On such questions science is neutral and proffers no intrinsic knowledge on humanity's goals or ends. The choice resides in the human realm of men, in their qualitative judgments, not in their quantitative ones. Only religion and art concern themselves with questions of value that arise from the predicament of man in a "situation" for which he is "not responsible." Such situations that demand choice reveal the potentialities of human beings. For it is only in the act of volition, often performed under stress, that people attain their noblest deeds or manifest their illimitable capacity for horror and tragedy. Art that turns from the realm of commitment is rightly viewed as mere diversion or fluff. Similarly, when science retreats into an autotelic complacency that disregards the possible effects of its discoveries on human beings, such as nuclear weapons or military research, it becomes a caricature of its highest potential. This is neither to gainsay the immense benefits of science nor to advocate Ludditism. It is to affirm the unity of human nature and the dire consequences of denying and dehumanizing the spiritual capacities of man.

The naive optimism that the nineteenth century had for science and for progress was more than undercut by the harsh horrors of the twentieth century, perpetrated with the Krupp machine gun, mustard gas, the aerial bombardment of civilian populations, the Nazi death camps (run with scientific efficiency), the nuclear bombing of

Hiroshima and Nagasaki, and the napalming of children. Such instruments of brutality brought the twentieth century approximately ten million dead human beings in World War I, fifty-five million dead in World War II, and twenty or more million slaughtered in the various regional and national conflicts since 1950. Added to this vast panorama of suffering are the sixty-six million or more of its own people that the former Soviet Union murdered for ideological reasons and the many millions who died either during the rise of communism in China or during its many subsequent upheavals. Excluding the long drawn out Napoleonic wars, these statistics should be contemplated in the light of the single most destructive war in the previous history of the world—the American Civil War, which, in comparison, resulted in the death of only approximately a half million people. Without the efficiency of science, the vast slaughter of modernity could never have been accomplished. Those who would contend there have always been nasty manifestations of man's capacity for brutality would do well to consider that the quantitative increase in the deaths of so many individuals constitutes an undeniably qualitative difference. It is this difference that has led to the frequent distrust of technology and to the fear of a nuclear or biological catastrophe that we might still fail to avert, given the threat of terrorism. Only the most naive would imagine that man is incapable, through either omission or commission, of such enormity.

Against such a background those who prattle about the non-referentiality of language and passing beyond humanism must be seen as one of the grossest distortions of the human spirit ever to happen along. Far from sinking further into an academic withdrawal from such realities, I believe, as a writer, I must recognize the overwhelming pressure of the reality of our time and reconnect art with life. Czeslaw Milosz identifies precisely the standard that criticism and poetry must acknowledge if they are to recover their equilibrium and to merit again the respect of the human family: "The twentieth century has given us a most simple touchstone for reality: physical pain." I take it as a sign of our times that criticism often fails to be intelligent enough to conceive of itself and poetry as involved in any way with life. But social conditions have changed so radically since the symbolists sanctified the doctrines of alienation and since the modernists and postmodernists began to extend them that they now reveal themselves for the tawdry clichés that they are. The blood of millions has washed them away. The struggle between oppression and federalism has been one of the most important characteristics of the last hundred years and only by recognizing this struggle and throwing off the autotelic, alienated singing robes of the decadents can literature again probe what it means to be a human being at this juncture of time and space. As Milosz suggests in the following excerpt from *The Witness of Poetry*, it is in the reality of physical pain and in the "fragility of those things we call civilization or culture" that the poet must again reclaim his social function:

> The poetic act changes with the amount of background reality embraced by the poet's consciousness. In our century that background is, in my opinion, related to the fragility of those things we call civilization or culture. What surrounds us, here and now, is not guaranteed. It could just as well not exist—and so man constructs poetry out of the remnants found in ruins.

The solipsism of postmodern poetry and criticism results from the paucity of "background reality" confronted by its practitioners. They revel so much in every form of "self-assertion" that they neglect the totality of human experience. Hence they spend their time on trivialities and the effete assumptions of nihilism. But "the remnants found in ruins" call out to us and lead us back to our senses. If science has proven anything, it is that life could "just as well not exist." As Pablo Neruda wrote, *"Yo vengo a habler por vuestra boca muerta."*

IV

. . . for then the Earth
Shall all be Paradise, far happier place
Than this of Eden, and far happier days.
John Milton

Criticism must take into account the major tendencies of modernity, the incessant "turn away from the origin," the long historical process that led through ever-deepening seas of blood. The touchstone of pain testifies to the inexorable process of events that has been tearing down the old world order of isolated, often monarchical peoples and nations, and slowly, steadily, despite all temporary setbacks, establishing the bonds of a new world order. Matthew Arnold's castigating of English provincialism and nationalism proves prescient beyond anything of which he could have ever conceived. The upheaval in creeds, traditions, and dogmas is but the preliminary to the welding together of the world. Arnold Toynbee perceives in his *Surviving the Future*, as throughout his work, the inevitable goal toward which modernity has been hurtling and understands the fundamental prerequisite for such a "revolution" is one in our "basic ideas and ideals":

The people of each local sovereign state will have to renounce their state's sovereignty and subordinate it to the paramount sovereignty of a literally world-wide world government. But this revolution in mankind's political organization can be brought about only as a consequence of a far more radical and more profound revolution in our fundamental ideas and ideals.

Modern history has been preparing for this "revolution" in our social structure by sloughing off allegiances to narrow commitments, by replacing them with a growing consciousness of the interdependence of all peoples, and by forging new modes of cooperation among formerly antagonistic peoples. Such revolution is not taking place, as Milosz observes, "without high cost." It took the so-called "war to end all wars" to lead to the first constructive step toward world federal governance: The League of Nations. Yet its aims were subverted by the virulent nationalistic passions that hamstrung its Covenant and the Treaty of Versailles. After World War II the United Nations, which rose out of the ashes of the hope of war-weary peoples for a lasting peace, was also hamstrung throughout the Cold War by the mutual suspicions and intrigues of its members.

As most of the major combatants of World War II turned to the interests of their own nations and most critics and poets were content to withdraw further into the self, one motley collection of people after another began their struggle for nationhood and claimed their independence. Despite exceptions and failures, much of the formation of unstable areas of the globe into sovereign states has been completed. Throughout South America, Africa, South East Asia, and the archipelagoes, new nations have arisen to play out their destiny on the global stage. The masses have further been brought together by the development of computer technologies and media that have culminated in the electronic global village, now nowhere more evident than in the vast potential of the Internet. Everywhere the peoples of the old order have assimilated or are assimilating the evolving new world culture that forms itself on the scientific and cultural achievements of Western civilization. Far from this being a negative development, this process has allowed, for the first time in history, one substantially unified, though not uniform, world human culture to begin to emerge. This process is still forging and consolidating the "ideas and ideals," the values, the principles of world federalism upon which globally minded people will ultimately establish lasting and universal peace.

This global process has not failed to make an impact on national cultures. In the United States World War II led to the weakening of the chains of bondage for many African-Americans who previously had been denied access to many sectors of the economy. With the entry of America into the war, many industries employed blacks in record numbers. Similarly women were also employed in record numbers and in jobs that were formerly reserved for men. The door opened to human equality and opportunity for millions of minorities and further swept aside a system of oppression that had roots reaching back into slavery. It is no coincidence that shortly after World War II institutional racism in America suffered some of its most lasting defeats. With the rise of the civil rights movement and such persons as Dr. Martin Luther King, Jr., America at last began to move, however reluctantly, toward the fulfillment of the true meaning of its Constitution and to prepare itself, however unwittingly, for its continuing role of offering the basic principles of federalism and human rights to the entire globe. In 1967 in *Where Do We Go From Here: Chaos or Community?* Dr. King understands the connection between the nonviolent struggle of the African-American and what he calls the community of the "world house" in the context of the United Nations:

> The United Nations is a gesture in the direction of nonviolence on a world scale. There, at least, states that oppose one another have sought to do so with words instead of with weapons. But true nonviolence is more than the absence of violence. It is the persistent and determined application of peaceable power to offenses against the community—in this case the world community.

I have long felt that for the first time in history the human being now stands on the threshold of becoming what only the rare individual, such as Socrates, dreamed of—a world citizen.

The forces that still work against such a vision becoming an actuality are immense and not languishing in passivity. Provincialism and bigotry embue each individual nation let alone the relations among sovereign states. More than vestiges of xenophobia linger. The difficulties that so often arise in the meeting of Western and Eastern peoples with one another, and with others of the globe, still hamper the thinking of many ordinary people, as well as those who conduct the international relations of their respective countries. Yet xenophobia is grounded in a provincial interpretation of other cultures that fails to appreciate both the beautiful diversity of human customs and the essential oneness of human nature, which "the prejudices of an age or country" leave untouched. Although numerous historical times exist around the globe and will continue to exist, their ultimate harmonization is readily conceivable and is taking place despite resistance. The barriers to understanding are diminishing often under the onslaught of dire international upheavals or incidents of terrorism that are compelling the proponents of provincialism to work together to find new means of cooperation. Such cooperative bodies and organizations as the European Community, the Conference on Security and Cooperation in Europe, the Council for Mutual Economic Assistance, the Central American Common Market, the Carribean Community and Common Market, the Association of South East Asian Nations, the League of Arab States, the Organization of American States, the Organization of African Unity, and the South Pacific Forum have all forged unprecedented relationships at a wider level than the nation-state. Similarly, the many conventions, treaties, and declarations of the United Nations, such as the Universal Declaration of Human Rights, the Declaration on Friendly Relations, the Declaration on Decolonization, the Convention on the Prevention and Punishment of the Crime of Genocide, the Non-Proliferation Treaty, the various pronouncements on discrimination based on race, religion, or sex, the attention drawn to the plight of millions of the world's children through numerous proclamations, as well as many other humanitarian and scientific efforts to promote the well-being of humankind, confronted with the peril of global warming, have all served to forge, despite politicization, a wider consciousness among the peoples of the world.

The reality of man is his thought, and it alone stands in the way of a peaceful world. Not only has it become possible for a world federation to evolve to protect humankind from its innate passions but it has also become inevitable. All roads lead to unity, even the devastating path of universal nuclear conflagration. The major barrier is our persistent failure to conceive of world governance as anything other than a form of fascism, socialism, or communism. In practical terms, the new world order can be established only on the principles of federalism. To do nothing constitutes a repudiation of the manifest destiny of America to become as "a city upon a hill" cooperating with and beckoning to all humankind the global path to political peace and stability. In *The Abolition* Jonathan Schell perceptively identifies the impasse at which the world still stands:

> The requirement for world government as the inevitable price for nuclear disarmament is at the heart of the impasse that the world has been unable to break through in almost four decades of the nuclear age.

Far from actually circumventing this requirement with the post Cold War arms reduction treaties, which leave plenty of weapons for overkill, we must recognize that world governance need not be any grotesque polity, as some members of the original American colonies had feared would become of the new world, but rather, if we but have the will, it can become the lasting haven of ourselves and the entire world, knit together by the highest ideals of the republican tradition. To imagine that we can remain indefinitely on the brink of annihilation without our choosing to follow the inevitable path of history through this putative impasse is the delusion of those who deny the direction of the vast horrors that mark the twentieth century and the portent of 9/11. Such a haven is possible, practical, and not a utopian vision. In the post Cold War world, history has not ended. Many inveterate problems will continue and endure, but, for the first time, they will receive the redress of the will of all the peoples of the planet. Wyndham Lewis once wrote, "A World Government appears to me the only imaginable solution for the chaos reigning at present throughout the world." Only within such a universal framework of value can society, literature, and criticism again find their bearings. The major powers must unequivocally recognize the global evolution of the international community toward unity, perceived by such champions of humankind as Woodrow Wilson, Franklin D. Roosevelt, and Dag Hammarskjold, and break through to a new path for the United Nations, one that fulfills the promise of its Charter to bring in the secure establishment of peace. No variation on the balance of power schemes of the past, the delusions of unilateral action, or a multipolar world will ever inaugurate the vision of the UN Charter, the instrument of the will of the Member States. Such UN initiatives as those in Kuwait, El Salvador, Cambodia, Mozambique, Bosnia, Kosovo, Haiti, East Timor, despite the at times impure motives of some of the participants, show we have already entered a new and welcomed stage in human history. And not even the retreat from and betrayal of the universal values of the United Nations, as was done by some member nations during the term of Boutros Boutros-Ghali, so devastatingly chronicled in his book *UNvanquished*, can in the long run stop this epic movement from reaching fruition.

Academic criticism that denies the moral, religious, and philosophical traditions of the Western world and passes "beyond man and humanism" to parasitic nihilism manifests the major upheavals of our time and highlights the impasse at which the nay-saying capacity of man has brought us. I know there is a truth to its negation, and it is that negation surrounds us. Similarly poet-critics who retreat into the self highlight the national isolation or flight from the responsibility that is our birthright from the earliest settlements upon our shores. Criticism must embrace this capacious perspective of global humanism because it is incontrovertibly true, consistent with the history of humankind, and the highest locus of value within the quotidian realm. Social conditions have more than sufficiently changed to necessitate a repudiation of the anti-values of modernism and postmodernism, of the cheap intellectual clichés of what Saul Bellow called the wasteland outlook. The dominant tradition of our literature and criticism has unabashedly been humanistic and dedicated to the fullest possible development of the individual within his cultural and historical context. Such development has always held supreme the capacities of humankind for transcendence, selflessness, nobility, and love of God, family, country, and kind. The distortions that have historically evolved between reason and belief, science and religion, society and the individual, need not preclude poets and critics from perceiving the invincible hand of God guiding the affairs of man, through glory and turmoil, into that promised day when swords shall be beaten into plowshares and mankind shall be gathered together.

Meditations in an Old Barn

We know no fuss or pain or lying
Can stop the moribund from dying,
That all the special tasks begun
By the Renaissance have been done.
                                        W. H. Auden

The AT&T tower on Madison Avenue was hailed as both an architectural joke and one of the most prominent examples of the postmodern trend in architecture. With its Chippendale highboy cutout, the tower was supposed to allude, unlike the modernist movement in architecture, to the historical past. But such ornamentation, though quaint and amusing, fails to conceal the same empty glass box that is the hallmark of modernist architecture. As the modernist movement in literature used synchronic forms to repudiate historical time, the International Style used cheap glass curtains fastened to a superstructure to lend its buildings an abstract appearance unrelated to the architectural past. Its crude functionalism, canonized in the maxim "form follows function," expresses the corporate debasing of human and aesthetic values to monetary terms. Far from constituting exponents of a revitalizing movement, postmodern architects have merely extended, as many postmodern poets have, the fundamental assumptions of modernism, with a little eclectic bric-a-brac thrown on the surface. But the resolving of major problems in architecture has always been accompanied or preceded by a new understanding of what it means to be a human being in a particular time and place. This is as true of literary as it is of architectural movements.

The thirteenth-century Chartres Cathedral reflects precisely a particular historical conception of human nature, reaching back to the Roman basilica. Far from symbolizing an absence, the cathedral symbolizes, even in Jacques Derrida's sense of the word, a presence. It was conceived, designed, and experienced as the representation of man's most profound understanding of himself and of the world; it was the manifestation of *splendor veritatis*, the radiance of truth; it was the image of the heavenly city, of Augustine's city of God, designed by the architect of the universe himself and inspired through the Virgin. Such reflection of ultimate reality was held to be the animating purpose of architecture, as well as of all art and literature, in an heroic attempt to grasp and express man's awe before the infinite mystery of life. Such awe is exactly what George Herbert expresses in these lines from his poem "The Church-Porch":

> When once thy foot enters the church, be bare.
> God is more there, then thou: for thou art there
> Only by his permission. Then beware,
> And make thy self all reverence and fear.

Here Herbert holds humility and self-effacement to be in harmony with the nature of the church and with man's relationship to God, a relationship which the physical structure of the church itself symbolizes. But throughout the entire modern era since the Renaissance and the Enlightenment there has been an incessant discrediting of such a spiritual conception of life, especially during this century, as Paul Johnson confirms in his Epilogue to *A History of Christianity*:

> During the past half-century there has been a rapid and uninterrupted secularization of the West, which has all but demolished the Augustinian idea of Christianity as a powerful, physical and institutional presence in the world. Of St. Augustine's city of God on earth, little now remains, except crumbling walls and fallen towers, effete establishments and patriarchies of antiquarian rather than intrinsic interest. . . . The Augustinian idea of public, all-embracing Christianity, once so compelling, has served its purpose and retreats—perhaps, one day, to re-emerge in different forms.

This secularization, worldwide in scope and also affecting all of the major religions, such as Hinduism, Buddhism, and Taoism, has been widely, if not universally acknowledged, though interpretations of it have varied from visions of atrophy to the postmodern "breakthrough," annunciated, for one, by Jacques Derrida, who says his *"affirmation . . . determines the non-center otherwise than as a loss of the center."* The retreat is so far advanced that many, if not most, postmodern poets fail to understand the historical substratum of the devolution that constitutes the period in which they live.

Matthew Arnold was the first poet fully to recognize and understand the loss of faith as the peculiarly modern problem. In "Dover Beach" Arnold proclaims that "The Sea of Faith / Was once, too, at the full," but all he hears is "Its melancholy, long, withdrawing roar, / Retreating, to the breath / Of the night-wind," the withering breath of secularization, as it were. Another poem, "Stanzas from the Grande Chartreuse," tells of the "Last of the people who believe," of the speaker's pilgrimage to the monastery of the Carthusian order. The opening stanzas recount the trek up the mountainside to the monastery and chapel as up the processional path of a nave to the high altar. From a distance he can see the "pointed roofs" through the twilight. Despite the austerity of the Carthusians, their harsh existence and beliefs, the speaker holds that "What we seek is here!" Yet he is so self-conscious that what is actually conveyed is his lack of belonging, his alienation, which he gives voice to in the line "What am I, that I am here?" He is excruciatingly aware that he has been a pupil of the "masters of mind," whom he correctly holds supreme. Even before T. S. Eliot, who decried "Make-Believe" but spent much of his life shoring it up, Arnold saw the old world as irrevocably dead, retreating before the bats of night. Like the speaker in "Dover Beach," who also "waits forlorn" and flees into the arms of his lover, the speaker in "Stanzas" flees, or tries to flee, into the arms of the Carthusians, "Till I possess my soul again."

The persona, though, does not prefer the "children rear'd in shade" to the gay, frivolous "sons of the world." He concedes the Carthusians are as lost in a desert as the children of action and pleasure. In a line W. B. Yeats was later to echo, the speaker owns the tragedy of his time and place: "The best are silent now"—silent before the on-rushing winds of cultural confusion and secularization as they "wait forlorn" for a new world "powerless to be born," a world in which the passions and the deepest perceptions can again be balanced. Yet Arnold, especially in his prose, must be held responsible for substituting culture and poetry for the "fallen Runic stone," for the dead world. His tears for the past were romantic ones.

Thomas Hardy wrote many poems about churches and cathedrals that demonstrate his awareness of and involvement in the increasing cultural confusion of his age. These poems are deeply influenced by his professional experience as an architect restoring churches. The poems range far beyond a merely journalistic, architectural documentation of the fading past, as in "The Impercipient," which is subtitled "At a Cathedral Service." The speaker manifests nearly the same tortured consciousness as Arnold's speaker in the "Stanzas." He is, even more than in Arnold, alienated from the "bright believing band," whose beliefs seem mere fantasies to him. Not knowing what to make of his plight, he calls it a "strange destiny," "a mystery." The title suggests not only that he is imperceptive but also that his "brethren" are imperceptive about the upheavals of the age and of the origin and validity of his doubts: "He who breathes All's Well to these / Breathes no All's Well to me." Such is the mystery that grieves the persona, as well as the charge by his brethren that "blessed things" he would "liefer not have be." To such self-righteous imputations, he answers,

> O, doth a bird deprived of wings
> Go earth-bound wilfully!

* * *

> Enough. As yet disquiet clings
> About us. Rest shall we.

Hardy, however, never attained "rest" or "ease" since he perceived fully the changes that were being wrought both inside and outside the cathedral. He reveals such a perception in this poem by suggesting that the bird has not "wilfully" chosen to be "earth-bound," restricted to the material realm. Rather, the bird has been "deprived of wings," and Hardy respects the truth enough to recognize the fact. In an early draft of the last lines, Hardy writes, "As yet confusion clings about us. We shall see." Such initial lines clearly indicate the impetus behind the poem to have been the exterior "confusion" and his determination to wait for the conundrum of his "strange destiny" to be resolved.

"A Cathedral Facade at Midnight" further probes the confusion outside the sanctuary and offers an explanation. The speaker stands at midnight before the western portal of a cathedral and intently, skeptically watches the "moonlight creeping" over the sculpted figures of the facade. I think of the Royal Portal of Chartres with its serene figures of lords and ladies who, perhaps, had deigned to offer their own labor to raise the hymn of the cathedral skyward; of the tympanum of Christ; of the spires on the magnificent towers; of the three lancet windows below the majestic, incomparable rose window, that opalescent emblem, which Dante used to such effect, on the breast of the Virgin's church—all painstakingly wrought out of the finest materials and with the most exquisite craftsmanship. But, to the speaker, the illuminated "stiff images" on the facade seem only to lament "the ancient faith's rejection":

> A frail moan from the martyred saints there set
> Mid others of the erection
> Against the breeze, seemed sighings of regret
> At the ancient faith's rejection
> Under the sure, unhasting, steady stress
> Of Reason's movement, making meaningless
> The coded creeds of old-time godliness.

In the darkness of midnight, in the "lunar look" of blanching moonlight, the pale, austere forms are revealed as a mere facade of sculpted rock and are discredited by the incessant march of reason and science. In another poem Hardy had speculated that "Perhaps Thy ancient rote-restricted ways / Thy ripening rule transcends."

Such hope is banished before the vision of reason and belief as diametrically opposed.

In Hart Crane's "The Broken Tower," which was the last poem he wrote before committing suicide, the possibility of the cathedral reflecting any reality other than the observer's own projected emotions has been completely swept away. The "dawn" of Crane's poem illuminates the "fallen tower" with the effusiveness of which only the American Adam is capable. Like Emerson or Whitman intoxicated with the ichor of nature, Crane's speaker wanders "the cathedral lawn / From pit to crucifix," from hell to apotheosis, from Concord to the Boston Common, from a blade of grass to the universe. Such revelation is always fitful for the American prophet-poet, and, though the "bells break down their tower," there is an "impasse" beyond which the bells cannot toll, as Crane's own poetry, his own "long-scattered score," achieves only "broken intervals" of substitution. The hubris and tragedy of his life in the "broken world" become evident when he imagines himself entering the world like Christ to restore harmony for at least an "instant in the wind."

As is typical of many American romantics from the transcendentalists to Robert Bly, the Jones Very of the postmodernists, Crane finds assurance in the inebriating "steep encroachments" of his blood, the afflatus of some vast and vague oversoul, whether it be called pantheistic, Jungian, or pre-Socratic matters little. Crane ends his poem with this conception of the "pulse" of "blood" and "heart":

> And through whose pulse I hear, counting the strokes
> My veins recall and add, revived and sure
> The angelus of wars my chest evokes:
> What I hold healed, original now, and pure . . .
> And builds, within, a tower that is not stone
> (Not stone can jacket heaven)—but slip
> Of pebbles,—visible wings of silence sown
> In azure circles, widening as they dip

The matrix of the heart, lift down the eye
That shrines the quiet lake and swells a tower . . .
The commodius, tall decorum of that sky
Unseals her earth, and lifts love in its shower.

Like some primordial man set down in the paradise of the new world, Crane stands in the torrent of revelation "healed, original now, and pure." Since the severed relationship between man and nature has been redeemed, the speaker can build "within, a tower that is not stone," but the pure edifice of the heart or soul which lifts "down the eye" to sanctify the physical "lake," "tower," "sky," and "earth" of this world, not a transcendent one. It is indicative of Crane's ungrounded plight that he thinks it necessary to point out parenthetically "(Not stone can jacket heaven)," for only someone adrift would ever conceive of a church or cathedral as enshrining deity, which is a thoroughly Greek and Roman idea. No pilgrim to Chartres fails to realize that the cathedral is a house of worship, a merely anagogical symbol of man's relationship to God.

By the middle of W. H. Auden's life few observers failed to perceive that an unprecedented dislocation from nearly everything Western civilization had once stood for had occurred. Whereas Augustine's confession "Our hearts find no peace until they rest in Thee" was held for hundreds of years as one of the most poignant utterances of the inviolable law of man's nature, as was his conception of the city of God, Auden perceived quite fully the dead world and the anxiety of the age. Yet he unequivocally affirmed the inescapably spiritual reality of man's nature, threatened, though it is, by our own bestiality and the nihilism of our times. After having quixotically declared in his Virginia lectures of March 1949 that the figure for our time must become "the builder, who renews the ruined walls of the city," Auden, compelled by honesty, wrote in June his poem "Memorial for the City," a memorial for its "crumbling walls":

Across the square,
Between the burn-out Law Courts and Police Headquarters,

Past the Cathedral far too damaged to repair,
Around the Grand Hotel patched up to hold reporters,
Near huts of some Emergency Committee,
The barbed wire runs through the abolished City.

Across the plains,
Between two hills, two villages, two trees, two friends,
The barbed wire runs which neither argues nor explains,
But, where it likes, a place, a path, a railroad ends,
The humor, the cuisine, the rites, the taste,
The pattern of the City, are erased.

The cathedral is, as a statement of fact, "too damaged to repair," as the "empty chapel" of *The Waste Land* is "only the wind's home." It has long been abolished though many cling to make-believe, make-shift substitutes, Augustan irony, or a pseudo-past that is only their own ahistorical expression of nostalgia. What now dominates the plain is the "barbed wire" of our raging will, of our confusion. And what is truly terrifying is that "the pattern of the City" has been erased, making all manner of abomination now permissible and the common experience of our daily lives. Similarly, the pattern of all the great religions has been obliterated.

It is precisely the function of Christianity as a pattern that Paul Johnson stresses in the following excerpt:

As an exercise in perfectionism, Christianity cannot succeed, even by its internal definitions; what it is designed to do is to set targets and standards, raise aspirations, to educate, stimulate and inspire. Its strength lies in its just estimate of man as a fallible creature with immortal longings. Its outstanding moral merit is to invest the individual with a conscience, and bid him follow it.

The ability of Christianity to serve as a model to inspire moral action is attested by nearly two thousand years of history and the now steadily increasing moral breakdown of Western civilization. It was in the cathedral that men once found the authoritative guidance for every activity of life, the unifying locus for the city or town itself around the cathedral square, the social, economic, legal, and educational succor for passage through the stages of life from birth to death.

Philip Larkin's "Church Going," written in 1955, attests, perhaps more than any other poem of the postmodern period, to the abolishing of the "pattern," to the "going" of the city. Such a realization characterizes the work of many postmodern poets, English as well as American, who, in their languid search for substitutes, often repeat, in one way or another, what Nietzsche's Zarathustra proclaims: "What does all the world know today? Perhaps this, that the old god in whom all the world once believed no longer lives." Actually, the poem goes even further, as do many postmodern poems, by assuming it, and asserts with Derrida that the "*non-center*," the vapid discourse, the chaos, does not constitute the "*loss of the center*":

> And what remains when disbelief has gone?
> Grass, weedy pavement, brambles, buttress, sky,
> A shape less recognisable each week,
> A purpose more obscure.

That is, "what remains" constitutes the postmodern "breakthrough," which is the logical outcome of Yeats's echoing of Arnold in his quatrain "The Nineteenth Century and After"—"The rattle of pebbles on the shore / Under the receding wave." At last, the truth, which now stands as a foregone conclusion of literary dogma, is that there is no truth. All is subjectivity, solipsism, alienation.

Larkin's speaker, "Bored, uninformed, knowing the ghostly silt / Dispersed," enters the church, in contrast to Herbert's counsel of reverence, full of self and hubris, partly because he has "no idea / What this accoutred frowsty barn is worth." He behaves like a gawking tourist, an antiquarian "randy for antique." After strolling about for some time, he reflects, "The place was not worth stopping for":

Yet stop I did: in fact I often do,
And always end much at a loss like this,
Wondering what to look for; wondering, too,
When churches fall completely out of
What we shall turn them into, if we shall keep
A few cathedrals chronically on show,
Their parchment, plate and pyx in locked cases,
And let the rest rent-free to rain and sheep.

Incapable of taking the cathedral seriously, deprived of a nurturing
social, cultural context, the speaker rambles about the church as
though he were browsing in a department store. Whereas once the
church plate, the chalices, patens, candlesticks, monstrances, and
pyxes had been used to celebrate Holy Communion, the persona can
conceive only of displaying them in "locked cases," as in a museum
or art gallery, which is the only function modern man can imagine
the cathedral or house of worship fulfilling. His sacrilegious
cynicism and irony attempt to dispel all vestiges of awe and mystery
from the ontologically transparent architectural metaphor and,
indeed, from life. "A few cathedrals," selected at random or for their
titillating specimens of "art," will "chronically" be exhibited for the
delectation of connoisseurs; the missals are "little books"; the high
altar and sanctuary are "stuff / Up at the holy end"; the silence of
the church echoes not reverence and worship but his sniggering. His
other conception of what to do with the church has systematically
been employed by more than one communist or fascist regime:
"accoutered frowsty barn" for "rain and sheep."

   As the persona derisively puts it, people will "forever" gravitate
to the barn, tend towards the lowest level, towards this "ground" or
worldly structure of church as merely physical object, solely out of
ignorant impulse, not because they submit to the Manifestation of
God:

It pleases me to stand in silence here;

A serious house on serious earth it is,
In whose blent air all our compulsions meet,
Are recognised, and robed as destinies.
And that much never can be obsolete,
Since someone will forever be surprising
A hunger in himself to be more serious,
And gravitating with it to this ground,
Which, he once heard, was proper to grow wise in,
If only that so many dead lie round.

The psychological, Freudian connotation of "compulsions" attempts to debase man's religious awe and worship of God to the mere impulse of bipeds, as does the nuance of "robed as destinies," which implies erroneous attribution of divine will. It is only in such a secular sense that the speaker can acknowledge the facet of man's nature that can never be "obsolete." Another subtly seductive stratagem Larkin uses here to drain piety of all rational respectability is his subverting the word "serious" into a pejorative term. Like so many other minor postmodern poets and critics, Larkin apparently imagines that anything truly serious is cause for laughter, skepticism, and decadent derogation. In a manner somewhat comparable to that of the Augustan poets, many postmodernists relish and excel at the play of trivial wit, which Larkin demonstrates superbly in the qualifying clause "he once heard," as though all were mere hearsay and subjective relativity, and in the closing hemistich "so many dead lie round," as though spirituality were in fact a type of death.

Henry Adams knew quite well what has died, as he wrote in *The Education*: "The religious instinct has vanished." Although he perceived perhaps better than any other modern writer what Chartres cathedral signified, his interpretation is ultimately tainted by his accepting the confusion, what he called "acceleration" and "multiplicity," as the powerhouse of the Dynamo, as the inner sanctum of human history. Such a belief informs his studying of his own mind, which almost earns him the right to be ranked as the first postmodern writer. But Adams still retained an implacable awareness of the outside world, of the historical changes that were affecting his time. And unlike the postmodernists, Adams could still trace the causes of the dislocation, though he drew the wrong conclusion, as can be seen in his treatment of Chartres cathedral in both *Mont-Saint-Michel and Chartres* and *The Education*, as though it were merely an aesthetic object or curio.

Nowhere does Adams approach the piety of George Herbert's "The Windows":

> Lord, how can man preach thy eternall word?
> He is a brittle crazie glasse:
> Yet in thy temple thou dost him afford
> This glorious and transcendent place,
> To be a window, through thy grace.

Herbert's love of God is uncorrupted by solipsistic nihilism, aestheticism, or skepticism. He knows that the cathedral is a "glorious and transcendent place" from firsthand experience of its luminous, anagogical reality. For him the cathedral is as a lead glass window allowing the light to stream through the pictured lives and deeds of Christ, the Virgin, the saints, as the light of divine grace streamed through their lives renewing the relationship of man to God. As Herbert suggests, the windows wrought by glass-makers are infinitely "brittle crazie glass" but may be suffered to serve as humanly limited symbols and metaphors of the invisible reality that lies beyond all creation. Perhaps more than the work of any other English poet, Herbert's poems testify to what has "vanished" from the soul of man. To find another poet of comparable spiritual purity and depth, I would have to turn to Attar, Wang Wei, or Basho.

In *The Devil in the Fire* John W. Aldridge identifies precisely the consequences of the vanishing of the past and its replacement by the crud of popular culture:

> We have created a ravaged society, composed of many millions
> of people who, in all their affluence or just because of it, are
> leading intellectually and emotionally impoverished lives, who
> have no resources beyond the material, who are plagued by
> feelings of aimlessness and boredom, and seemingly can find life
> tolerable only by keeping themselves anesthetized on diversion
> and trivia.

That we now stand, or stagger, in the midst of a "ravaged society,"
thoroughly deprived of any spiritual sanction that can provide a
coherent conception of value, authority, reason, and purpose, is a
universally recognized fact—one powerfully recognized by such
dystopian writers as Evgeny Zamyatin, Aldous Huxley, Arthur
Koestler, and George Orwell. This state of affairs renders intelligible
much of popular culture, which is basically pre-packaged, easily
digestible "diversion and trivia" that "anesthetizes" people from the
past, the dimmed reality of their nature, and the brutal, horrifying
confusion that now surrounds us all.

The city has been swept away and through the fenestration no light
shines. Rather, light now glances off the sides of the sleek glass
curtains that shroud our cold, flat-topped boxes, which aspire to
nothing but the scraping of profit from the bleak, enclosing sky.
Postmodern architecture's eclectic decorating of facades with
bric-a-brac can prevent few thoughtful observers from perceiving
the same empty, ahistorical conception of human nature that informs
the International Style, a style which now reflects the emptiness of
the soul in every major city on the face of this earth. Strangely
enough, through representing, almost mimetically, the emptiness of
modern life, architecture has conveyed what it means to be a human
being in our particular time and place. Similarly, writers, often
despite themselves and contrary to their stated purposes, have also
proclaimed the spiritual malaise that ravages the human psyche in
our time. Regardless of the substitutes many writers have concocted
to fill the void, regardless of whether their work is a symptom or a
contemplation of the "*non-center*," their testimony has been that we
cannot go back, that the dead world of Christianity, as well as the

other traditional world religions, is beyond restoration, though many have tried and are still trying to restore it. Arnold perceived with perhaps the clearest vision the tragedy of the modern era, the tragedy of the interregnum: man caught between a dead world and one incapable of being born. Yet here in the interregnum, here a hundred and some years after Arnold, here at the beginning of the twenty-first century, the social disintegration has reached such undeniably vast proportions, such anarchy, it must surely herald a new world in a different form now struggling to emerge, now struggling to be born.

The American Journey into the Land of Ulro

A tempest has swept aside much of the Judeo-Christian tradition that for so long undergirded life in America as throughout Western civilization. Yet what has taken its place often inspires apprehension for the present and for the foreseeable future. Whereas rapacious individualism was once mollified and rechanneled by religion into service of the public good, it now often goes unbridled and wreaks havoc in both the public and private domains. This decline has been amply reflected in American literature from the Puritans to the work of the writers of the last forty years. Now the reigning ideology is one of relentless nihilism, nominalism, and solipsism. Many writers and critics accept as a foregone conclusion that we cannot know anything about our world, refer to it in any meaningful way with language, or hold any higher standard than unmitigated reveling in the passions of the self. Often they accomplish these reductions by rejecting the history of American social, religious, and literary traditions, the American experiment itself. For them time becomes chaos. I find it difficult to imagine a greater depth of decadence to which literature might sink. Yet writers are merely reflecting the general malaise that afflicts the prevailing culture, and they are doing so with greater integrity than those who would imagine such fundamental problems do not exist. Writers, perhaps more than any other group of people, have been aware of what Czeslaw Milosz observes in his *Land of Ulro*: "since the eighteenth century something, call it by whatever name one will, has been gaining ground, gathering force." All too often American writers have abetted this process, while their work has been merely a symptom of it or a landmark on our journey into the land of Ulro, into the wasteland of modernity.

The Puritans brought with them on their "errand into the wilderness" an indomitable belief in God and in revelation. They held, as have Jews and Christians throughout history, indeed as have all the revealed religions, that God is outside the universe, takes an active interest in the affairs of man, intervenes through history, and reveals His will through such figures as Moses and Christ so that man shall never go unguided. Through prayer the Puritans believed man experiences a mystic link with God that can become the impetus for service to his fellow human beings and for the leading of a moral life. John Winthrop, the first governor of the Massachusetts Bay Colony, manifests many of these beliefs in his lay sermon "A Model of Christian Charity," which he delivered on the deck of the Arbella somewhere in the middle of the Atlantic in 1630:

> We shall find that the God of Israel is among us . . . when He shall make us a praise and glory, that men shall say of succeeding plantations: "The Lord make it like that of New England." For we must consider that we shall be as a city upon a hill, the eyes of all people are upon us. . . . if our hearts shall turn away so that we will not obey, but shall be seduced and worship other gods, our pleasures and profits, and serve them, it is propounded unto us this day, we shall surely perish out of the good land whither we pass over this vast sea to possess it.

Winthrop exhorts the Puritans that "the eyes of all people are upon us" to remind his brethren that they have a commission from God for the purpose of vindicating religion in the face of the corrupted faiths of Europe and England. He draws his language almost directly from the jeremiads of the Books of the Prophets, who tirelessly castigated the Israelites for backsliding and for serving false gods. To Winthrop it was clear that the new world was to be "as a city upon a hill," which could not be hid, manifesting obedience to God, the covenant, and the search after salvation. As the Puritan *Shorter Catechism* was soon to phrase it in 1647, "Man's chief End is to Glorify God, and to Enjoy Him for ever." "I am the way, the truth, and the life" suffuses his thinking and his society.

Edward Taylor, the foremost poet of the Puritans, subscribed to this belief regarding man's chief duty. In a poem of 1685, "Huswifery," Taylor uses the image of a Christian housewife working on a spinning wheel for the slow evolution of the soul. The persona invokes God to make her a "Spinning Wheele compleate" and the "Holy Worde" the raw wool or material from which a

garment may be woven to embellish the cloth of her life with
"Flowers of Paradise." This goal is "Man's chief End":

> Then cloath therewith mine Understanding, Will,
> Affections, Judgment, Conscience, Memory,
> My Words, and Actions, that their shine may fill
> My wayes with glory and thee glorify.
> Then mine apparel shall display before yee
> That I am cloathd in Holy robes for glory.

Taylor conceives of grace suffusing the attributes of man and
transforming them into "Holy robes for glory," into spiritual
"apparel." This belief, essentially the doctrinal belief in conversion,
is presupposed throughout the literature of the Puritans as by
Winthrop: "He shall make us a praise and glory."

In Taylor's poem "Upon a Spider Catching a Fly," grace is
opposed to another major Puritan belief, the innate depravity of
man. The poem begins with the observation of a spider netting and
killing a fly and then proceeds to a meditation on the import of the
incident. "Hell's spider" weaves his web

> To tangle Adams race
> In's stratigems
> To their Destructions, spoil'd, made base
> By venom things
> Damn'd Sins.
>
> But mighty, Gracious Lord
> Communicate
> Thy Grace to breake the Cord, afford
> Us Glorys Gate
> And State.
>
> We'l Nightingaile sing like
> When pearcht on high
> In Glories Cage, thy glory, bright,

> Yea, thankfully,
> For joy.

The "venom things," like the venom of the spider or that of a snake, are the "Damn'd Sins" of man, which debase and limit "Adams race." Yet the speaker conceives of grace breaking "the Cord" and providing man with "Glorys Gate / And State." Indebted to the English metaphysical tradition, Taylor proclaims the elected will rapturously sing like a nightingale "For joy." His certitude is that of another world from ours. Barely fifty years after Taylor's poems were written, in the face of widespread rejection of the harsh, intolerant Puritan order, Jonathan Edwards tried to reaffirm the grace of conversion and the Puritan way of life. Men were beginning to turn from theism to moralism, such as Franklin's. The "something" noticed by Czeslaw Milosz was "gaining ground."

Thomas Paine's *Age of Reason* of 1794 fully vents the loathing many deists of the Enlightenment, especially the *philosophes*, such as Voltaire and Rousseau, had for revealed religion during the eighteenth century. Following the *Zeitgeist*, Paine states, "It is only by the exercise of reason that man can discover God." Unlike the Puritans, he dismisses revelation and intuitive knowledge and applies only the criterion of reason to the three major revealed religions:

> Every national church or religion has established itself by pretending some special mission from God, communicated to certain individuals. The Jews have their Moses; the Christians their Jesus Christ, their apostles and saints; and the Turks their Mahomet; as if the way to God was not open to every man alike. Each of those churches shows certain books, which they call revelation, or the Word of God. The Jews say that their Word of God was given by God to Moses face to face; the Christians say, that their Word of God came by divine inspiration; and the Turks say, that their Word of God (the Koran) was brought by an angel from heaven.

His rationalistic skepticism festers in his choice of the word "pretending," as does his arrogance in the clause "as if the way to God was not open to every man alike." Revelation presupposes that the way to God is indeed not open to every man in the way that it is open to a Manifestation. Rather, man ranks below such a figure as Christ or Moses and is absolutely debarred the access to deity with which they are blessed; hence, the unequivocal dependence on the mediator and on the Word of God, both of which inform man of the laws of his own being and counsel against hubris. Paine, though, denies revelation as mere "hearsay," "second hand" knowledge that is "limited to the first communication" and is worthless beyond it. His confusion of the difference in the station of man and of the prophets reflects the increasing confusion of the human and the divine. Yet given the historical background of religious tumult during the sixteenth and seventeenth centuries, Paine was more than justified in calling for tolerance: "let every man follow, as he has a right to do, the religion and worship he prefers."

As Thomas Jefferson evinces in his *Notes on the State of Virginia* in 1784, such tolerance is infinitely preferable to the senseless religious and social strife of the past. After describing the intolerance of the New England Puritans and the early Anglicans of Virginia, Jefferson asserts,

> It does me no injury for my neighbor to say there are seventy gods, or no god. . . . Reason and free enquiry are the only effectual agents against error. Give a loose to them, they will support the true religion, by bringing every false one to their tribunal.

I doubt any American can read this passage and not feel its justice and sanity. Roger Williams had been one of the earliest settlers upon these shores to begin to realize, as he put it, the necessity of tolerance for "the most paganish, Jewish, Turkish, or Antichristian consciences and worships." Williams' banishment to Rhode Island by the Puritans is one of the earliest lessons in our history of the viciousness of self-righteous religious intolerance and its deleterious effect on the social order. Jefferson's wise affirmation of tolerance is the only reasonable solution to the perennial problems of religious bigotry and the freedom of the individual conscience. Without respect, deep, real, sincere respect, for the religious convictions of others, for the sanctity of the human conscience, for its protection under commonly binding law, America would be reduced to ashes, as devastated as Beirut or Yugoslavia at their worst. We must never doubt for even a single moment that religious freedom is one of the greatest principles and achievements of Western democracy.

Despite his laudable emphasis on tolerance and freedom of conscience, Jefferson's sole standard in *Notes on the State of Virginia*, beyond the utilitarian maintenance of social order, is deistical reason. Such a standard is already far removed from the totality of human experience and marks a further curtailment of the theocentric universe. For Jefferson, the spectator of the natural beauty of Virginia stands in rapture before the creation of the watchmaker God, not before a world Edward Taylor and Jonathan Edwards found imbued with spiritual import, signs, and emblems. Such implicit Enlightenment repudiation of man's intuitive capacities could not but contribute to the rationalistic *Zeitgeist* that eventually gave rise to transcendentalism.

More than any other American writer of the nineteenth century, Ralph Waldo Emerson tried to reassert intuition in the face of reason, science, industrialization, and "corpse cold" Unitarian religion. In *Nature* in 1836 he excoriates the "unrenewed understanding" for regarding only "things" and opposes to this "animal eye" the spiritual "eye of Reason," which, when it opens, estimates the true value of the material world by seeing through it to the "instantaneous in-streaming causing power." Nature becomes not merely a sign or emblem of the spiritual—spirit and nature become one. Such new pantheistic eyes will lead to the realization that the "bruteness of nature is the absence of spirit." Such an "advancing spirit" will suffuse the world with beauty "until evil is no more seen." Whereas Edwards had tried to turn back the historical process and the deists had taken a skeptical attitude toward ultimate questions, Emerson stepped forward as "a newborn bard of the Holy Ghost."

Nowhere is his self-election more evident than in his "Divinity School Address" to seniors at Harvard in 1838. He urges upon them the "eternal revelation in the heart," which Christ, Moses, the prophets, all saints and holy men have experienced and which, he claims, might be theirs. Yet the idea of revelation is so discredited that it appears "as if God were dead." He exhorts them that "the need was never greater of a new revelation than now" since all can readily detect a "universal decay and now almost death of faith in society." The cause of this decline, Emerson thinks, is "The soul is not preached." After remarking on the passing of the Puritan creed, he warns "none arises in its room." On this prospect Emerson laments the modern loss of religion and expresses the desperation he feels for the social dislocations the loss has caused:

> And what greater calamity can fall upon a nation than the loss of worship? Then all things go to decay. Genius leaves the temple to haunt the senate or the market. Literature becomes frivolous. Science is cold. The eye of youth is not lighted by the hope of other worlds, and age is without honor. Society lives to trifles.

He rhetorically asks what can be done and answers that the remedy can be found in the contrast he has repeatedly drawn between the church and the soul: "In the soul then let the redemption be sought." Like Emerson, the divinity students are to "love God without mediator" and "acquaint men at first hand with Deity." Emerson, the "man without a handle," wanders from the biblical deity to a pantheistic oversoul in one sentence to another, while his essentially prophetic ejaculations fail to convey convincingly the "new revelation," its promised eradication of evil, or the remedy for the crisis of which he is so deeply aware. Thrown back on his own devices he became the first American writer "to make his own" by blending together every vague God-mysticism he could find.

Emerson discloses further his realization of how serious the modern crisis is in the concluding paragraph of "The Divinity School Address":

> I look for the hour when that supreme Beauty, which ravished the souls of those Eastern men, and chiefly of those Hebrews, and through their lips spoke oracles to all time, shall speak in the West also. . . . I look for the new Teacher, that shall follow so far those shining laws . . . and shall show that the Ought, that Duty, is one thing with Science, with Beauty, and with Joy.

This passage echoes down the halls of American literature and religious thought, resonating like Virgil's great prophecy in the fourth Eclogue. Despite Emerson's religious excesses, his choice to leave the church was the right one, since his search for the transcendental in the face of the "gathering force" was the motivation of his life, a search he intuited could only find fulfillment in the fullness of time.

Emerson completes his romantic deification of the writer in his essay "The Poet," which he published in 1844. He avers that what he calls "sacred history" "attests that the birth of a poet is the principal event in chronology"; that is to say, all prophets of God are mere poets and "the religions of the world are the ejaculations of a few imaginative men" who reveal "Logos." The poet achieves revelation by "resigning himself to the divine aura which breathes through forms," through nature, and on which he can draw if he but suffers "the ethereal tides to roll and circulate through him." Drawing on the "true nectar," he becomes a "liberating god," as was Swedenborg. Though Emerson concedes he looks in vain for such a poet who is capable of revealing "the new revelation," he insists America "dazzles the imagination" and "will not wait long for metres." The pattern became set for aberrant mystics from Thoreau and Whitman to Hart Crane, Allen Ginsberg, and Robert Bly.

Walt Whitman was one of the first cosmic bards to swallow the glowing coal from Emerson's lectures and essays. Whitman knew, as he writes in the early lines of "Song of Myself," that "creeds and schools" were "in abeyance" and sought in the soul, as Emerson had instructed, the remedy. His *Leaves of Grass* was to have been the new bible, his revelation from "nature without check with original energy." Through him the afflatus would surge and surge, "the current and index" of "All." He immodestly conceives his task as

Lithographing Kronos, Zeus his son, and Hercules his grandson,
Buying drafts of Osiris, Isis, Belus, Brahma, Buddha,
In my portfolio placing Manito loose, Allah on a leaf, the
   crucifix engraved,
With Odin and the hideous-faced Mexitli and every idol and image,
Taking them all for what they are worth and not a cent more,
Admitting they were alive and did the work of their days....
Accepting the rough deific sketches to fill out better in myself.

Like Emerson, drawing from the East and West, Whitman confuses all distinctions, sees them all as merely doing "the work of their days," and steps forward to "fill out better" in himself the "rough deific sketches" that he himself hopes to bestow on "each man and woman." Antinomianism achieves its apex. Whitman launches "all men and women forward" with him "into the Unknown." The "spear of summer grass" becomes the flag of his expansive, "hopeful green" disposition, his yearning for what he calls elsewhere, "Passage, immediate passage" to confront God himself face to face. In 1871 in *Democratic Vistas*, his fullest prose treatment of his tenuous "Idealism" and "Personalism," Whitman announces, in a manner reminiscent of Matthew Arnold, "The priest departs, the divine literatus comes."

Emily Dickinson too drank at the Emersonian fountain, stating once, Emerson "is sweetly commended." She, however, continued under the Puritan worldview in her poems to a much greater extent than either Whitman or Emerson. Many poems evince her fairly orthodox aura of Christian sensibility, as in "1052": "I never spoke with God / Nor visited in Heaven— / Yet certain am I of the spot." Such an aura, though, can be deceptive. As a young woman she could not fit in with the orthodox routine of Mount Holyoke and wrote of her family in 1862 to T. W. Higginson that "They are religious—except me—and address an Eclipse, every morning—whom they call their 'Father.'" Late in her life in about 1882 she could write scathingly in "1545": "The Bible is an antique Volume— / Written by faded Men." The volume is not only antiquated but also further debilitated by the exhausted, male chauvinist hands that wrote it. Thick with sarcasm, the poem hammers at the major subjects of the Bible and opposes the captivating poems of Orpheus, metaphorically her own, to Puritanic condemnation.

The struggle in Dickinson's soul between Puritanism and the emerging modern worldview finds the clearest, fullest expression in "1551":

> Those—dying then,
> Knew where they went—
> They went to God's Right Hand—
> That Hand is amputated now
> And God cannot be found—
>
> The abdication of Belief
> Makes the Behavior small—
> Better an ignis fatuus
> Than no illume at all—

"Those dying" are people living back "then" under the full sway of the Puritan religion. Given Calvin's doctrine of election, they knew with certitude where they were going after their earthly life: "to God's Right Hand." Already here in 1882 Dickinson has sensed or picked up in her reading, perhaps from a secondary source on Darwin, the loss or amputation of religious belief: "God cannot be found." She achieves in this poem her most poignant expression of this loss, a loss she does not accept placidly in the last stanza. The Puritan side of her soul implies that the renouncing of belief leads to immorality and decadence, small brutish behavior unworthy of human beings. Yet she cannot revert to the "Eclipse" and "antique

Volume." She has already moved too far toward the modern era for that to happen. In these closing lines of her career, torn within, she turns to her usual sweet substitute of Emersonian transcendentalism. The pathos of this turn reveals itself in the mind of this brilliant woman through her choice of words: "ignis fatuus." She understood what she was doing and that for her there was no other choice.

In 1907 in *The Education of Henry Adams*, Adams chronicles the further demise of the old New England morality from his great-grandfather, President John Adams, who loathed Emerson, to President Grant and on to the twentieth century: the "disappearance of religion puzzle[s] him most." Everywhere Adams sees a weakening of the old moral bonds of the world and an increasing emphasis on material civilization and success. For him the new dynamos of the Paris Exposition of 1900 symbolize the material energy or force of the modern world: "As he grew accustomed to the great gallery of machines, he began to feel the forty-foot dynamos as a moral force, much as the early Christians felt the Cross. . . . Before the end, one began to pray to it." Adams, an early modern, becomes a worshiper of the very entropy and chaos he perceives but cannot fathom: "Nihilism has no bottom." As he observes in his reflections on the ganoid fish,

> Every one had probably lived and died in the illusion of Truths which did not amuse him, and which had never changed. Henry Adams was the first in an infinite series to discover and admit to himself that he really did not care whether truth was, or was not, true.

This nihilism inevitably leads Adams to his dynamic theory of history, to his worship of change, multiplicity, and "the stupendous acceleration after 1800." Subsequent literature confirms he was one of the first "in an infinite series" to peer into the bottomless depths of the void. He recognizes what Emerson and Whitman fail to perceive: If man becomes his own prophet or god, he is left in a relative universe of illimitable illusion with no objective basis by which to gauge truth. Under such conditions the possibility of any divinity becomes the first belief to be repudiated, which is what Nietzsche learnt from Emerson. Yet even Adam's method for establishing acceleration and entropy remains bound to an objective standard—the Virgin of Chartres Cathedral, which represents for him the force of the love of God as expressed through unity. By taking the thirteenth century "as the unit from which he might measure motion down to his own time," he arrives at the perception of twentieth century multiplicity: "Except as reflected in himself, man has no reason for assuming unity in the universe, or an ultimate substance, or a prime-motor." Adams is one of the first writers to demonstrate that, in the modern world unity can be found only in the study of one's own mind.

It is in the modern prison of the mind that T. S. Eliot confronts the wasteland. As he quotes F. H. Bradley in his notes to *The Waste Land*, "The whole world for each is peculiar and private to that soul." Shorn of all tradition, unity, and faith, the isolated spectator of Eliot's poem wanders through the flow of his consciousness from one discrete incident to another, perceiving past, present, and future in a welter of simultaneous chaos. Instead of "the glory of the Lord" that appeared to Ezekiel, Eliot's "Son of man" knows "only / A heap of broken images" that are desiccated and lifeless, while a "famous clairvoyante" substitutes for the veracity of revealed religion: "I do not find The Hanged Man." In place of Civitas Dei looms the "Unreal City," the residence of modern man devoid of all spirituality. In the section "What the Thunder Said," Eliot evokes Christ's agony in the garden of Gethsemane, his crucifixion, and his death in the modern world: "He who was living is now dead" and "We who were living are now dying." Eliot substantiates this loss throughout the poem, as in the debased, bestial relations of the lovers in "A Game of Chess" and "The Fire Sermon." Despite Eliot's hint of resurrection in the passage on Christ's appearance to the disciples on the road to Emmaus, which begins with the line "Who is the third who walks always beside you," the burden of the poem is the horror that he does "not find The Hanged Man." Eliot obscures this fact by using the Indian *Upanishads* as a substitute, yet his spectator is ultimately left "in his prison / thinking of the key": "aethereal rumours" that might "revive" him, though only "for a moment," before leaving him alone on the shore with the fragments of his ruins, and with the fragments of the modern world. As an old man Eliot repudiated and downplayed this vision, but his overly intellectualized *Four Quartets* nevertheless fail as poetry, which by definition must contain one's deepest experience of life in order for the emotions to be engaged as well as the intellect. Far from the *Four Quartets* standing as a monument to the reality of man's spiritual nature, they stand as ironic witness to its loss.

Whereas Eliot laments the loss that marks the modern world, Wallace Stevens, closer to the sensibility of Henry Adams, defines the change, as many people have, as not a loss but an advance: "If one no longer believes in God (as truth), it is not possible merely to disbelieve; it becomes necessary to believe in something else": "The poem of the mind in the act of finding / What will suffice," in the act of consciously creating an ersatz, a "supreme fiction." In "Sunday Morning" Stevens discovers "What will suffice" for him throughout the rest of his career—a hedonistic, Sybaritic wallowing in sensation. The persona dreamily lingers in her dressing gown "in a sunny chair":

> Shall she not find in comforts of the sun,
> In pungent fruit and bright, green wings, or else
> In any balm or beauty of the earth,
> Things to be cherished like the thought of heaven?
> Divinity must live within herself.

By finding comfort in the things of the earth, in its sensual abundance, she suggests the "something else" to which she has turned. Her subjective sensations are equated with divinity in much the way antinomians once took the promptings of their own impulses for the voice of deity. Unlike the Puritans, her "chief End" is not "the thought of heaven" but her own individualistic "moods" and "passions," "all pleasures and all pains" that are solipsistically "within herself": "These are the measures destined for her soul."

When man and the world become the measure of all things, earth is increasingly construed as the only paradise and nothing exists beyond it. "Death," she says, "is the mother of beauty," and not the mother of meditation on the spiritual ground of Being. Humankind find solace in the sensuality of nature as do the "maidens" and the "ring of men" who "chant in orgy." She eventually hears on the luxuriant water of the day,

> A voice that cries, "The tomb in Palestine
> Is not the porch of spirits lingering.
> It is the grave of Jesus, where he lay."

Christ, which all nature shouts for the deaf to hear, is nothing but a mere man consigned to an earthy grave. Humankind live "in an old chaos of the sun," of a wholly physical existence that is "unsponsored" by any god. Stevens drives home this point in the closing lines of the poem by describing "casual" or chance "flocks of pigeons," not doves, that make "Ambiguous undulations as they sink" down to the darkness of the earth, where the woman wallows in the Sunday morning sun.

Ernest Hemingway boasted of his living in the darkness of the earth, a darkness of which he knew nothing else. In his short story "A Clean, Well-Lighted Place," published in 1933 in *Winner Take Nothing*, Hemingway distills, from one of his own potable bottles of booze as it were, the quintessence of modern nihilism. Set in a bar in Spain, the story tells of an old man and two waiters lost in the abyss of modernity. The old man is sunk in despair, and neither waiter lives for anything of substance though only the older one realizes it, which he manifests while reflecting on the meaning of life to himself:

> It was all a nothing and a man was nothing too. It was only that
> and light was all it needed and a certain cleanness and order.
> Some lived in it and never felt it but he knew it all was nada y
> pues nada y nada y pues nada. Our nada who art in nada, nada
> be thy name thy kingdom nada thy will be nada in nada as it is

in nada. Give us this nada our daily nada and nada us our nada
as we nada our nadas and nada us not into nada but deliver us
from nada; pues nada. Hail nothing full of nothing, nothing is
with thee.

Here Hemingway subverts the Lord's Prayer into a paean to the lord
of our times in order to give the true meaning of the modern
meaninglessness of life its clearest, most succinct expression. As
Saul Bellow said about this story in his Jefferson lecture, "nihilism
acknowledges the victory of the bourgeois outlook." This nihilism
pervades Hemingway's writing from *The Sun Also Rises* and *A
Farewell to Arms* to *The Old Man and the Sea*. His ability to give
this nihilistic vision contemporary expression partly explains the
immense resonance of his work with Americans in all walks of life.
Whether the masses consciously, rationally understand the
philosophical implications of Hemingway's writing or not, they, as
well as intellectuals who do, sense the faithfulness of this hymn to
modern experience.

   After an initial phase of Catholicism, Robert Lowell increasingly
awoke to the modern world. Almost all of Robert Lowell's
Collected Prose, published in 1987, was written after the
mid-fifties. The few exceptions, especially a 1943 review of T. S.
Eliot's *Four Quartets* and a 1944 essay on Gerard Manley Hopkins,
demonstrate Lowell's early fervent Catholicism, which undergirds
his first book of poems, *Land of Unlikeness*. In other reviews during
the late forties and early fifties, Lowell concentrates on minor poets
and critics associated with or influenced by the formalistic New
Criticism. His earlier religious affirmation is conspicuously absent.
By 1959 when he publishes *Life Studies*, his most widely acclaimed
book, Lowell's work has already taken on, to recall the epigraph of
his first book, "a likeness which is no longer like its original . . . no
longer like itself." As he writes in the poem "Beyond the Alps," he
has "left the City of God" and has planted his feet on what passed
with him for "terra firma."

   Like most of the minor poets of the last forty-five years, Lowell
turned to the self as substitute for religious belief. In *Life Studies* he

ransacked his personal life and family for what thin sustenance he could extract, setting, thereby, an example that Anne Sexton, Sylvia Plath, and others followed to their detriment. The novelty of his method has long seduced many into overrating the book. By 1967 Lowell could write in his loose re-creation of *Prometheus Bound* by Aeschylus, "I have little faith now, but I still look for truth, some crumbling momentary foothold." He concedes in 1969 in *Notebook* that he has become a "poet without direction." His hero becomes the "nihilist" who "has to live in the world as is." The quality of his poems continues to decline until, in his last book, *Day by Day*, one reads them, if at all, largely out of a tepid sense of duty. Lowell knew, as he remarks in one of two interviews reprinted with his prose, "we've gotten into a sort of Alexandrian age."

Like Stevens and Hemingway, Lowell, in a poem of 1967, "Waking Early Sunday Morning," suggests the demise of revealed religion. The poem's opening stanza recounts a naturalistic dream of a salmon breaking loose from the earth and climbing a ladder or run "to clear the top on the last try / alive enough to spawn and die." Yet the persona curtails the association of human aspiration and backs off to wake "before the day's begun." "Creatures of the night," of his archetypal dreams, grind on while the sun of the unconscious mind is bitten back by the dawn of the workaday world, leaving the "fireless mind, running downhill," with "business as usual in eclipse." In what is perhaps an echo of Emily Dickinson's lines "Better an ignis fatuous / Than no illume at all," the persona reflects "Better dressed and stacking birch, / or lost with the Faithful at Church," singing "stiff quatrains" that speak of peace but "preach despair." This route of aspiration is also rejected with an emphatic "No" in favor of "old clothes" and rummaging in the unconscious, pre-Socratic "woodshed for / its dregs and dreck."

There the persona discovers primitive debris "banished from the Temple," "damned by Paul's precept and example," and "banned in Israel." In one of Lowell's most direct meditations on the sweeping aside of the Judeo-Christian tradition, he asks,

When will we see Him face to face?
Each day, He shines through darker glass.
In this small town where everything
is known, I see His vanishing
emblems, His white spire and flag-
pole sticking out above the fog,
like old white china doorknobs, sad,
slight, useless things to calm the mad.

The darkening of the Pauline glass goes unperceived by many of the "Faithful at Church" in the "small town" where everything else is, as one might predict, "known." "His vanishing / emblems" protrude above the obscuring "fog" like knobs on doors that offer no exit, partly because the relationship to God is misconstrued as one in which man himself should "see Him face to face." All emblems have become "useless things to calm the mad," such as Lowell himself. Through a long historical process, the impulse of the romantics for "immediate passage" proves to lead ultimately to the asylum, to the point where the individual, as Lowell writes in "Stars," "only has to care about himself."

For Lowell mere power-politics survive into the present, where there are no longer "weekends for the gods." War continues as it has for thousands of years with "no advance":

Only man thinning out his kind
sounds through the Sabbath noon, the blind
swipe of the pruner and his knife
busy about the tree of life . . .

Lowell asserts the "blind" brutality of "small war on the heels of small war" as the only constant in history. All joy and sweetness are gone from the planet earth, which orbits like a ghost "forever lost / in our monotonous sublime." The kingdom of ennui, nihilism, and solipsism replaces the kingdom of God. Lowell awakes to what he writes in "Since 1939," in lines that sum up his work and the entire modern and postmodern periods: "If we see a light at the end of the tunnel, / it's the light of an on-coming train." He tells us, in "Night in Maine," "Fire once gone, / We're done for."

How long are we to ignore the cause of the "gathering force," the origin of the "on-coming train"? Regardless of how frivolous, aberrant, and mad some poets have been during the postmodern period, I hold it must be acknowledged that they accurately reflect the decline of Western culture, the decline of the unique value of the human being, for which the less thoughtful, including many literary critics, are partly responsible. The incontrovertible history of our culture and our literature has been the waning of belief in God and in revelation and the substituting of ever-increasing forms of secular understanding based on the isolated, hedonistic, and, often today, therapeutic self. Far from demonstrating the primordial fantasy of God's existence, this tempest, this vast historical process declares, as resoundingly as the histories of the Old Testament, man's utter dependence on God—the transcendent Essence all the great religions have recognized. When man turns to his own devices, the inevitable outcome is the degrading of both the public and private domains. God guides humankind through revelation and through the ineffable mystic love that binds man to his creator. It is as Pascal writes, "We come to know truth not only by reason, but still more so through our hearts." But we cannot return, not that any intelligent person would think it desirable to return, to the world of the Puritans or the Catholicism of the thirteenth century, and all human attempts to restore the Judeo-Christian tradition will indubitably continue to fail. That world is gone forever, and we cannot go backwards. We stand in need of revelation, and it cannot come from ourselves.

Postmodern American Poets:
Debauchees of Dew

The Alexandrian poets, especially Callimachus and Apollonius, brought about a revolution in classical poetry. For the first time in Western history poets wrote almost exclusively for a coterie. The ancient public epic and tragedy disappeared; the expression of the laws, customs, and values of the polis disappeared; the Hellenistic bridge between two worlds was under construction. But the concomitant social upheavals were not reflected in the work of the poets who frequented Alexandria and its colossal library. Instead, poetry became the pastime and the echo of an entirely personal imagination—no longer was it a voice for those who otherwise had no voice—poets were interested only in themselves. The quotidian, the banal, whatever was personal in origin and vacuous or absurd in conception and intent, consumed their time. Unsurprisingly, given the loss of respectable content, the Alexandrians and their successors the Neoterics were unparalleled technicians, who distinguished themselves by vying with one another in the creation of new meters, forms, rhythms and other baubles, which not until Virgil were put to effective use. In short, their lack of attention to what was happening outside themselves deprived their poetry of the most profound and human themes. American poetry since 1950 supplies a striking analogue to the Alexandrians and Neoterics.

Yet even the Alexandrian paradigm fails to offer a perspective capacious enough for comprehending some contemporary American poetry. What must be taken into consideration is that these poets are working within a tradition that can be traced back to our Puritan founders and, a little more recently, to Emerson, Emily Dickinson, as well as other transcendentalists. Perry Miller identifies accurately the impulse that animated the transcendentalists who left the Puritan fold:

These New Englanders . . . turned aside from the doctrines of sin and predestination, and thereupon sought with renewed fervor for the accents of the Holy Ghost in their own hearts and in woods and mountains. But now that the restraining hand of

theology was withdrawn, there was nothing to prevent them ...
from identifying their intuitions with the voice of God, or from
fusing God and nature into one substance of the transcendental
imagination. Mystics were no longer inhibited by dogma. They
were free to carry on the ancient New England propensity for
reeling and staggering with new opinions. They could give
themselves over, unrestrainedly, to becoming transparent
eyeballs and debauchees of dew.

Although, strictly speaking, contemporary poets are not
transcendentalists, the form of their thinking is often the same. The
ambrosia, however, may be phenomenology, blends of arcane
disciplines, religions that are largely dead in the lands of their birth,
but the rhetoric of salvation remains the same: one sudden draught
from the blessed fountain will work a metamorphosis in the very
quintessential foundation of existence. New opinions abound.
Antinomian romanticism still rules the day.

And yet the net must be thrown even wider in order to consider a
fundamental shift in poetic sensibility that assured contemporary
poets would one day raise their minor voices in antiphony to the self:
the loss of mimesis—or the beginnings of its loss in the nineteenth
century—a loss which can be perceived in the work of Emerson and
his predecessors and contemporaries on both sides of the Atlantic.
What came to replace mimesis was the most distinguishing feature
of the romantics: their expressive theory of poetry. They believed a
poem was the internal made external, the "spontaneous overflow of
powerful feelings." This shifted attention from objective
phenomenon and the influence poetry had on the audience to the
personality of the poet, to his intense ability to express himself
genuinely, and to his creative and much-worshiped imagination.

The result of this shift was to cut poetry off from any claim to
authority or truth. Previously, poets had always had the bedrock of
mimesis to rely on: the incontrovertible signified that their mimetic
signifiers referred to. The reader also had recourse to tradition and
verifiable experience. But Alexandrianism returned. Poetry could no
longer battle Medusa. It could only cower in the corner and pretend

life would magically get better, deride what it did not understand, or loathe the bourgeoisie. Poets themselves abetted this change by turning on conceptual, rational modes of cognition, by denying the ability of poetry to have an impact on other men, and by withdrawing into a protective cork-lined sensibility that they held to be, or that was in effect, beyond logical understanding and beyond social commitments and responsibilities. M. H. Abrams comments on the ultimate result this change had on modern poetry:

> The purpose of producing effects upon other men, which for centuries had been the defining character of the art of poetry, now serves precisely the opposite function: it disqualifies a poem by proving it to be rhetoric instead.

The romantics, New Criticism, Eliot, Auden, most contemporary poetry and criticism, share, to one degree or another, this redefinition of the art of poetry, as if mimesis were dead and done with.

Although much of the foregoing discussion is applicable to most postmodern poets on both sides of the Atlantic, a few American poets who gather around what they are fond of calling the "buffalo wallow," or a variant of it, will be concentrated on here. Galway Kinnell is one of these poets and one of the heirs and purveyors of the aforementioned redefinition of poetry. Like many contemporary poets, Kinnell simplifies the cause and effect relationship between the conscious, rational mind and the historical evils and failures of Western civilization. According to his essay "Poetry, Personality, and Death," the rational mind has lost touch with the "life of the planet" and "thwarts our deepest desire, which is to be one with all creation." Eventually he writes, "We now know that science is the trouble." To him the conclusion is clear: the rational mind and its offspring *scientia* must go. It has apparently never occurred to Kinnell that the trouble is not *scientia per se* but what particular men have chosen to do with systematic knowledge at particular junctures in time. His work also reveals very little awareness of anything outside the self—little awareness of the benefits that the objective mind has brought about—instead, we are to be "reborn more giving, more alive, more open," and yes, "more related to natural life." Like the work of the transcendentalists, Kinnell's is so amorphous I never really know precisely what he is suggesting, though promises of transformation are abundant.

An early poem by Kinnell (written before 1954) that uses the convention of a journey in quest of an epiphanic, transformative union with the unconscious is "In the Glade at Dusk." The persona travels or returns to a glade obediently, as if called:

> The glade catches fire, and where
> The birds build nests they brood at evening
> On burning limbs. Spirit of the wood, dream
> Of all who have ever answered in the glade at dusk—
> And grass, grass, blossom through my feet in flames.

Kinnell's voyaging or questing self typically knows no social connection or responsibility. His only interest is his journey. Abruptly, suddenly, "The glade catches fire," but an insubstantial fire that is reminiscent of alchemical fire imagery and Yeatsian theosophy, and then an apostrophe to the "Spirit of the wood"—primordial, primitive Pan. All this sets the scene for the epiphany of the final line, but it becomes no more historically defined than Emerson's moment of satori on the Boston Common or Dickinson's draught of "liquor never brewed."

James Wright's poem "A Blessing" has much in common with Kinnell's poem. Wright's persona too journeys into the "life of the planet," into nature as embodied by two Indian ponies. The blatant erotic description of these ponies indicates their relation to the same buffalo wallow, the same primitive and unconscious aquifer that Kinnell praises when he invokes "primal," "cosmic sexuality." After caressing one of the ponies, the persona says,

Suddenly I realize
That if I stepped out of my body I would break
Into blossom.

The blessing of "The Blessing" comes from a peculiar and intuitive
source that "Suddenly," inexplicably, makes the axis of vision
coincident with the axis of things. The dichotomy between the body
and self, the surrealistic, irrational image of breaking into blossom
are almost obscured by the portentousness with which Wright
suffuses this poem. Auden's lines come to mind: "Vague idealistic
art / That coddles the uneasy heart."

In a poem that discloses Robert Bly's affinity with Kinnell and
Wright, Bly writes about our "Evolution from the Fish," the second
and last stanza of which is quoted in its entirety:

What a joy to smell the flesh of a new child!
Like new grass! And this long man with the student girl,
Coffee cups, her pale waist, the spirit moving around them,
Moves, dragging a great tail into the darkness.
In the dark we blaze up, drawing pictures
Of spiny fish, we throw off the white stones!
Serpents rise from the ocean floor with spiral motions,
A man goes inside a jewel, and sleeps. Do
Not hold my hands down! Let me raise them!
A fire is passing up through the soles of my feet!

As the first unquoted stanza of this poem tells us, the persona is one
who "is moving toward his own life," a solipsistic quester, a
primitive swatch of "mammoth fur" that "moves toward the
animal"; the last stanza concerns itself primarily with epiphany, with
union with the "life of nature." Yet the phoniness of the epiphany
barely conceals itself behind the inept exclamation marks. The
convention, however, holds: "In the dark we blaze up," "throw off
the white stones," which are no longer black, due to, it would seem,
some type of illuminating experience, and "a man" (anybody,
everyone) "goes into a jewel, and sleeps"; that is, enters or returns

to the cave of the mysterious unconscious, where he raises his hands in thankful prayer for the blessing of encountering the irrational "life of nature" that is passing up, absurdly, through "the soles of his feet." What we have here is so clearly a stock convention that I would think any self-respecting contemporary poet would be embarrassed to use it, and embarrassed to advance such a trivial conception of evolution as our history. It is the same vague and simplistic abuse and ravaging of the past that leads Bly to commit the banalities of his so-called men's movement.

But one poet has found a way to out-Bly Bly; at least, that is what Robert Hass seems to be trying to do with his own fishy poem "San Pedro Road." Hass opens the poem with a description of fishing at the mouth of a creek that empties into a "leaden bay":

> A carcass washes by, white meat,
> spidery translucent bones and I think I understand,
> finally dumb animal I understand, kick off boots,
>   pants, socks,
> and swim,
>   thrashing dull water to a golden brown,
> terrorizing the depths with my white belly, my
>   enormous length,
> done with casting, reeling in slowly, casting . . .

The persona seeks here what he earlier in the poem calls the "great white bass," not quite a stone (Hass does get in "bones") but still representative of primordial forbears in "muddy bottoms." And though the poetic diction has changed, the rhetoric remains the same: he advances an irrational, epiphanic experience. Like Wright's persona, Hass's takes action: he strips off the habiliments of rational civilization, kicks aside all social ties and obligations, and joins the fish in the irrational "depths" of the mind.

W. S. Merwin also uses the same convention of a journey into the unconscious and is well known for the predictability with which it appears in his poetry. Most of his customary techniques can be found in the poem "Bread," which plays on the old saying about the bread of life. Here, though, the bread of life is a slice of the irrational forces that Merwin worships as primitive peoples worship the moon:

> Each face in the street is a slice of bread
> wandering on
>
> searching . . .
>
> have they forgotten the pale caves . . .
> have they forgotten the ragged tunnels
> they dreamed of following in out of the light . . .
>
> to be sustained by its dark breath
> and emerge
>
> to find themselves alone
> before a wheat field
> raising its radiance to the moon

"Each face" keeps dreaming of following the "ragged," abandoned tunnels "in out of the light," while the unconscious impulses of humankind persist in knocking at the doors of consciousness, inviting fallen rational man to enter and be redeemed, "be sustained by its dark breath." Once this happens they "emerge" to find themselves, true to the self-centeredness of the tradition, "alone" before a field that raises its radiance to the moon. Although the journey has been from light to dark to light, the light of the moon is surrounded by darkness and is merely another example of the convention: the bread of life (an entire field of the raw stuff) is the darkness of the bestial mind. This is the radiance these misguided and foolish poets advance for our salvation.

What these poets fail to take into account can be found in these excerpts from *Genocide* and *The Fate of the Earth*:

The burning had reached a pitch that night. Every chimney was disgorging flames. Smoke burst from the holes and ditches, swirling, swaying and coiling above our heads. Sparks and cinders blinded us. Through the screened fence of the second crematory we could see figures with pitchforks moving against the background of flames. They were men from the special squad turning the corpses in the pits and pouring a special liquid so that they would burn better. A rancid smell of scorched flesh choked us. Big trucks passed us trailing a smell of corpses.

They held their arms bent forward . . . and their skin—not only on their hands but on their faces and bodies, too—hung down. If there had been only one or two such people . . . perhaps I would not have had such a strong impression. But wherever I walked, I met these people. . . . Many of them died along the road. I can still picture them in my mind—like walking ghosts. They didn't look like people of this world.

Such are the fruits of the unconscious mind when it goes uncontrolled by rational, civilized restraints. That these poets play only into the hands of the general mindlessness instead of struggling to come to grips with it and to challenge it with a world aesthetic economy is an outrageous abdication of moral and social responsibility.

Those poets who feel the burden of complicity upon their backs will not withdraw into a dreamlike phantasmagoria of the unconscious self; they will confront the gruesome realities of human nature that have manifested themselves more horrifyingly during the last hundred years than at any time in the past and will halt the long drift from a sober but healthy mimesis to a decadent and solipsistic literature that impresses one only by the appalling spectacle of its own lamentable degeneracy. To understand what a world aesthetic economy would entail, we must again commit literary heresy and look outside the self at the real world that Jonathan Schell describes in his *Fate of the Earth*:

National sovereignty lies at the very core of the political issues that the peril of extinction forces upon us. Sovereignty is the "reality" that the "realists" counsel us to accept as inevitable, referring to any alternative as "unrealistic" or "utopian." If the argument about nuclear weapons is to be conducted in good faith, then just as those who favor the deterrence policy . . . must in all honesty admit that their scheme contemplates the extinction of man in the name of protecting national sovereignty, so must those who favor complete nuclear and conventional disarmament . . . admit that their recommendation is inconsistent with national sovereignty; to pretend otherwise would be to evade the political question that is central to the nuclear predicament. The terms of the deal that the world has now struck with itself must be made clear. . . . Our choice so far has been to preserve that political organization of human life at the cost of risking all human life. We are told that "realism" compels us to preserve the system of sovereignty. But that political realism . . . is nihilism in every conceivable sense of that word. We are told that it is human fate . . . that, in obedience, perhaps, to some "territorial imperative" . . . we must preserve sovereignty and always settle our differences with violence. If this is our fate, then it is our fate to die. But must we embrace nihilism? Must we die . . . I do not think so. . . Our present system and the institutions that make it up are the debris of history. They have become inimical to life, and must be swept away.

A world aesthetic economy would take into account the teleology of human history that is now perceivable. Where once only disorder and confusion could be discerned, a goal can now be seen. And the scientific development over the past one hundred years can at last be seen as merely the prerequisite to the creation of a global infrastructure. From the earliest scattered bands of Neanderthals, the first clans, tribes, and incipient cities, from the first tentative steps toward empire and nationhood, humankind has steadily been progressing toward the highest possible level of social organization attainable on this planet: a Trust of sovereign and independent nation-states that recognizes at last that the well-being of each nation-member can be obtained only through mutual allegiance to one supreme international governing federation. Even as the forces of lethargy and nationalistic provincialism struggle to prevent it from occurring, destiny impels humankind to rise to a higher level of consciousness and unity.

Today no poet can conceive of a higher goal than the recognition and further establishment of what is already an operational fact: the unity of all peoples and nations. To the artist these still only dimly acknowledged realities offer themselves as grist for his mill only if he also takes account of the unprecedented horror we have become: We ourselves are hell. "I look around me, and, lo! on every visage a Black Veil!" "I still see sin, new sin, mixing itself with the best of that I do." "'Is there but one spider in all this spacious room?' then the water stood in Christiana's eyes, for she was a woman quick of apprehension; and she said, 'Yes, Lord, there is more here than one. Yea, and spiders whose venom is far more destructive. . . .'" "Human kind can not bear very much reality." All this Shakespeare knew:

> Out, vile jelly!

> O damn'd Iago! O inhuman dog!

> One may smile, and smile, and be a villain.

> Comfort's in heaven, and we are on the earth,
> Where nothing lives but crosses, cares, and grief.

This is that Shakespearean axis, that Hawthornean blackness that Melville knew and stalked and probed—"Evil is the nature of mankind"—that which "no deeply thinking mind is always and wholly free." But what we get in most postmodern poets is sentimental banalizing of human nature. They cleave, as simplistically as Bly often does, humanity into the rich, the executives, the "darkening armies" and scientists versus the innocent, the poor, the poet, the male lovers of nature and all those who are incapable of confronting harsh realities; and they extricate all from the guilt that drips from their and our hands like the blood and gore that tainted the streets of Hiroshima, Cambodia, Vietnam. These are the fruits of nationalism, our nationalism, all nationalism. For if today poets do not call for international order, we stand tacitly opposed to thousands of years of human history and, all the more egregiously, opposed to hundreds of thousands of years of history that might yet be.

On the act of international injustice mimesis makes its stand. And out of the act of international injustice, incontestable universal human values return. As a young poet studying with Robert Hayden, I know he perceived these truths and the direction in which we are inevitably heading. He once explicitly indicated so in an interview:

> History or events, seem to be pushing us toward internationalism, a world view. The Bahai Teachings assure us that America will be an instrument for peace in the future. I think that maybe America is being prepared for that as a result of having all the races, cultures, and nationalities of the world in one way or another in the country.

Here is a vision that in its sane perception of social realities and possibilities stands in stark contrast to the return-to-the-life-of-nature crowd, to an America reveling in "primal," "cosmic sexuality," to the unconscious and anarchic passions that seek always to destroy the civilizing forces of our country. Our duty is still to be as a city upon a hilltop. "Where there is no vision, the people perish."

In the closing pages of *Mimesis*, Erich Auerbach also perceived the direction in which we are moving:

> We can not but see to what an extent—below the surface conflicts—the differences between men's ways of life and forms of thought have already lessened. The strata of societies and

their different ways of life have become inextricably mingled. There are no longer even exotic peoples. A century ago (in Mérimée for example), Corsicans or Spaniards were still exotic; today the term would be quite unsuitable for Pearl Buck's Chinese peasants. Beneath the conflicts, and also through them, an economic and cultural leveling process is taking place. It is still a long way to a common life of mankind on earth, but the goal begins to be visible.

But those poets and critics who are too purblind to see the goal would have us expend our energies on lesser matters, would lead us down irrational paths that assure disaster by lulling us into a false sense of security and by freeing us of the share of guilt and complicity that is ours. Or they would try to dissuade us from confronting the social complexities and responsibilities of our age by foisting an exhausted literary doctrine on us; a doctrine that claims, as Auden wrote, "Poetry makes nothing happen"; a doctrine canonized variously in the effete criticism of structuralism, deconstruction, reader-response, the new historicism, and so on ad nauseam—so much of which is characterized by what Andrei Sakharov calls in *My Country and the World*, the "leftist-liberal faddishness" of the intelligentsia of the West.

Now when a quantum leap is required in cognitive and emotional development, art, too, as always, will be at the forefront of such change. It is worth recalling that Yeats once criticized Shelley for his failure to conceive of the world as a continual conflict, for his lack of a Theory of Evil. And it is precisely this failure that deprives many postmodern poets of any lasting interest. In following their postmodern equivalent of the "ancient New England propensity" for magical transformation, amelioration, and conversion, they trivialize the perdurable antinomies of human nature. Postmodern poets have repeated the romantic experience.

Poets since 1950 (including many poets not mentioned here) have tended to address an ever more specialized and personal audience, if not an academic or MFA coterie. Perhaps overwhelmed by the ponderous burden of guilt and horror that the modern world has proven so capable of producing, most poets have largely turned away from their society and have written, for themselves and a few epigones, poetry permeated with mystification and couched in language calculated to obfuscate the fatuity of their vision. And, while they developed in some cases into masters of the technicalities of new forms, meters, and rhythms to accomplish their effects, they drifted further and further away from any respectable, intellectual and emotional, conceptual content. At the same time these poets manifested a concern with the self that obscured, paradoxically, their essential indifference to social stability, which is achievable only through collective participation and cooperation in the continuing struggle for peace and justice. In short, they did what Americans have too often done when cut off from any respectable ground of value: they became antinomians, transparent eyeballs, devotees of some vast and vague abyss, seeking a liquor that was never brewed.

Mimesis

We are on the way toward the unification of our planet.
Czeslaw Milosz

During the last two hundred years poets have steadily been turning away from mimesis and have increasingly been substituting subjective modes of understanding. This devolution has been widely discussed and has often been held to have begun with the romantics, who turned away, in a sense, from nature and substituted an expressive, prophetic conception of poetry that idolized the poet and his imagination. Modernist poets also chose to turn away from nature by emphasizing the synchronicity of the present and the past and the resulting autonomous artifact. Postmodern poets, lost in a cesspool of anomie, have turned, almost without exception, to the minutiae of daily life and of the self, and they have often sought refuge in the banal, irrational, evanescent emotions of the unconscious mind. Today many younger poets are even clinging more tenaciously and thoughtlessly to the surface of the prosaic self. This turning away from the profundity of the objective world occurs, paradoxically, during a century when the pressure of international tragedy has made itself felt unprecedentedly on the consciousness of all the diverse peoples of the world. It is as if, because poets have failed to make any sense of the external world, they have despaired of any rational, conceptual understanding and have been retreating further and further into the triviality of the quotidian and of themselves. But the pressure refuses to lessen. It makes itself known most emphatically in the egregious, heinous acts of international injustice and terrorism that mark our times. This pressure finds succinct formulation in the following excerpt from Wyndham Lewis's *America and the Cosmic Man*: "speculations about the future of the world at large are imposed on one by the atomic developments which are responsible for a situation without precedent in human life." I believe the hegemony of subjectivity must give way to the overwhelming objectivity of international tragedy, terrorism, and the continuing thermonuclear peril, which wrench us from our dreams and demand mimetic contemplation.

Subjectivity takes as its standard of understanding and knowledge the feelings and arbitrary inclinations of the subject—the self becomes the measure of all things, instead of the totality of experience. This forcing of the subject into the center precludes a mimetic confrontation with the object and thereby isolates the subject from its complement, which is existent independent of thought. The former is the bastion of solipsism, the latter the citadel of mimesis, for the object is tantamount to that which is universally valid, whereas the subject, in isolation, is prone to unmitigated myths and absurdities. Daniel Bell corroborates much of this evaluation in *The Cultural Contradictions of Capitalism* and identifies further the subjective malaise that afflicts modern art and literature:

Modernism is the disruption of mimesis. It denies the primacy of an outside reality, as given. It seeks either to rearrange that reality, or to retreat to the self's interior, to private experience as the source of its concerns and aesthetic preoccupations. The origins of this change lie in philosophy, primarily in Descartes and in the codifications of the new principles by Kant. There is an emphasis on the self as the touchstone of understanding and on the activity of the knower rather than the character of the object as the source of knowledge. . . .

Instead of the "activity theory of knowledge," of "making and doing," of function, process, discourse, and play, the overwhelming object of the tragedies of this century and the still possible "outside reality" of the charred remains of millions demand referential, mimetic contemplation, which is not a crude journalistic copying of reality, but a selective interpretation, a search for meaning and understanding.

Such a shift from the subject to the object is based on more than impulse—it is based on the already-spilled blood of millions. For the modern era has largely been a subjective one as the mass emotionalism of fascism, communism, and other forms of irrationality demonstrate. Goethe was well aware of the historical perniciousness of subjectivity, as he indicates in this passage from Eckermann:

> All eras in a stage of decline and dissolution are subjective; on the other hand, all progressive eras have an objective tendency. Our present time is retrograde, for it is subjective: we see this not merely in poetry, but also in painting, and much besides. Every healthy effort, on the contrary, is directed from the inward to the outward world; as you see in all great eras, which were really in a state of progression and all of an objective nature.

We must move "from the inward to the outward world," move out of our ethnocentricism. The acts of the last hundred years and the objective, historical threat of nuclear weapons necessitate a stark realism that acknowledges the pressure of both the blast wave that constitutes half the energy released in a thermonuclear explosion and the thermal wave that unleashes a third of the energy and vaporizes everything within its radius. Further, it acknowledges the local and global fallout that could destroy millions of people through a variety of radiation sicknesses, such as the crippling of the central nervous system, the gastrointestinal tract, and hematopoiesis. It is upon such Aristotelian objects of contemplation, on such a real existent, on such actions of men, that the subject must find the source of human knowledge, for there are in such objects universal concepts—a conceptualized essence in the existent itself. This shift would constitute, in Goethe's words, a "healthy effort."

Given the presence of such pressures, even Jacques Derrida, legerdemain not discounted, acknowledged the referential power of mimesis, as is evidenced in an issue of *Diacritics* on nuclear criticism:

> If we are bound and determined to speak in terms of reference, nuclear war is the only possible referent of any discourse and any experience that would share their condition with that of literature. If, according to a structuring hypothesis, a fantasy or

phantasm, nuclear war is equivalent to the total destruction of the archive, if not of the human habitat, it becomes the absolute referent, the horizon and the condition of all the others. . . . Literature and literary criticism cannot speak of anything else, they can have no other ultimate referent, they can only multiply their strategic maneuvers in order to assimilate that unassimilable wholly other.

The pressure of this absolute and ultimate referent proclaims both the sovereignty of the referentiality of mimesis and the human treason of the entire structuralist and poststructuralist bag of tricks for the specious, academic playthings that they are. Reader-response criticism, hailed by some, only concentrates more unrelentingly on the subjectivity of the individual reader. No amount of chicanery, no amount of whoring after tenure, can substitute for the primacy of not the author, the text, or the reader, but of nature, the undeniable center of fear and consciousness.

One outcome of this central referent is the beginning of the establishment of new human values. Ervin Laszlo, former Director of the United Nations Institute for Training and Research (UNITAR), makes this point in his book *The Inner Limits of Mankind*: "A new phase in history is now beginning. This age is . . . a global one marked by new conditions and the corresponding need for new values. But most of mankind fails to see it is upon us." Norman Moss, in *Men Who Play God*, perceives this same shift in the locus of value and locates the "motive force" for such a shift partly in the pressure of nuclear weapons:

Ultimately, the prevention of thermonuclear war will probably require some new international system, to replace the present one of competing sovereign nation-states. . . .

The pressure of the "absolute referent" is unquestionably accomplishing this change, though haltingly, erratically, and while "most of mankind fails to see it is upon us." Such change, of course, as Moss remarks, will be "subtle, undramatic and limited." As he also says, the object of the creation of a new international system "would be to avoid massacre" not to affirm the utopian oneness of man, though out of such an object of value must arise the realization that "we are all part of one another" and that our history impels us toward a wider stage of social responsibility and organization, while preserving the integrity of individual nation-states.

Another outcome of the "ultimate referent" is its incessant pressure toward rationality, toward the power of human reason, while many continue to wallow in their escapist cesspools of subjectivity. Such escapism is a byword for modern culture, which, in its greedy cooptation of ever-multiplying forms of triviality, discloses its lack of critical, conceptual capacity and its blatant, post-bourgeois nihilism. Brand Blanshard acknowledges in his book *Reason and Belief* the reasonable, practical goal toward which all nations and peoples are impelled:

> Nations must give up some part of their independence; they must believe in a reason that transcends prejudices and international boundaries; and they must be willing to hand over to a super-national government the control of the major weapons of destruction. That the 130 governments now in the United Nations, and particularly the half dozen most powerful ones, can be induced to take this line before the outbreak of Armageddon does not seem very probable. However that may be, there is only one way out of anarchy, whether individual or national.

Such voices, attesting to the ineluctable necessity of "a reason that transcends prejudices and international boundaries," merit much more consideration. The problem facing such champions of humankind is not only the disillusionment, nihilism, and preoccupation of the masses, but also the alienation of many of the best minds, who are all too obsessed with form, theory, language, technique, self, and ahistorical pedantry. Fundamental to this problem of scholasticism is the failure to believe the human mind can struggle its way through the pervasive quagmire of horror, terror, and anomie that have reached such prodigious international proportions as now to be routinely accepted as the only possible state of affairs. Blanshard's doubt notwithstanding, fear and love of our kind must unify and impel us to recognize unequivocally the truth that there is "only one way out of anarchy."

One notable example of the current escapist irrationality, because it brings together and uncritically mouths so many of the sophistries that today pervert so much academic criticism and literary theory, is the following passage from Mihai Spariosu's *Mimesis in Contemporary Theory*:

Being opposed to mimesis as good simulation (or imitation), mimesis as bad simulation replaces Being with Non-Being or the infinite play of simulacra in which copies no longer turn into models, but, on the contrary, dispense with them altogether while still remaining copies. . . . Although both good and bad simulation originate from Platonic mimesis, one reinforces Being and Truth and implies eternal presence without absence, while the other one disinstalls Being and Truth and implies eternal absence without presence, which is perpetually deferred. In terms of my thesis that mimesis and play are both instruments of a power-principle in Western culture, this scheme actually describes the internal movement of philosophy and science, which sees a reversal in its dialectic of Myth and Reason, or a "return" to play as authority or as a means of reinforcing Western power-configurations. In this context, mimesis has also reversed its function: it is no longer an instrument for subordinating (dionysian) play to knowledge and truth, but, on the contrary, an instrument for subordinating the latter two to the former.

What is emphasized here is the subject as substitute for the object, which "is perpetually deferred" or ignored in favor of "Non-Being or the infinite play of simulacra." This Derridean play or myth is tantamount to the worst nihilism and relativism and advances itself as "authority" in place of any intelligent, reasonable understanding, or social, conceptual knowledge and truth. It is this type of "mimesis as bad simulation," as a perversion of all modes of reasonable discourse for and among human beings, that inspired Plato to banish charlatans from the city-state. For power is an inescapable condition of human existence that demands self-control, self-mastery, and an object-centered awareness of history and duty to assure, within the limitations imposed on human nature, its consecration to the social, public good, about which postmodern sciolists could clearly care less. The work of the poststructuralists is not only decadent in and of itself but is also a symptom of the malaise that vitiates much of world-culture at the very moment when it needs the most to establish the supremacy of power subordinated to the rights and well-being of all nations and peoples.

René Girard's work on mimesis has concentrated precisely on its relationship to power, especially in his specialized meaning of mimetic rivalry, conflict, desire. He holds that this "conflict is observable in animals" and, in human beings, "tends toward interminable revenge." It is exactly the dread specter of such revenge that impinged on the consciousness of the peoples of the world. In "To Double Business Bound" Girard affirms the objective pressure of the nuclear threat:

> It would be sheer madness to expect from now on that the escalation of mimetic strife will bring back some tolerable order. We know only too well that our destructive power already exceeds or will soon exceed the ecological tolerance of the terrestrial milieu.... The dynamics of destructive power in our world must coincide with the dynamics of cultural awareness, as demanded by the very nature of the foundation now emerging into the light not so much in our books as in that absolute technological threat we are busy creating with our own hands.

It is the fear of exceeding the "ecological tolerance of the terrestrial milieu" that is creating "the dynamics of cultural awareness," which, emerging in nature, at previously unknown levels of social unity, call out for a critical, referential confrontation, "in our books," with the objective, external, given world of reason, not myth. "Our destructive power," "the bomb," is, as Derrick De Kerckhove writes in *Diacritics*, "the first truly active principle for the creation of a planetary consciousness." Without counteraction, without a practical criticism to "coincide with the dynamics of cultural awareness," lethargy and alienation will continue to be our fate.

As far back as the formation of the League of Nations there have been observers who have called for international order. Ominously, the wobbling, infantile steps that have been made required World War I and II to shake humankind from its inveterate provincialism. The vision of Albert Einstein after World War II is still noteworthy because of the subsequent hamstringing of the Charter of the United Nations, which could have been prevented, along with the Cold War and the arms race, had his plea been heeded:

> The only hope for protection lies in the securing of peace in a supranational way. A world government must be created which is able to solve conflicts between nations by judicial decisions. This government must be based on a clear-cut constitution which is approved by the governments and the nations and which gives it the sole disposition of offensive weapons.

"The sole disposition of offensive weapons," the constitutional power to maintain observance of its adjudications, on behalf of all peoples and nations, is the authority still required by the United Nations to become, at last, the protector of humankind against the subjective, selfish dictates of barbarous individuals and nations. With varying degrees of emphasis, Jonathan Schell affirms this same position in *The Fate of the Earth* and *The Abolition*. It is lamentable that when so many observers have announced the failure of both the Left and the Right, those humanists who ought to declare the universal human values that rise out of the lifeblood of millions, that could rise out of the blood of millions more, cower in perplexed decadence, isolated in their shrouds of self like madmen in straitjackets.

The inevitable goal of humankind now unveils the cultural ferment of the last one hundred and fifty years or so for what it was—the purgative tempest requisite for the creation of a global infrastructure, requisite for the creation of an international community. This widely perceived teleology restores intelligible historical progression and purpose to time and space, annunciates the urgency of the hour, reveals the highest locus of objective human value, and orders the conflicting passions and self-seeking impulses of both aberrant individuals and nations, while it upholds the discrete integrity of all nation-states and recognizes the non-utopian, recalcitrant nature with which it must contend. Everywhere the dying cries of the old world order can now be heard. As eventually out of the fractious Greek poleis, the deep-seated hatreds of the Italian city-states, the clashing interests of the separate thirteen colonies of America, a wider loyalty is already and irrevocably forming despite the impotent, retrograde forces that conspire to impede its manifestation from the realm of intellectual and humane conception into the ultimate haven of a much-divided, disillusioned, and war-torn humanity.

Writers who choose to remain clinging to the old world order like blood-suckers to a decaying corpse doom themselves to ineffectuality and alienation from the steadily emerging center of value, from the steadily emerging world community. They also deprive themselves of the untapped possibilities of a new mimetic use of language and of the most comprehensive perspective for criticism our time now affords, which E. B. White perceived long ago in the pages of *The New Yorker*. Whatever they choose to substitute in its place, esoteric myths, moribund traditions, dissection of their familial relations, self-flagellating personal confession, "deep" images, fascination with "the thing itself," with the trivialities of life, all these will lead to nothing and will finally be left on the discard of facile coteries. Only by recognizing our complicity and by confronting and exploring it can the darkness of human nature be reconciled with the glory of this vision, this inevitable, objective reality. This duty requires the artist, as craftsman, as maker of aesthetic artifact fundamentally different from but based on life, to disenchant, to hold up to nature a stark but corrective mirror that will, with a devastating shock wave, destroy the vestiges of the old order by representing life and men as they are, wrapped in their bigoted, nationalistic sins of omission and commission. Those who loathe the old provincialisms will hold high the pluralistic love of diversity, of the splendor of the essential form of humankind, of its universal, collective unity and beauty. Such a world aesthetic economy, such a new area of life put under aesthetic examination and judgment, restores objective, intellectually respectable content and purpose to the imitation of human character in all its ambiguity and complexity.

With the rejection of subjectivity, nihilism, and nominalism, with the accurate assessment of and confrontation with external reality, the sovereign power of mimesis returns, challenges mass banality and complicity, illuminates human actions and history, establishes an enlightened, authoritative global humanism. Only by becoming accountable to all humankind, driven there by international tragedy, terrorism, and the fear of thermonuclear peril, by its possible onslaught, if not by love, can a serious standard worthy of contemplation be established once more and merit the central, interpretive, evaluative position in the world community.

Poetry in the Nuclear Age

For too long nuclear weapons have threatened a quarter of a million years of human development on this planet. No other threat to human well-being has ever posed such possibly dire consequences. Much of what humankind has ever produced can still be blasted away in no more than a few hours. As modern human beings, we take it for granted that not only are the artifacts of civilization imperiled but also the environment itself and most forms of plant and animal life. For many of the survivors of such a catastrophe, life would barely be worth living. Since the late 1940s our threat to ourselves has steadily mounted to the inconceivably destructive nuclear arsenal of many times the overkill of the entire planet. Even after the implementation of the arms reduction treaties, since the collapse of the Soviet Union, more than enough weapons remain to overkill much of the human species. I believe we should remember with respect the general direction of the Acheson-Lilienthal-Baruch Plan following World War II. No greater pressure challenges our inveterate provincialism than the proliferation of the nuclear threat, which necessitates a reaffirmation of fundamentally humane values. A global humanism would give us a new critical perspective from which to view our history. During most of the postmodern period, poets largely conformed to the inclination of the age to withdraw into the self and sought refuge there from the increasing pressure of the external threat by extending the autotelic conception of literature of the modernist poets and critics. Now that the Cold War has receded into the past and we stand at the beginning of a new century, literature must reclaim its ancient duty to confront directly the objective world. During the last fifty years a few poets have managed to preserve the mimetic power of language, and a few, who are firmly in the solipsistic tradition, have managed to break through, at least momentarily and with varying degrees of success, to grapple with the harsh horror of nuclear annihilation.

In her "Three Poems of the Atomic Age," Edith Sitwell was the first poet of stature to perceive and respond to the implications of the nuclear threat. The first poem, "Dirge for the New Sunrise," evokes, after a brief dream of safety, a vision of the destruction of Hiroshima:

But I saw the little Ant-men as they ran
Carrying the world's weight of the world's filth
And the filth in the heart of Man—
Compressed till those lusts and greeds had a greater heat than that
 of the Sun.

And the ray from that heat came soundless, shook the sky
As if in search for food, and squeezed the stems
Of all that grows on the earth till they were dry—
And drank the marrow of the bone:
The eyes that saw, the lips that kissed, are gone—
Or black as thunder lie and grin at the murdered Sun.

The living blind and seeing Dead together lie
As if in love. . . . There was no more hating then,
And no more love: Gone is the heart of Man.

These lines, written in 1948, remain one of the most haunting contemplations of the horror of the nuclear age. They demonstrate Sitwell's awareness of the thermal pulse that has a temperature greater than the center of the sun, greater than 10,000,000°C, and that vaporizes, depending on megatonnage, everything at ground zero and as far away as several miles in only ten to twenty seconds. The thermal pulse or heat wave would desiccate, if not incinerate, "the stems / Of all that grows on earth" and would drink "the marrow of the bone." Whatever plants would escape vaporization in a full-scale nuclear war would surely be so thoroughly irradiated with beta and gamma rays that the long-term survival of many forms of vegetation is highly doubtful. The irradiation of bone marrow, to say nothing of the whole body, would lead to the ionization of hematopoiesis, anemia, a higher susceptibility to all infections, and a disruption of the manufacture of platelets, which cause the clotting of blood and thereby prevent bleeding to death from other injuries.

These maladies would come about, as Sitwell suggests, only if "The eyes that saw, the lips that kissed," survive the initial radiation, the thermal wave, and the blast wave. It is more likely that most eyes and lips, in an instant, would be "gone," or "black as thunder," charred to scar-fried corpses that "grin at the murdered Sun."

In the second poem "The Shadow of Cain," Sitwell connects "the filth in the heart of Man" with the biblical murder of Abel by Cain, of man by his brother. Like the biblical passage, she uses the particularity of violence to suggest universal disequilibrium:

> . . . there came a roar as if the Sun and Earth had come
>   together—
> The Sun descending and the Earth ascending
> To take its place above . . . the Primal Matter
> Was broken, the womb from which all life began,
> Then to the murdered Sun a totem pole of dust arose
>   in memory of Man.

This "Sun" is both Christ as Son of God and the splitting of the atom that unleashes the "Primal Matter" of the universe, the stellar furnace that once forged the atoms of all life. Such a vast disruption of natural order finds its emblem in the "totem pole of dust," the mushroom cloud as cross upon which hangs vaporized humankind.

Sitwell identifies the cause of the cataclysm with the lust of Dives for gold and material attachments, with the lust of perhaps armament manufacturers and aggressors:

> To Dives: "You are the shadow of Cain. Your shade is the
>   primal Hunger."
> "I lie under what condemnation?"
> "The same as Adam, the same as Cain, the same as Sodom,
>   the same as Judas."

Such "primal Hunger," such greed that sells humankind for gold, Sitwell equates with original sin, with fundamental limitations of human nature. Compared with the frequently sentimental conceptions of postmodern poets, Sitwell's recognition of limitation in the "heart of Man" manifests, whatever one might think about the doctrine of original sin, a soberly just estimation of the Aristotelian actions of man in the twentieth century:

And the fires of your Hell shall not be quenched by the rain
From those torn and parti-colored garments of Christ, those
    rags
That once were Men. Each wound, each stripe,
Cries out more loudly than the voice of Cain—
Saying, "Am I my brother's keeper?" Think! When the last
   clamor of the Bought and Sold,
The agony of Gold,
Is hushed. . . . When the last Judas-kiss
Has died upon the cheek of the Starved Man Christ, those
   ashes that were men
Will rise again
To be our Fires upon the Judgment Day!
And yet—who dreamed that Christ has died in vain?
He walks again on the Seas of Blood, He comes in the   terrible
Rain.

Sitwell holds that nothing can quench the hell of hate in the heart of man but Christ, whom she uses as a symbol of the "ashes that were men" at Hiroshima, as in the cries of "Each wound, each stripe," the "clamor of the Bought and Sold, / The agony of Gold," the "Judas-kiss" that is the last one because of atomic annihilation, which she joins with the "Judgment Day."

    She explicitly makes this correlation in her Preface to *The Collected Poems*:

This poem is about the fission of the world into warring particles, destroying and self-destructive. It is about the gradual migration of mankind, after that Second Fall of Man that took the form of the separation of brother and brother, of Cain and Abel, of nation and nation, of the rich and the poor—the

spiritual migration of these into the desert of the Cold, towards
the final disaster, the first symbol of which fell on Hiroshima.

Sitwell evinces a diachronic, historical conception of the "migration
of mankind" from time immemorial "towards the final disaster,"
which she believes Hiroshima heralds. Although her conception of
redemption and last judgment is a traditionally Christian one,
Sitwell's originality lies in her identifying such imagery with the
horror of nuclear war, as in the last line in which Christ "walks
again on Seas of Blood, He comes in the terrible Rain." This
"terrible Rain" is the rain of retribution, the local and global fallout
of radioactive particles.

In the last poem "The Canticle of the Rose," Sitwell draws on the
medieval myth of a rose growing out of fire and ash. The rising of
the rose on its stem is symbolic of Christ, of the ephemerality of life,
and of rebirth. A woman emphasizes the evanescence when she
sings, "All things will end— / Like the sound of Time in my veins
growing . . . / Yet will the world remain!" Sitwell follows this song
with these lines:

The song died in the Ray. . . . Where is she now?
Dissolved and gone—
And only her red shadow stains the unremembering stone.

Although the atomic bomb dropped on Hiroshima was only 12,000
kilotons, a mere firecracker by the standard of megatonnage, the
only trace left of many human beings was the "red shadow" of their
outline on the stone benches they were sitting on. Out of the fires of
such a ray, out of the vaporization of millions, Sitwell suggests will
come a horribly tragic rebirth of a spiritual understanding of man's
nature and a wiser recognition of human limitations:

But high upon the wall
The Rose where the Wounds of Christ are red
Cries to the Light—
"See how I rise upon my stem, ineffable bright

Effluence of bright essence. . . . From my little span
I cry of Christ, Who is the ultimate Fire
Who will burn away the cold in the heart of Man.
Springs come, springs go. . . .
'I was reddere on Rode than the Rose in the rayne . . .'
'This smell is Crist, clepid the plantynge of the Rose
  in Jerico.'"

"The Wounds of Christ are red" underscores the typology that the shadows on the stone imitate. The light is conceived of as both a divine one and the flash of light that is brighter than the sun. The light is, to Sitwell, in both senses, "the ultimate Fire / Who will burn away the cold in the heart of Man" and restore man's power of scent.

Edwin Muir's "The Horses," which T. S. Eliot called "that terrifying poem of the 'atomic age,'" presents a more pastoral restoration. The speaker of the poem recounts that less than a year after nuclear war "the strange horses came" and that by then the few survivors had made their "covenant with silence," with the devastation of any outside world with which to communicate. Warships and planes, in the early days, wander past with their dead pilots slumped over the controls, the radios pick up nothing, the nations lie asleep, tractors rust about the fields. The speaker grants what would probably be the plight of most of the world after nuclear war:

We make our oxen drag our rusty ploughs,
Long laid aside. We have gone back
Far past our fathers' land.

Civilization would be pushed back far past the level of hundreds of years ago. What economy might survive, if enough people did, would surely be at least initially a medieval agricultural one, since the complex modern economy would never be able to operate with the means of production and distribution devastated. This collapse of the economy would deprive "farmers" of the benefit of hybrid seeds, fertilizers, pesticides, and fuels that support modern agribusiness. Hence Muir's poem makes recovery sound too easy. It is unlikely that people who have always relied on a highly interdependent world economy could create within a year a system of supplying the food, shelter, heating, and so on needed for their survival in the midst of a global radioactive dump that would poison almost anything they managed to grow, raise, or produce. Instead of Muir's vision of a saving remnant reduced to idyllic medieval farming, I would more realistically expect to find wandering bands of forest dwellers, of hunters and gatherers, though little would remain for which to forage.

Muir ends the poem with the coming of horses and the vision of a refuge or "Eden" in the "broken world":

In the first moment we had never a thought
That they were creatures to be owned and used.
Among them were some half-a-dozen colts
Dropped in some wilderness of the broken world,
Yet new as if they had come from their own Eden.
Since then they have pulled our ploughs and borne our loads,
But that free servitude still can pierce our hearts.
Our life is changed; their coming our beginning.

Writing in 1956 Muir can be excused the failure of even the scientific community to realize the lethal dose of gamma radiation for most animals ranges from about 200 to 1,000 rads. For the oxen dragging the ploughs, it would take to kill them about 180 rads; for the horses, about 350 rads; for the colts, probably less, if they survived their birth defects; for the "farmers" themselves, radiation sickness would begin at about 150 rads, fifty percent survival possible at 450 rads, and almost one-hundred-percent fatalities at 600 rads. In the first few weeks following a one megaton explosion, radiation can be expected easily to reach more than 3,000 rads as far as a hundred miles from ground zero and to cover thousands of square miles. If only a relatively small percentage of megatonnage still available today were detonated, it is quite possible the level of global radiation could reach lethal doses even after the most dangerous period of approximately two weeks. It is doubtful any horses would survive to change lives by offering their "free servitude" to man. In Hiroshima, dead horses were a common sight.

In her sequence of poems of 1957 "Time Hinder Not Me; His Arms Reach Here and There," Muriel Rukeyser states, with a more soberly informed tone than Muir, "I realize what was done in the desert, at Alamogordo." In the following passage Rukeyser focuses on the underlying physics involved in a nuclear explosion:

> The work in the loss of mass.
> The work in the lifetimes of the fixed stars.
> The work in ideas of unstability:
> > divisible and transmutable as matter,
> > divisible and transmutable as idea,
> The inner passage of lifetimes and of forms.
> Relations of stars and of the stages of life.
> The half-life of the forms.
> The laws of growth and form.

"The work in the loss of mass" alludes to Einstein's equation $E=mc2$, the conversion of mass into energy. In fission bombs the critical mass required to start a chain reaction that splits the atoms can be as little as a few pounds of uranium 235. In the Hiroshima bomb the amount was merely a few ounces compressed by a triggering explosion to begin the chain reaction, the same reaction that occurs in "fixed stars." It was "The work in ideas of unstability" that led to the use of uranium 235, the least stable isotope.

This atomic reaction is the fundamental energy of the stars in which all atoms of matter and life were once forged and in which, one day, millions of years in the future, all atoms will be reforged:

> The universe passes along a way of cycles.
> A process of matter dissolving in the stars,

> Turned into radiation, passing through forms
> Again to matter; again, perhaps, to birth.

We are, as the astronomer Robert Jastrow wrote, from star-stuff and to star-stuff shall we return. Yet Rukeyser's hopeful vision of the cycles of the universe melting down all atoms to reconstitute life and of time not hindering anybody is hardly a consoling thought, though an undeniable aspect of "Nature, red in tooth and claw," raised to the nth degree. She counterpoints this quality of nature with her "central belief" that humankind "are children of God / That their lives come first and are sacred."

Robert Lowell's "Fall 1961" is more responsive than Rukeyser to the actuality of the threat of nuclear war. The historical background of its composition was the Berlin Crisis in late summer and early fall of that year. Lowell is, therefore, confronting, as uncharacteristic of him as it may be, an objective historical crisis that, as was widely feared, might very well have triggered a nuclear war:

> All autumn, the chafe and jar
> of nuclear war;
> we have talked our extinction to death.
> I swim like a minnow
> behind my studio window.
>
> Our end drifts nearer,
> the moon lifts,
> radiant with terror.
> The state
> is a diver under a glass bell.

The overwhelming pressure of the threat forces itself on the isolated speaker's consciousness. The public discussion of the possibility of extinction has been too much in terms of abstractions, statistics, probabilities. Confronted with the objective threat, the individual is reduced to the small powerless figure of a minnow, which is absurdly seeking refuge from the blast wave behind the flimsiest of structures. The terrifying prospect of devastation is projected on and reflected from the moon, "while our end drifts nearer."

The powerlessness of the individual and of the mass of people is emphasized in the next stanza:

> A father's no shield
> for his child.
> We are like a lot of wild
> spiders crying together,
> but without tears.

The inability of the father to protect his child discloses the utter powerlessness of the individual to fulfill the most basic duty when faced with the devastation of nuclear war. The "wild spiders" suggest humankind's ineffectuality and fragility before the immensely destructive force of nuclear weapons. As time runs out the "tock, tock, tock" of "the grandfather clock" marks the passing of lopsided historical time and the urgency of the crisis. Compared with the placid hopefulness of Rukeyser and Muir, Lowell's suffering speaker offers a much more accurate mimetic representation of reality, of the stakes involved in the world outside his own mind. It is this poignant dramatization of every human relationship and facet of nature at risk that gives the poem its intensity. Most "studio windows" would be blasted out as far away as twenty miles. After the heat wave, the greatest threat to people caught in the open would be from flying debris from which almost nothing could "shield" them. One of the most common injuries at Hiroshima was lacerations from flying glass, which, because of reduced ability to ward off infection and to produce platelets, often proved fatal.

Robert Hayden's "Zeus over Redeye," written in 1970, recounts a visit to the Redstone Arsenal in Alabama. The poem begins with the speaker establishing a historical perspective by comparing the "new mythologies of power" with the old mythologies of Greek and medieval myth. He also ironically reflects on the rockets "named for Nike" and "for Zeus, Apollo, Hercules— / eponyms of redeyed fury." Unlike Lowell's passive speaker, Hayden's persona visits the Redstone Arsenal with a member of the staff from whom he seeks to understand the implications of the "energy and power":

> Ignorant outlander, mere civilian,
> not sure always of what it is
> I see, I walk with you among
> these totems of our fire-breathing age,
> question and question you,
>
> who are at home in terra guarded like
> a sacred phallic grove.
> Your partial answers reassure
> me less than they appall.

His persistent questioning testifies to the pressure on his consciousness of the distinctive mark of our time, the "totems of our fire-breathing age." The old mythologies are also extended to the new one by describing the missile fields as a sacred grove, as though the arsenal were at a Greek shrine, such as Delphi or Oedipus' grove of the Eumenides. The partial, guarded answers of the guide "appall" him with the implications of annihilation, as they would any sane, informed, rational person.

Though not in a time of public crisis, Hayden's speaker shares with Lowell's an intense fear of devastation, which is based on his firsthand experience of the undetonated potentiality of the weapons:

> I feel as though invisible fuses were
>
> burning all around us burning all
> around us. Heat-quiverings twitch
> danger's hypersensitive skin.
> The very sunlight here seems flammable.
> And shadows give
> us no relieving shade.

One of the greatest barriers to confronting the nuclear threat is the feeling of impotence a person has before the "invisible" danger of holocaust. Nearly all missile fields are far from populated areas and access to them is restricted. Since nuclear war has fortunately never been waged, other than the tragedies of Hiroshima and Nagasaki, few people have any experience of what such a war would be like. This permits most people to remain oblivious of the danger. It is only by a rational, compassionate exertion of the human will that a quarter of a million years of human evolution on this planet can be assured of at least as many more years of further development. As Jonathan Schell writes in his book *The Fate of the Earth*, it is "only by descending into this hell in imagination now that we can hope to escape descending into it in reality at some later time." The issues are as complex as the appalling sophistries of the human will. Although the shadows of that will "give / us no relieving shade," what can be willed can be unwilled—we can break through the abstractions of annihilation, feel imaginatively the heat wave "burning all around us," know its possibility, and stand against what Hayden once called "the technology of disaster," stand for what is humane and enduring.

Denise Levertov takes such a stand, descends into the hell, in her poem "On the 32nd Anniversary of the Bombing of Hiroshima and Nagasaki," written in 1977. The speaker recalls having been told as a young twenty year old, "With this / the war is over." As was typical of most people at the time, she did not truly understand the implications of the bombing and "the technology of disaster" in which it would result. Levertov's speaker remarks on the "quantum leap" of death statistics: "eighty-seven thousand / killed outright by a single bomb, / fifty-one thousand missing or injured." Somehow in youthful preoccupation, this unprecedented reality, "This we ignored."

Unlike the resurrected rose of Sitwell's poem, Levertov holds out no hope of rising from the ashes but simply presents the statistics of devastation, which the speaker took no notice of at the time, having been caught up in the jubilation over the end of the war and the "vague wonder, what next? What will ordinary / life be like, now ordinary life as we know it / is gone?" Along with ordinary life the lives at Hiroshima were incinerated, vaporized into the stone by the heat wave, into the conscience of succeeding generations:

> the shadow,
> the human shadowgraph sinking itself
> indelibly upon stone at Hiroshima
> as a man, woman or child was consumed
> in unearthly fire—

The shadow "cries out to us to cry out," digs its nails "into our souls / to wake them," proclaims

> . . . something can yet
> be salvaged upon the earth:
> try, try to survive,
> try to redeem
> the human vision
> from cesspits where human hands
> have thrown it, as I was thrown
> from life into shadow. . . .

The horror of vaporization is counterpointed with the capacity to save "the human vision" from the degradation to which humankind has debased it. Although Levertov shares some of the shortcomings of postmodern poets, her ability to uphold a human vision distinguishes her work at times from the more decadent solipsists of the period. Her poem brings to mind Masuji Ibuse's *Black Rain* which poignantly acknowledges the tragic complicity of both the Japanese and Americans.

Richard Eberhart bears witness in "Testimony," written in 1984, to a similarly high vision of humankind, a "vision of immateriality":

> We are the materialists of the atom bombs,
> Fear seizes us in the joints,

We think a vision of immateriality
Must have no meaning, none,

In our teeter and balance before annihilation,
The end of us,

When it comes, when it comes, the blast,
Destruction of the best and worst,

We wanted to look in the eye of God,
We got six feet of radioactive sod.

Eberhart asserts "We are the materialists of the atom bombs," the children, the offspring of Einstein's theory of relativity, which has been put to nihilistic purposes Einstein himself never held or intended. What has become the "normative" vision of our age is the meaninglessness of life, the absurdity of existence, the corruption of all human intentions. Such nihilism, when not explicitly stated by many postmodern poets, is implied by the lack of respect with which any vision of man's more noble, humane capacities is treated. Eberhart connects, as Levertov and Hayden do to a degree, this debasement of man into a mere expendable animal with our fear and precarious position "before annihilation." He extends this suggestion in the line "Destruction of the best and worst," which may allude to Matthew Arnold's "The best are silent now" and to W. B. Yeats's "The best lack all conviction, while the worst / Are full of passionate intensity." According to Eberhart, the threat under which we suffer is but the reflection of a cosmic disequilibrium, a disruption that could lead to a radioactive grave.

  Yet Eberhart is probably too hopeful about our needing or receiving "six feet of radioactive sod." It is unlikely that enough people would survive to bury all the millions of charred and decaying corpses or enough would be able to spend what little energy and resources they might have left to do so. It is precisely the materialism and the lack of caring, the lack of love, that Eberhart confronts in "Fantasy of a Small Idea":

Maybe it is time before atomic holocaust
To fantasize that any small act of love,
Say any goodwill eye-flash to a passer-by
Is just possibly a great gain to humanity,
That to love anybody is a triumph of instinct
And if there are enough small acts of love to save us
We might outwit perhaps dream-bombing scientists,
Even take care of our planet without stabbing and killing.

Disdain for a transcendent human vision so thoroughly poisons the atmosphere like fallout that the small idea of love, announced, as Eberhart says, by the ancient fifth-century Greeks, Christ, Muhammad, and Buddha, indeed by all the great religious figures, has been struck down by the cynicism of Freud and the "Satanic Hitlers and Stalins." Although there is a tenuously nostalgic quality to Eberhart's avowal of love, although it relies on vaguely romantic good intentions, as is demonstrated by his relegating scientists to the one-dimensional world of "dream-bombing," he soberly acknowledges the reality of the pressure of the threat by undercutting his vision with the word "fantasy" and by contrasting his desire to "look in the eye of God" with the harsh horror of "radioactive sod." Such acknowledgments toughen, at least to a degree, his humane vision of love, testify to his awareness of what is at stake, and indicate somewhat his recognition of the historical upheavals that have culminated in the potential holocaust, whether global or to local isolated cities, that threatens us all.

Whatever one may think of any spiritual vision, whether it emanates from a traditional revealed religion or a cranky, postmodern American Adam or Eve, a humane, transcendent understanding of our basic human oneness proffers a much needed standard from which to evaluate the still immensely destructive stockpile we have built up in defense of national sovereignty. Although the Soviet Union has been swept aside, I believe we must remember that the nuclear age is not over. We still stand on the edge of the abyss while many continue to split hairs over their risible systems of nominalism, while others wallow in subjective worlds of trivia, while most are becoming less capable of confronting the spiritual crisis of the prevailing international culture that is taking place outside our narcissistic heads. Our age is one of anarchy, confusion, and receding hope and belief in the sanctity of the individual and of human life in general. After a quarter of a million years of human evolution, no greater fear troubles the psyche of the diverse peoples of the globe and drives home to us our common humanity, our common frailty, than the still enormous and dangerous national arsenals of nuclear weapons and the proliferation of nuclear materials to rogue states and perhaps terrorists. Chernobyl is a mere foretaste of what the world could suffer. Only the principles of a global humanism, channeled through such cooperative institutions as the International Atomic Energy Agency, can protect us from nuclear weapons of mass destruction, as well as chemical and biological weapons. Only a quantum leap from the level of the nation to the oneness of the globe, as it has been routinely viewed from the heavens, can prevent "final disaster" from becoming a ghastly reality, here on the threshold of the twenty-first century, in some possibly unpredictable way, outside in the given world.

Yeats's "Vision of Evil"

W. H. Auden once wrote that he was incapable of considering Yeats's theosophy and spiritualism "as anything but a joke." Such criticism was actuated by more than mere animus, by more than puerile jealousy. Even during Yeats's lifetime there were many writers and critics who similarly indicted him. There has always been speculation that Yeats's system is nothing but a very clever hoax—metaphors for poetry that he himself had enough sense not to believe in. Other observers have held that Yeats derived a certain amount of pleasure from the sight of people taking his fancies seriously. In "Yeats as an Example," Auden noticed another very peculiar fact:

> In most cases, when a major writer influences a beginner, that influence extends to his matter, to his opinions as well as his manner—think of Hardy, or Eliot, or D. H. Lawrence; yet, though there is scarcely a lyric written to-day in which the influence of his style and rhythm is not detectable, one whole side of Yeats, the side summed up in the Vision, has left virtually no trace.

Although this observation was true enough in 1948, it is not true of subsequent poets. Of course, no postmodern poet has slavishly embraced his theosophy. But what T. S. Eliot called "the spectacle" of Yeats has indeed exerted a formidable influence on postmodern poets. Though Auden may have recognized it by the end of his life, he could not have foreseen this influence in 1948. The malignancy was only setting in. That is, "the spectacle" of Yeats's concocting a substitute based on some sort of vague spiritualism has made more of an impact than the content of his system. As Auden remarked, the content is a joke.

Eliot made a similarly perspicacious observation on Yeats's system in *After Strange Gods*:

> Mr. Yeats's "supernatural world" was the wrong super-natural world. It was not a world of spiritual significance, not a world

of real Good and Evil, of holiness or sin, but a highly sophisticated lower mythology summoned, like a physician, to supply the fading pulse of poetry with some transient stimulant so that the dying patient may utter his last words.

Yeats's world is not one of "real Good and Evil" but a vague and affected "Vision of Evil." The term itself is suffused with romanticism and evinces the strain of Yeats's summoning it out of the phantasmagoria of his mind. His inveighing against Shelley and other romantics for lacking a "Vision of Evil" reflects Yeats's own half-hidden realization that he too was creating a substitute for "a world of spiritual significance." Repeatedly throughout his career he revealed that his conceptions were merely "a highly sophisticated lower mythology" and that his "Vision of Evil" was merely a stratagem.

In "Yeats as a Realist," Stephen Spender also perceived the same moral and spiritual shortcomings:

Yeats' poetry is devoid of any unifying moral subject, and it develops in a perpetual search for one. Although he has much wisdom, he offers no philosophy of life, but, as a substitute, a magical system, which, where it does not seem rhetorical, is psycho-analytic, but not socially constructive. Reverent as he is, he does not convey any religion; instead, we are offered . . . an aristocratic faith.

Spender's emphasis on Yeats's lack of a constructive social vision applies not only to Yeats but also to most postmodern poets who often went to even greater lengths than he to remain oblivious of the harsh horrors of the twentieth century and to concoct their own solipsistic substitutes. Like Yeats's, their poetry "develops in a perpetual search" for a respectable "unifying moral subject" or "world of spiritual significance"—that is, when it does not develop through a perpetual affirmation of nihilism.

Most of Yeats's own comments on good and evil redound to his own detriment. In 1919 in "If I Were Four and Twenty," Yeats himself belongs in, and may have included himself in, his category of "any modern writer":

> When we compare any modern writer . . . with the writers of an older world, with, let us say, Dante, Villon, Shakespeare, Cervantes, we are in the presence of something slight and shadowy. . . . The strength and weight of [these older writers] come from their preoccupation with evil. In Shelley, in Ruskin, in Wordsworth . . . there is a constant resolution to dwell upon good only; and from this comes their lack of the sense of character, which is defined always by its defects or its incapacity, and their lack of the dramatic sense; for them human nature has lost its antagonist.

What could be more "slight and shadowy," what could dwell more on sentimental good, than most of Yeats's work up to 1919? It was only in 1914 that he began to cast off his coat "Covered with embroideries / Out of old mythologies," which were cautiously replaced in 1919 with the beginning of new mythologies in *The Wild Swans at Coole*. Such new mythologies, however, failed to make an advance toward the recognition of real good and evil and the concomitant sense of character that demonstrates comprehension of the ineradicable defects and flaws in human nature. Yeats continually swept away the antagonist by the sensuously entrancing assertion of his own fancies.

A statement by Yeats on Shelley in *A Vision* more clearly establishes that these failures are Yeats own abiding failures:

> Dante . . . was content to see both good and evil. Shelley, upon the other hand . . . found compensation for his "loss" . . . in his hopes for the future of mankind. He lacked the Vision of Evil, could not conceive of the world as a continual conflict, so, though great poet he certainly was, he was not of the greatest kind. . . . perhaps all at some time or other, in moments of fatigue, give themselves up to fantastic, constructed images, or to an almost mechanical laughter.

Yeats includes himself in Phase 17 of his system along with Shelley. Incorrectly, he places Dante in this Phase. Dante, however, had seen real good and evil and not a phantasm of it as Shelley and Yeats concocted out of their own imaginations. For Dante saw the evil that men perpetrate on one another, while Shelley and Yeats are merely playing around with literary props or tenuous dualisms that extricate the individual from his share of the burden of guilt and sin that pervades human nature. No gaiety could be more hollow than Yeats's, which is based on his "fantastic, constructed images" and "mechanical laughter," all of which he summons to console himself and his readers at the very moment when he might have at last confronted the horrifying limitations of human nature. Dante never separates art from life. But Yeats's theories hurry him first from moribund Irish mythology, to theosophy, spiritualism, automatic writing, and, eventually, to fascism, the logical end of his nihilistic, aristocratic faith.

One of the earliest indications of the direction in which Yeats was irrevocably heading was the fervor of his reading of Nietzsche, whom he called "that strong enchanter" in a letter to Lady Gregory in 1902. From then on, Yeats continued to read Nietzsche, as Mrs. Yeats confirmed, until the end of his life. Many observers have pointed out that Yeats, like Rilke, was a Nietzschean from his earliest years. This is undeniable since many poems and passages in his prose smack of similar ideas. Some of the peculiar places in which Yeats found his ideas have already been mentioned. A place or passage that is remarkable for its foreshadowing of Yeats's theories can be found in *Thus Spake Zarathustra*:

And yet once more Zarathustra began to speak. "O my new friends," he said, "you strange higher men, how well I like you now since you have become gay again. Verily, you have all blossomed; it seems to me such flowers as you are require new festivals, a little brave nonsense, some divine service and ass festival, some old gay fool of a Zarathustra, a roaring wind that blows your souls bright."   (tr. Walter Kaufman)

Yeats supplied, as had Nietzsche, "new festivals," new mythologies, folderol for those who could not see through it. He accomplished this feat partly by emphasizing an intellectually vacuous but arcane substitute that hid its underlying nihilism. By the end of his life he realized he believed in neither good nor evil and, following the example of Nietzsche, pitched all belief aside and sought refuge in an irrational, "gay" celebration of chaos and brute domination. What T. S. Eliot remarked about Nietzsche can also be profitably applied to Yeats: "Nietzsche is the most conspicuous modern instance of cheering oneself up. The stoical attitude is the reverse of Christian humility." This "cheering oneself up," this denying the reality of good and evil, this flaunting of a "stoical" gaiety, marks the inevitable end of Yeats's spectacular career.

Unsurprisingly, given the influence Nietzsche had on Nazi Germany, Yeats too ended up a fascist. Like Ezra Pound, that other great modernist creator of botched substitutes, Yeats at least only briefly developed a personal affection for a particular despot, for "Moose." In the thirties Yeats began to put away his "new festivals" and to disclose his true self: "I think the old Fenian in me would rejoice if a Fascist nation or government controlled Spain." In "I Am of Ireland," Auden commented on Yeats's unmasking:

> At the very end of his life, in pamphlets like "On the Boiler," Yeats came out into the open: "I must lay aside the pleasant paths I have built up for years and seek the brutality, the ill-breeding, the barbarism of truth."

Stepping out into the open had been a long process for Yeats, but, when he finally found the courage to make the move, few people failed to recognize the old Yeats who had always existed just below the surface of his work. Stripping away the masks in 1939 in "On the Boiler," Yeats unveiled his unmitigated scorn for the "gangrel stocks," for "forcing reading and writing on those who wanted neither," for Ireland's "representative system" of government. At the same time, he affirms that it may become "the duty of the educated classes to seize and control" the necessities of life, to limit the families of "the unintelligent classes," to embody violence in "our institutions." Of this last assertion, Yeats writes, "Desire some just war, that big house and hovel, college and publichouse, civil servant—his Gaelic certificate in his pocket—and international bridge-playing woman, may know that they belong to one nation." I need only recall the many despots who harkened to such Machiavellian advice to perceive Yeats's "barbarism of truth." Yeats never outgrew his provincialism—never could conceive of anything international besides bridge-playing. Incapable of understanding the ramifications of international good and evil, incapable of seeing the real evil that fascism posed to millions of people, Yeats remained to the very last blinded by his passionate devotion to "one nation" and thereby failed to apprehend both the human treason of his own system and the inevitably increasing devotion of our age to the well-being of all nations—only such an Economy can now safeguard the integrity of any particular nation. And no variety of fascism employing the risible methods of eugenics or spiritualism can do anything for the welfare of humankind as is attested by the horrifying and tragic slaughter of World War II.

In the poems "The Gyres" and "Lapis Lazuli" Yeats greeted the beginning of that slaughter with the Nietzschean words "Rejoice!" and "Their ancient, glittering eyes, are gay." While Mussolini was invading Ethiopia in 1936 and dramatizing the ineffectuality of the League of Nations, while fascist Italy and Germany were perfecting their savage methods in Spain, William Butler Yeats sat down and wrote

> What matter though numb nightmare ride on top,
> And blood and mire the sensitive body stain?
> What matter? Heave no sigh, let no tear drop,
> A greater, a more gracious time has gone;
> For painted forms or boxes of make-up
> In ancient tombs I sighed, but not again;
> What matter? Out of cavern comes a voice,
> And all it knows is that one word "Rejoice!"

"The Gyres" stands in relation to the fascist tract "On the Boiler" as the *Commedia* does to Dante's *De Monarchia*. That the former poem is the embodiment of the most repulsive political chicanery of the twentieth century is not an insignificant fact. Rather it shows that literary symbols and language are not arbitrary signifiers locked in a world of linguistic relativity but can have reference to erroneous ideologies and assumptions that in fact eventually incinerated upwards of six million human beings and resulted in the deaths of many millions more. Such "blood and mire" have seldom been hailed by even remotely intelligent and feeling human beings as worthy of any kind of rejoicing whatsoever. It is difficult to think of a more egregious example of a poet's failure to distinguish between real good and evil, between suitable literary mythologies and treason to humankind—excluding, that is, Ezra Pound. The claim by Yeatsian devotees that the language of this "coarse" poem expresses a moral position amounts to nothing but a stratagem to rescue Yeats from the unequivocal condemnation he deserves. And his horrendous abdication of artistic responsibility becomes even more evident if compared to Pablo Picasso's exemplary confronting of the horror of evil, despite his own foolish Marxism, in "Guernica."

Similarly, "Lapis Lazuli" is, as one academician writes, "against both nature and the social order, and perhaps against reason also." Yeats wrote the poem in July of 1936, and it achieves by sheer force of its poetry two sleights of hand: it equates with the hysterical, philistine women anyone who might refuse to applaud Yeats's conception of tragic joy and the whole-sale slaughter of innocent human beings; and it misreads Shakespeare so that Lear and Hamlet become prototypes of the Yeatsian tragic hero. These stratagems aid Yeats in pulling off the main assertion of the poem: "All things fall and are built again, / And those that build them again are gay." In this general context, the propensity of Yeats for folderol has also been justly criticized: "Inhumane nonsense is not always the best foundation for aesthetic judgment, and perhaps we might be a little wary of 'the message of affirmation' Yeats is bringing us." Nobody who has truly seen into the darkness of what human beings are capable of perpetrating can possibly "imagine," as Yeats does, that to stare inhumanely down on all the evil, "all the tragic scene," merits the distinction of such a word as gaiety.

The spectacle of "Lapis Lazuli," more than any other single poem by Yeats, had a formidable influence on postmodern poets. By its turning away from the awful horror of contemporaneity and imagining a non-existent aesthetic substitute that is devoid of moral choice and human responsibility, it legitimizes brute power and domination and thereby served as a seductive precedent for the wallowing of postmodern poets in ever more insidious worlds of solipsism and isolation from humane, social duty. This abdication by Yeats, which is paralleled by a similar abdication in much of modern literary criticism, accounts for his consistent cheering up of himself and his readers by suggesting that evil resides entirely outside the perceiver, who may serenely look on in gaiety without the least ruffling of his bourgeois, aristocratic, or, as is often the case, especially in regard to Yeats, academic complacency.

T. S. Eliot and "The Horror! The Horror!"

For, in certain moods, no man can weigh this world,
without throwing in something, somehow like Original Sin,
to strike the uneven balance.
Herman Melville

In his review of Hawthorne's *Mosses from an Old Manse*, Melville confesses his fascination with that "mystical blackness" which pervades Hawthorne's work as though it were "a touch of Puritanic gloom." Not only does Melville admire "the infinite obscure of his background," but also he connects it with Shakespeare's "quick probings at the very axis of reality," probings that Melville drew heavily upon when his own "hypos" got the upper hand. T. S. Eliot also recognized the "blackness" in Hawthrone and once approvingly remarked in a lecture on Hawthorne's "profound sensitiveness to good and evil" and his uncanny ability to convey horror. Unfortunately, these qualities have become rarer and rarer to the point that, in much postmodern literature, they are virtually non-existent. I find instead a pervasive sentimentality that robs humanity of its capacity for illimitable "blackness," treachery, and tragedy. This puerile sentimentality has done much to weaken the portrayal of character and has driven writers further and further from any intellectually respectable, referential confrontation with "the axis of reality" into ever more vague forms of nihilism, nominalism, and other modes of artistic castration. Although many young poets are choosing to go even further into the prosaic, it would be wise to look more closely at Eliot's "background" instead of rejecting him out of hand, as has too often been done during the last thirty years or so. His sense of "blackness," of horror, remains unequaled by any other poet of this century. It allows him to struggle with and confront the evil within his own soul and to see the external chaos for what it is—a manifestation of the internal. His Christian faith not only gave intellectual depth to his life and work but also gave him a sound perspective from which to view the social upheavals of his time.

Many have acknowledged Eliot's sense of horror but usually only as the insignificant element that he rushes past on his way into the blinding light of redemption. Some observers, however, have been more perceptive. E. M. Forster, for one, indicated his awareness that there "is much more in his work than black followed by white." Paul Elmer More in 1932 was more explicit though uneasy about the same thing when he referred to "a cleft in Mr. Eliot's career" between the poet who sees chaos and the critic who sees "the steady decrees of a divine purpose." Eliot was well aware of the charge of inconsistency and answered More in *After Strange Gods*:

> My friend Dr. Paul Elmer More is not the first critic to call attention to an apparent incoherence between my verse and my critical prose.... It would appear that while I maintain the most correct opinions in my criticism, I do nothing but violate them in my verse; and thus appear in a double, if not a double-faced role.... I should say that in one's prose reflexions one may be legitimately occupied with ideals, whereas in the writing of verse one can only deal with actuality. Why, I would ask, is most religious verse so bad.... Largely, I think, because of a pious insincerity.... People who write devotional verse are usually writing as they want to feel, rather than as they do feel. Likewise, in an age like the present, it could only be poetry of the very greatest rank that could be genuinely what Dr. More would be obliged to call "classical"; poets of lower ability—that is all but such as half a dozen perhaps in the world's history—could only be "classical" by being pseudo-classical; by being unfaithful and dishonest to their experience. It should hardly be necessary to add that most of us would not recognize a classical writer if he appeared, so queer and horrifying he would seem even to those who clamour for him.

Here Eliot states clearly that poetry must honestly "deal with actuality," with the "blackness," while prose may contemplate "ideals." But what is of more interest in this passage is his describing the classical writer as "queer and horrifying," a description that can be profitably compared with Eliot's allusion in 1916 to T. E. Hulme's belief that "The classicist point of view has been defined as essentially a belief in Original Sin." Eliot, in effect, is suggesting that More has failed to recognize the appearance of a poet in the classical tradition and has been seduced by what is actually the main virtue of his work: the conscious choice not to commit sentimental, "pious insincerity."

Eliot revealed the same thinking in his statement about I. A. Richards's charge, which Eliot thought was wrong, that *The Waste Land* effected "a complete severance between poetry and all beliefs":

> It [Richards's charge] might also mean that the present situation is radically different from any in which poetry has been produced in the past: namely, that now there is nothing in which to believe, that Belief itself is dead; and that therefore my poem is the first to respond properly to the modern situation and not call upon Make-Believe.

This statement is by far the most, if not the only, illuminating one that Eliot ever made about *The Waste Land*. It patently connects the poem to the unique historical situation of the modern age, to the loss of what Matthew Arnold called the "Sea of Faith" (in Derrida's vaguer terminology *"the loss of the center"*). This excerpt also demonstrates Eliot's refusal to fabricate a system, "Make-Believe," as Yeats did, to replace it. For Eliot would have the horror of "actuality" or nothing.

The epigraph "The Horror! The Horror!" from Joseph Conrad's *Heart of Darkness*, which Eliot initially chose for *The Waste Land*, also connects the poem to "actuality" much more effectively than the one he eventually selected. Eliot himself was reluctant to delete it and, of course, sought to convince Ezra Pound of its worth by referring to it as "much the most appropriate that I can find, and somewhat elucidative." Lyndall Gordon asserts that the epigraph indicates Eliot's ". . . horrifying discovery of innate depravity and the associated fear that few have the stature to transcend it." The impact that such a reading has on *The Waste Land* is tremendous, and it transforms the poem from "a personal and wholly insignificant grouse against life," or against Eliot's first wife, Vivien, or the speculation surrounding Jean Verdenal, into a profound and devastating "probing of the axis of reality." This reading is also what Helen Gardner has in mind when she writes in *The Waste Land: 1972* that

> The peace invoked at the end as a blessing is the peace that comes from discovery and acceptance of the truth in all its horror: the truth of human failure and of human need.

Eliot's career can be properly viewed as a sustained attempt to recognize and portray the limitations of human nature.

Despite the "peace invoked at the end," *The Waste Land* deals almost exclusively with such limitations by presenting concrete examples of dryness, infertility, and those who are "Distracted by distraction from distraction." These range from the implacable memories of "The Burial of the Dead" to the cloying relationship of "A Game of Chess" with its own "planted corpse": "The chemist said it would be all right, but I've never been the same"; to the increasing awareness in "The Fire Sermon" of the all-consuming inferno of lust and complicity: "But at my back in a cold blast I hear / the rattle of the bones, and chuckle spread from ear to ear"; to the dousing of the fire of dryness in "Death by Water"; and, in what is perhaps the most terrifying passage in Eliot's poetry, the horrifying evocation of "blackness" shortly before the blessing of the thunder:

> What is that sound high in the air
> Murmur of maternal lamentation
> Who are those hooded hordes swarming
> Over endless plains, stumbling in cracked earth
> Ringed by the flat horizon only
> What is the city over the mountains
> Cracks and reforms and bursts in the violet air
> Falling towers

> Jerusalem Athens Alexandria
> Vienna London
> Unreal

The "Murmur of maternal lamentation," which suffuses the entire poem, is the ancient lamentation for the horror of the whole human condition as embodied by the primitive "hooded hordes," who perceive only "the flat horizon" that rings, encircles, imprisons them in their bestial state, whether on "the endless plains" or in the "Unreal" and "Falling" cities. This cracking, reforming, bursting lamentation manifests itself at every stage of Eliot's career, and it is not one that he restricted only to his verse.

The lamentation exists more subtly in Eliot's earlier poetry but can be found there nonetheless. For example, in "Portrait of a Lady" a hostess squirms under the cruel, detached observation of a young visitor. To him she reveals momentarily her true belief about her life that is composed of vapid "odds and ends": "[For indeed I do not love it . . . you knew? You are not blind! How keen you are!]" Although she attempts to moderate the disclosure through irony, she knows that she, as well as he, is alone in a tomb, which, with or without friends, is *"cauchemar!"* As if in recognition of primitive mysteries, under his own social superfluities, inside his own brain "a dull tom-tom begins." This same nightmare pervades the "Preludes," which especially strip away the "masquerades" of time: "One thinks of all the hands / That are raising dingy shades / In a thousand furnished rooms." The horror of these lines comes from the synecdoche of "hands" and from the metaphorical identification of "dingy shades" with cheap, sordid "rooms" or lives. These "images" symbolize the condition of humankind: "The notion of some . . . / Infinitely suffering thing."

Primitive mysteries also "tom-tom" below the surface of "Rhapsody on a Windy Night," in which "Every streetlamp . . . / Beats like a fatalistic drum, / And through the spaces of the dark / Midnight shakes the memory." This "fatalistic drum" is akin to those in Conrad's *Heart of Darkness* and similarly shakes up the memory, returns to consciousness the repressed and "supreme moment of complete knowledge." This is the meaning of the exclamation "Memory!" near the end of the poem and the matter-of-fact recognition "You have the key." Eliot's statement that *The Revenger's Tragedy* expresses "an intense and unique and horrible vision of life" applies equally well to this poem: "I could see nothing behind that child's eye." This same perception is made by Webster in "Whispers of Immortality," in which he sees "the skull beneath the skin; / And breastless creatures under ground / Leaned backward with a lipless grin." Donne is privy to a similar insight:

> He knew the anguish of the marrow
> The ague of the skeleton;
> No contact possible to flesh
> Allayed the fever of the bone.

Although these lines are intended to have sexual connotations and draw on Eliot's idea of the "dissociation of sensibility," they also exude horror at "our lot" and at the unlikelihood of ever allaying the "fever" and "anguish of the marrow." And the Sweeney poems are worth mentioning in passing as good examples that exude these same ideas regarding "our lot," while more than a trace can also be found in poems that follow *The Waste Land* but precede *Four Quartets*.

Often *Four Quartets* have been treated as the culmination of a "lifetime's effort" in the sense of Eliot's having attained to something like spiritual peace and calm. Though this would not be entirely inaccurate, they retain much more of his sense of "actuality" than is sometimes acknowledged. In "East Coker" the same fire that rages in "The Fire Sermon" is symbolically evoked:

> Until the Sun and Moon go down
> Comets weep and Leonids fly
> Hunt the heavens and the plains
> Whirled in a vortex that shall bring
> The world to that destructive fire
> Which burns before the ice-cap reigns.

The comets' weeping suggests irremediable cosmic woe as well as disruption of the natural order. This idea is developed further in the vortex that shall bring creation to the destructive inferno and may be echoed partly in the subsequent description of "the quiet-voiced elders" whose wisdom was "only the knowledge of dead secrets / Useless in the darkness into which they peered / Or from which they turned their eyes." Melville also knew there are those who either skim the pages or turn from what they cannot face. In another section the poem returns to this theme:

> Our only health is the disease
> If we obey the dying nurse
> Whose constant care is not to please
> But to remind of our, and Adam's curse,
> And that, to be restored, our sickness must grow worse.

Eliot's choice of the adjective "dying" is not fortuitous but in accordance with his loathing for "Make-Believe," which he proves again by not turning his eyes away from "our, and Adam's curse." The "sickness" that must grow worse, in Kierkegaard "the sickness unto death," is the one that leads from the destructive flames to the "purgatorial fires."

Eliot states, in *After Strange Gods*, "The perception of Good and Evil—whatever choice we may make—is the first requisite of spiritual life." "The Dry Salvages" begins with the natural world by describing the river as a brown god which is "sullen, untamed, and intractable," "first recognized as a frontier," a region of experience that is largely unexplored. Once men learn to circumvent and refuse the river, it quickly becomes "almost forgotten," though it endures to serve as a "reminder / Of what men choose to forget." Stephen Spender appropriately identifies this river with Rilke's "hidden guilty river-god of the blood" since Eliot suggests this in the hemistich "The river is within us." The natural world is further described in Eliot's typically primitive sea imagery of starfish, hermit crabs, whale bones, pools, sea anemones, and so on.

The second section of "The Dry Salvages" relates that there is no end "To the drift of the sea and the drifting wreckage" of mariners upon it. These cycles approach the same symbolic meaning as the river itself and gloss further what "is almost forgotten by the dwellers in cities":

> I have said before
> That the past experience revived in the meaning
> Is not the experience of one life only
> But of many generations—not forgetting
> Something that is probably quite ineffable:
> The backward look behind the assurance
> Of recorded history, the backward half-look
> Over the shoulder, towards the primitive terror.

The speaker does not commit the error so common among the city-dwellers. His intention is not to escape the "past experience," "the hidden guilty river-god," but to glance towards "actuality," "the primitive terror." That many generations have shared in this experience authenticates it and exposes "the assurance / Of recorded history." The preserving of the guilty past, however, requires recollecting the "bitter apple and the bite in the apple," for it is this "ragged rock" that looms always threateningly in the sea despite the best machinations to glaze over or conceal it—that ancient rock remains "what it always was."

F. O. Matthiessen said of *Four Quartets* that "Essential evil still constitutes more of Eliot's subject-matter than essential good." One passage which brings out the purgatorial burning of essential evil is the magnificently rendered meeting with a dead master. The meeting occurs in a world of fire—both the scourge of the destructive air raids of World War II and the scourge that refines. The latter fire presupposes elemental wrong through which the "exasperated spirit / Proceeds." Despite the well-intentioned admonitions of the dead master, the interlocutor betrays that his nature is similar to that of the city-dwellers in "The Dry Salvages" by stating from the first, "speak: / I may not comprehend, may not remember." On the sounding of the air horn, the old master fades—unheeded—back into the "waning dusk," the shadow world from which he came.

The black undertone is again sounded in the next section of "Little Gidding" in the words "Sin is Behovely"; that is, necessary, inevitable, kneaded into the very marrow and heart of existence for the predetermined reason of detaching man from the world and leading him to the refining fire, which rages throughout "The Fire Sermon" and many of the earlier poems, identified with a pervasive, primordial fire that burns deep in the heart of creation. This "intolerable shirt of flame" cannot be removed, though it may be ignored or "almost forgotten." The dove that descends is contrasted with the pernicious dove, the dive-bomb of destruction in an earlier section. The dove as Pentecostal flame strikes terror into existence because of its horrifying annunciation. The dark tones that hedge in the shadowed regions quail and despair before this knowledge—a knowledge too terrible for many to bear. Eliot, however, discloses his own horror by his choice of words: "torment" and "intolerable."

Eliot again handles this theme of terrible knowledge in *Murder in the Cathedral*. In fact, the subject of the play is precisely original sin. Although much of the play revolves around Becket's involvement with the four tempters and four knights, they all actually function to dramatize Becket's own internal battle with temptation and pride. Similarly, the chorus of the women of Canterbury, who are devoted to Becket, unveil, by their horrified reaction of the tempters and knights, Becket's increasing knowledge of humanity. Eliot pours into one speech by the chorus all the primitive sea imagery that he had been perfecting for decades and then has the chorus go to the heart of the matter:

It was here, in the kitchen, in the passage,
In the mews in the barn in the byre in the market-place
In our veins our bowels our skulls as well
As well as in the plottings of potentates
As well as in the consultations of powers.
What is woven on the loom of fate
What is woven in the councils of princes

Is woven also in our veins, our brains,
Is woven like a pattern of living worms
In the guts of the women of Canterbury.

The pronoun "it" has no clear antecedent in context but is preceded by about thirty lines of lobsters, crabs, whelks, and other crustacean imagery. What the women are recognizing is "In our veins our bowels our skulls" and in the intrigues of despots as well as in the well-intentioned consultations of legitimate, respectable powers. To see such things in the "guts" of the world, Becket tells them, is to see and "accept" their "share of the eternal burden."

After Becket has been killed by the knights, the chorus recoil in horror:

We are soiled by a filth that we cannot clean,
    united to supernatural vermin,
It is not we alone, it is not the house, it is not the
    city that is defiled,
But the world that is wholly foul.
Clear the air! clean the sky! wash the wind! take the
    stone from the
stone, take the skin from the arm, take the muscle from the
bone, and wash them. Wash the stone, wash the bone, wash
the brain, wash the soul, wash them wash them!

It is the irony and futility that permeate the last four lines which make them particularly effective. The chorus, overwhelmed by terror, seek to extricate the "brown guilty river-god" from the dark crevices in which it abides. Of these choruses Spender writes that Eliot "touches the utmost depths of horror that he knows, which we find in "Prufrock," *The Waste Land, Sweeney Agonistes*—indeed, throughout his work."

These depths can also be found in *The Family Reunion*, which has often been read as a gloss on *The Waste Land* and Eliot's life in general. Harry or Lord Monchensey imagines he has pushed his wife off an ocean liner, though it is eventually disclosed that he suffers from a feeling of guilt for having often contemplated doing it. The darkness thickens when it is uncovered that his wish for her death parallels his own father's sin of wishing for Harry's mother's death. Harry, therefore, bears the unacknowledged burden of sin from the past that plagues him and his entire family:

> It's not being alone
> That is the horror—to be alone with the horror.
> What matters is the filthiness. I can clean my skin,
> Purify my life, void my mind,
> But always the filthiness, that lies a little deeper...

Regardless of whether or not Harry expresses Eliot's distaste for women and marriage, the play does hinge on the inescapable guilt of the past driving a man to seek expiation.

The charge regarding the "cleft in Mr. Eliot's career" between the verse and the prose cannot, however, be made about all his prose. There are many instances in which the seeming incoherence does not exist—many instances in which "actuality" plays as large a role as in the verse. Eliot of course dismissed the charge in *After Strange Gods* and in the same book his critical remarks on Ezra Pound again evince his belief that poetry must not commit "pious insincerity" by glazing over the dark depths. It is possible that Eliot's criticism of Pound may have been influenced partially by Robert Browning's interest in "the soul under stress" and what decisions and choices are made. Regardless, Eliot's criticism remains perhaps the best that has ever been written about Pound and is applicable to much of modern and postmodern literature—for with the disappearance of the idea of original sin, or as Melville put it, "something, somehow like" it, human beings have indeed become "more and more vaporous." Eliot's concern in Pound with the lack of what Matthiessen calls "essential evil" implies that Eliot regards the chaos, even in his prose, as deep within "our veins our bowels our skulls" and that it cannot be left out of the balance when a writer seeks to create a character that even remotely approximates the dynamic struggle that constitutes life. Writers like Pound who commit sentimental simplification of the foundation of our being, the contemporary lie that evil is entirely outside us and not within, prostitute themselves to a banal complacency that seeks only to be released from its share of the burden of guilt and horror that seethe deep in the "guts" of "actuality."

Shortly after his criticism of Pound, Eliot makes some insightful remarks on W. B. Yeats and perceptively detects the sentimentality that lies at the bottom of Yeats's theories and visions. The only effect of Yeats's dualism has been to free some of his less perceptive readers from the burden of guilt and complicity that is theirs. Of course, another effect has been the creation of some of the most "vaporous" characters and ideas of this century. It is of this type of dualistic mistake made by Yeats and others that Eliot is thinking in the following excerpt from *The Idea of a Christian Society*:

> We are accustomed to make the distinction (though in practice we are frequently confused) between the evil which is present in human nature at all times and in all circumstances, and the evil in particular institutions at particular times and places, and which, though attributable to some individuals rather than others, or traceable to the cumulative deflection of the wills of many individuals throughout several generations, cannot at any moment be fastened upon particular persons. If we make the mistake of assuming that this kind of evil results from causes wholly beyond the human will, then we are liable to believe that only other non-human causes can change it.

Here Eliot is addressing the problem of Manichaeanism, or a variety of it, such as Yeats's, which looks only to the mechanical cycles and gyres to make their rounds. And within the overall discussion of Eliot's book, he may have been thinking of communism and fascism. Of course any polity is capable of the "cumulative deflection of the wills of many individuals throughout several generations." This emphasis on the will is precisely what prevents Eliot's thinking from falling into the intellectually flaccid determinism of Yeats's system. The human will, the capacity for volition, for choosing to acknowledge and accept the burden, always rules supreme in Eliot's thinking. Witness, for example, his earlier comment on Pound regarding "moral and spiritual struggle" and "individual responsibility." But, and this is the point of the preceding passage, the human will is always capable, egregiously capable, of "deflection" and self-deception.

This same capacity for self-deception is brought out again later in *The Idea of a Christian Society*:

> He [the secular reformer or revolutionary] conceives of the evils
> of the world as something external to himself. They are thought
> of either as completely impersonal, so that there is nothing to
> alter but machinery; or if there is evil incarnate, it is always
> incarnate in the other people—a class, a race, the politicians, the
> bankers, the armament makers, and so forth—never in oneself.

By now it is evident that Eliot is applying in his prose the same principle that undergirds much of his poetry. The indictment of the secular reformer or revolutionary is identical with his indictment of Pound's Hell, which "is a perfectly comfortable one for the modern mind to contemplate" since the evil is all in "other people."

In 1949 Eliot published *Notes Towards the Definition of Culture*. This book and *The Idea of a Christian Society* are the only works of social criticism by any poet of this century that are worthy of serious consideration because Eliot's balanced sense of literary, social, and religious concerns provides him with a sound and intellectually inviolable perspective from which to view "the immense panorama of futility and anarchy which is contemporary history." As *After Strange Gods* and *The Idea of a Christian Society* demonstrate, even when Eliot writes in his prose, his work retains "a touch of Puritanic gloom." *Notes Towards the Definition of Culture* is no different:

> What we ordinarily mean by understanding of another people,
> of course, is an approximation towards understanding which
> stops short at the point at which the student would begin to lose

some essential of his own culture. The man who, in order to understand the inner world of a cannibal tribe, has partaken of the practice of cannibalism, has probably gone too far: he can never quite be one of his own folk again.

To this droll statement Eliot appends the note: "Joseph Conrad's *Heart of Darkness* gives a hint of something similar." No better gloss could be had than Spender's general observations on Conrad and Eliot: "The country of the mind described by Conrad is a country of pure horror. Eliot is usually thought of as a sophisticated writer, an 'intellectual.' For this reason, the feeling of primitive horror which rises from the depths of his poetry is overlooked." I might add here, from the depths of his social criticism as well. For the "hint" that Eliot clearly has in mind is a glimpse of the unfathomable horror that resides deep below the surface of social superfluities. Both Kurtz and Marlowe in *Heart of Darkness* achieve this same recognition and are never quite one of their "own folk again." And this is so because to voyage into the heart of darkness is to come back as metamorphosed as Kafka's Gregor. It is instructive that in this extract Eliot is discussing at the same time the confrontation of one culture with another and the dark light that may blaze out from the interstices between them. Although Eliot never experienced a radically different culture, as Conrad and Melville had for instance, he spent extended periods in Europe and may even have felt the shaking of cultural facades in England. It is not unexampled for exposure to relatively similar peoples to culminate in such "hints"; how much more revealing is exposure to peoples who, though not in the least "primitive," observe conventions so dissimilar as to allow one to glimpse, with previously unknown clarity, the essential human nature that all men share.

Eliot was aware, though, that such glimpses were not contingent on travel. His essay on Baudelaire in 1930 focuses on basically the same recognition:

But actually Baudelaire is concerned, not with demons, black masses, and romantic blasphemy, but with the real problem of good and evil. . . . In the middle nineteenth century . . . an age of bustle, programmes, platforms, scientific progress, humanitarianism and revolutions which improved nothing, an age of progressive degradation, Baudelaire perceived that what really matters is Sin and Redemption. . . . the recognition of Sin is a New Life.

Perhaps it needs to be said that Eliot is cognizant of both sides and not merely the more lugubrious one. He is, like Baudelaire, concerned with "the real problem of good and evil," for, as Abdu'l-Baha recognized, evil "continues and endures." Eliot knew that the acknowledgment and the acceptance of sin are not self-flagellating affairs (debased and confused in the modern popular imagination with mental illness), but lead, through the refining fire, to a New Life. This recognition, however, is one that is easier in word than deed—for the soul is capable of the most pernicious stratagems and sophistries to gainsay its complicity and to extricate itself from the quagmire of its own actions.

Leszek Kolakowski in his book *Religion* summarizes well the classicist position that pervades Eliot's poetry and prose:

Christians have never been expected to believe in the story of the fall as retold and travestied by rationalists. It is not even material to genuine religious understanding whether or not they accepted in a literal sense the biblical account of what happened in the primeval garden. The history of Exile, one of the most powerful symbols through which people in various civilizations have tried to grasp, and to make sense of, their lot and their misery, is not a "historical explanation" of the facts of life. It is the acknowledgment of our own guilt: in the myth of Exile we admit that evil is within us; it was not introduced by the first parents and then incomprehensibly imputed to us. . . . Instead of devolving the responsibility for our misfortunes on a pair of ancestral figures we admit, through the symbol of our Exile, that we are cut out of warped wood (to use Kant's metaphor).

This "symbol of Exile" distinguishes Eliot from his sentimental contemporaries as well as the postmodernists, most of whom bent every effort to conceal this dark but emancipating knowledge from themselves and from their readers. If poetry is to free itself from ever more banal forays into the prosaic and quotidian, if it is to confront the interminable ambiguities of human volition, I believe it must return to the classicist perspective or "something, somehow like" it. Anything else is a dead end—one that results increasingly in a contemptibly trite, suburban solipsism. Only the realization that man is indeed a spiritual being fraught with complexity and compelled to struggle for mortal and infinite stakes can restore even a modicum of profundity and intellectual respectability to the literature of our time.

At the Dark Tower

Robert Lowell, Sylvia Plath, James Wright, Robert Bly, as well as other postmodern poets, place varying but pervasive emphasis on irrational psychic forces. Their work stands in marked contrast to that of older poets. In Robert Browning, while he perceives the irrational as part of human nature, he regards it as a force against which one must struggle, not indulge and wallow in. Like so much of Browning's narrative work, Browning's "Childe Roland to the Dark Tower Came" is, as he himself wrote, "about the development of a soul, little else is worth study." His characters believe in God because he himself did—his comment in a letter to Ruskin corroborates this: "A poet's affair is with God, to whom he is accountable, and of whom is his reward." Despite his religious belief, Browning held that man cannot achieve absolute knowledge of or attainment to God in this world, which is by definition not the divine one, but the theater of the struggle of the soul to reach him. As with any poet, Browning's poems can never be separated from his life and beliefs without doing violence to his work. The fact that our age has, to its detriment, largely lost belief in the veracity of the spiritual life constitutes no justification for projecting onto Browning's work the vague fantasies that have been concocted by many poets and psychologists.

Browning reveals the real struggle of "Childe Roland" in the following lines:

> No! penury, inertness and grimace,
> In some strange sort, were the land's portion. "See
> Or shut your eyes," said Nature peevishly.
> "It nothing skills: I cannot help my case:
> 'Tis the Last Judgement's fire must cure this place,
> Calcine its clods and set my prisoners free."

"The land's portion" is the inmost recess of the soul through which Roland travels—through which all men must travel whether they choose to shut their eyes or not to the "starved ignoble nature." Kierkegaard affirmed that this portion was the *sine qua non* of

Christianity: "the consciousness of sin." In this stanza Browning irrefutably sets the poem in a Christian context by referring to the Last Judgment and by capitalizing "Nature" to draw attention to the word and to indicate that it is the original nature of man that is being alluded to when "Nature" speaks: "It nothing skills: I cannot help my case." For "Nature" knows nothing can be done to eradicate the innate problem, nothing but the symbolic "last Judgement's fire" will redeem the human soul.

This refining fire returns later in the poem: "Burningly it came upon me all at once, / This was the place!" This place, the Dark Tower, which is the soul, the place of sin, guilt, and transgression, stands not only for all human nature but also for Roland as an individual: "Without a counterpart / In the whole world." The Dark Tower also stands for death, the end of the journey of life. Roland, like so many aspiring knights, is caught unawares by the Last Judgment, even "After a life spent training for the sight"; that is, partially, if not entirely, for the sight of God. In the last moment before death, Roland sees all those who died loyal to the quest ranged on the hillsides to witness his last heroic deed:

> in a sheet of flame
> I saw them and I knew them all. And yet
> Dauntless the slug-horn to my lips I set,
> And blew. "Childe Roland to the Dark Tower came."

Enwrapped in a "purgatorial fire," Roland steps toward the development of his own soul. Though he goes down before the ineradicable enemy, he goes down dauntlessly with open eyes—a rarity among men and worthy of the notice of "The Band," all of whom had failed, as all men ultimately fail. But, as Roland says early in the poem, "just to fail as they, seemed best / And all the doubt was now—should I be fit?" This is the utmost to which a knight can aspire; or as Browning once told an interviewer, "He that endureth to the end shall be saved," or "just about that."

Much of the poem hinges on the doubt, despair, and hopelessness that Roland feels. He knows he is defeated before he begins.

Nevertheless, he chooses, often feebly, to persevere. That doubt exists in the citadel of sin and guilt explains the evil, horror, and grotesqueness of the poem. He finds about him what he finds within: "The horror! The horror!" In the beginning, after his meeting with the cripple, Roland turns aside, perhaps from living with "shut eyes," a less conscious form of quest:

> Yet acquiescingly
> I did turn as he pointed: neither pride
> Nor hope rekindling at the end descried,
> So much as gladness that some end might be.

Initially his frame of mind is one of acquiescence. He takes neither pride nor hope in the quest because he knows he will ultimately fail, though at least his failure will put an end to his torture and suffering, an end that he desires. Witness the manner in which he finally turns away from the cripple: "quiet as despair." Or witness his descriptions of the landscape which always manifest despair and a "starved ignoble nature": The docks's leaves are "bruised as to balk / All hope of greenness"; his way is a "darkening path"; willows fling themselves over into the little river "in a fit / Of mute despair, a suicidal throng"; the "mere earth" is "desperate"; a "palsied oak" gapes at death; finally, the "ugly heights and heaps" of the soul come into view just before he is about to give up.

In the context of the poem, these external horrors are as terrifying as they are because Roland views them from the conscious self, which is capable of acts of volition and capable of discerning good and evil, its own and that of others. Again and again in the poem, he consciously chooses to push onward though often near the brink of despair. We have already seen that he turns "acquiescingly" from the cripple, who on the literal level of the poem requires Roland to change his direction. Once Roland pledges himself to the plain, "the safe road" of his past disappears and the horror of the present engulfs him. When he can endure no longer the reality around him, he says, "I shut my eyes and turn them on my heart." But "It nothing skills." The horror remains the same. This turning is the same as that pointed out by the cripple—a turn inward to the heart of darkness and evil. Roland's journey is both a journey through life to the Dark Tower of death and one through the recesses of his heart or soul. Instead of finding encouragement or a "draught of earlier, happier sights," he discovers Cuthbert, whose reputation is besmirched by "one night's disgrace," and Giles, on whose breasts "hang-man hands" pin a declaration of his hypocrisy—"poor traitor, spit upon and curst!" Such are the terrifying sights of a man who consciously, discriminately, looks into his own heart. Aught else is but the deception of "the safe road."

Now far from that road, Roland's world of horror and evil spurs him on repeatedly, though like most consciously honest knights, he knows himself to be more than a little faint-hearted, so unlikely is success, so incapable of it is he deep down. And the grotesqueness of the landscape forms the dark background against which he forges on. The inexplicable waste, the seemingly unjustifiable agony of the various creatures he encounters, the frightful possibility that he too might end a traitor, serve to inspire him to gird up the loins of endeavor, to die at least in the throes of mortal (immortal) combat. On a deeper level the pervasiveness of evil, which Roland discovers, indicates the truth of the words spoken by "Nature": "I cannot help my case"; that is, neither Roland nor any one else can eradicate the flaws that are intended to detach man from this world and lead him to God. The only cure is the ancient one. In his only unqualified act of heroism in the poem, Roland chooses dauntlessly to confront the sheet of flame that already purifies "all the lost adventurers" and thereby redeems the meager hope that has somehow sustained him on the way.

Browning never defined his thoughtfully held but abiding belief that man is a spiritually rational being in such a way as to include the type of irrational experience so many postmodern poets have indulged in. Shamanism, druidism, anti-intellectual reveling in the unconscious forces of the mind, vague sentimentality of the worst kind, have marked their work, with no awareness of good and evil, no awareness that the choices made in life are fought for, are complex and labyrinthine as the corridors of the inmost recesses of the soul. Unlike "Childe Roland," their work often lacks all significance because it is built on the tenuous emotions that flit aimlessly across the surface of the brain.

While many postmodern poets have fled the sanctuary of the rational, historical, conscious mind, what they have turned to is seldom clear. Some appear to have adopted antedated religions that are even dead in the lands of their birth; some have tried to revive nebulous forms of nature-mysticism weirdly mixed with equally peculiar schools of psychology; others have entirely abandoned the conscious mind and climbed onto the junk-heap of popular culture to celebrate the maladies of Western and modern civilization—maladies they themselves are symptoms of; still others have tried to live like blood-suckers off the decaying corpse of the already-written. Most of these shortcomings are due to a fundamental failure of moral imagination and spiritual vision. In contrast to Browning, who attempted to plumb the depths and development of the soul, postmodern poets and critics have largely directed their attention to the more mundane minutiae that distract them from the world outside their own limited realm of self-absorption, as in the poetry of Donald Hall. Browning looked out at the world and saw it for what it is.

T. S. Eliot perceived the beginning of this change in sensibility that has culminated in solipsism and the disappearance of real men and women from postmodern literature in *After Strange Gods*:

> The human beings presented to us both in poetry and in prose fiction today . . . tend to become less and less real. It is in fact in moments of moral and spiritual struggle depending upon spiritual sanctions . . . that men and women come nearest to being real. If you do away with this struggle, and maintain that by tolerance, benevolence, inoffensiveness and a redistribution or increase of purchasing power, combined with a devotion, on the part of an elite, to Art, the world will be as good as anyone could require, then you must expect human beings to become more and more vaporous. This is exactly what we find of the society which Mr. Pound puts in Hell, in his Draft of XXX

Cantos. Mr. Pound's Hell for all its horrors, is a perfectly comfortable one for the modern mind to contemplate, and disturbing to no one's complacency: it is a Hell for the other people, the people we read about in the newspapers, not for oneself and one's friends.

It is only by consciously turning, as Roland turned, out of the safe way of banality, to face the horrifying depths of darkness that seethe below the surface in the locus of "moral and spiritual struggle," that even a modicum of profundity can be restored to the mimetic representation of human character, of "the soul under stress. We live in an age that is willing to do anything to deny its own sin, guilt, and complicity in order to extricate itself from the burden of moral choice. To use the figure of Edwin Arlington Robinson, one of the truly great American narrative poets who learnt, along with Robert Frost, from Browning, we, like children who have not yet mastered the splendor of brightly colored building blocks, point the finger at "other people," accusing the outside world of harboring the monotone evil of the universe. But the Bell still rings. The band still gathers in the refining fire. The hills lie chin on hand "to see the game at bay":

Dauntless the slug-horn to my lips I set,
And blew. "Childe Roland to the Dark Tower came."

Sophocles and the Plague of Modernity

Wandering between two worlds, one dead,
The other powerless to be born.

Matthew Arnold

In discussing *Oedipus Rex*, Aristotle stresses the perfection of the plot and hamartia, Freud emphasizes incest as representative of the deepest yearnings of men and women, and other commentators underscore the inexorable operation of the forces of fate. Each interpretation, though accounting for a facet of the play, fails to take a broad enough view of the issue Sophocles is actually dramatizing. For his focus is not merely on the tragic flaw of Oedipus, the act of incest, or the destruction of human folly under the grinding wheels of fate. Rather, I believe Sophocles, devotee of Apollo, highly conscious of the increasing social confusion of Periclean Athens, is primarily concerned with the relationship of the people to the gods.

At the very beginning of the prologue Oedipus listens to suppliants before the palace who implore him to save the city from sundry afflictions: the crops are blighted, the herds are diseased, children are dying in the womb, and plague is ravaging the entire population. Oedipus proclaims he is grievously aware of the suffering of the city and has already sent Creon to Delphi to seek Apollo's directive. The threatened condition of the city is the motivating force of the play and undergirds all action, as when Oedipus resolves to search for the cause of the suffering: "an old defilement we are sheltering" (trans. Fitts and Fitzgerald). This defilement refers not only to Oedipus' own terrible acts but also to the corruptions perpetrated when the people themselves fail to discover Laius' murderer and to oppose Oedipus' ascension to the throne. Only Oedipus, as the elder priest tells him, "Wisest in the ways of God," in whom a god had once breathed to set the people free from the Sphinx, can root out the source of the plague and restore the proper relationship to the gods.

Although Oedipus does suffer from his quick temper, which is demonstrated in his confrontations with Tiresias and Creon, he is fervently attempting to save the city, trying to safeguard his people against anarchy and the intrigues of all possible enemies. And although Oedipus is fated to suffer, what is crucial about his suffering is that it is intended to reaffirm for the people the omnipotence of the gods and the nothingness of man, even the noblest and wisest one, who, contrary to appearances, is the very source of the plague that afflicts them all. In the second stasimon, which is central to the meaning of the play, the chorus succinctly presents the issue with which Sophocles is concerned. In the first strophe they pray for reverence and that their "words and actions" may "keep the laws of the pure universe / From highest Heaven handed down." Their emphasis on law, characteristic of the Greek milieu, presupposes the violation of the laws of the universe, which has resulted in the plague and disequilibrium of the relationship between the human and the divine. In the first anti-strophe the chorus next warns the tyrant against becoming drunk with hubris, recklessness, and vanity because such vices will bring about his fall from power and the disruption of the polis. They end by beseeching divine protection for the ruler "Who will fear God, and on His ordinance wait."

The second strophe of the ode expresses outrage at the hubristic impulse, at "any mortal who dares hold / No immortal Power in awe." Such flagrant self-assertion against both the divine and the community assures that such a person "will be caught in a net of pain." This strophe clearly alludes to the unknown killer of Laius and, ironically, to Oedipus, who has been entangled in the net of incest and fate woven by the gods. The second and closing anti-strophe, which is suffused with the chorus's own fear and doubt, focuses on what is truly the crux of the play:

> Shall we lose faith in Delphi's obscurities,
> We who have heard the world's core
> Discredited, and the sacred wood
> Of Zeus at Elis praised no more?
> The deeds and the strange prophecies
> Must make a pattern yet to be understood.
> Zeus, if indeed you are lord of all,
> Throned in light over night and day,

Mirror this in your endless mind:
Our Masters call the oracle
Words on the wind, and the Delphic vision blind!
Their hearts no longer know Apollo,
And reverence for the gods has died away.

Here the chorus calls upon Zeus to vindicate his laws and oracles, the latter of which were discredited by Jocasta near the end of the second epeisodion. Yet the people and Oedipus have also gainsaid the truth of the oracles, the people by turning only to Oedipus, and Oedipus by attempting to avoid the oracles. Both Laius and Jocasta had tried to escape them by exposing the infant Oedipus on Mt. Cithaeron. What is of abiding importance to the chorus and to Sophocles is that "Their hearts no longer know Apollo, / And reverence for the gods has died away." Somehow, the chorus affirms, there must be a "pattern" or design inherent in the course of events that remains still too obscure to detect but which will reveal itself in the fullness of time.

Design manifests itself in the climax of the play when Oedipus exclaims "Ah God! It is true! All the prophecies!" This discovery not only humbles Oedipus but also vindicates to the community the indisputable sovereignty and reality of the gods. Like the Book of Job, what the gods have done to Oedipus finds its meaning and resolution in its educative purpose for the community, which learns to say with Oedipus, "I am sick / In my daily life, sick in my origin." The chorus drives home this recognition of pollution and limitation in the closing lines:

Men of Thebes: look upon Oedipus.

This is the king who solved the famous riddle
And towered up, most powerful of men.
No mortal eyes but looked on him with envy,
Yet in the end ruin swept over him.

Let every man in mankind's frailty
Consider his last day; and let none
Presume on his good fortune until he find
Life, at his death, a memory without pain.

Here Sophocles does not emphasize Oedipus' tragic flaw, fate, or incest, but rather the utter nothingness and frailty of mankind before the mystery of death and the omnipotence and inscrutability of the gods. Oedipus, innocent and incomparable in suffering, a scapegoat for the welfare of the community, has served to restore the proper relationship of man to the gods and achieves further understanding of his suffering in *Oedipus at Colonus*, entering the sacred grove.

It is a commonplace of historiography and literary criticism that "reverence for the gods" was rapidly dying out in fifth-century Greece, and Sophocles certainly bears witness to such a loss in *Oedipus Rex*. Although Euripides was only slightly younger than Sophocles, Euripides had already moved on to express the common skepticism and the tendencies that heralded what was to come. Matthew Arnold may very well have had Sophocles in mind when he wrote the following lines in "Stanzas from the Grande Chartreuse" about his pilgrimage to the monastery of the Carthusian order:

Not as their friend, or child, I speak!
But as, on some far northern strand,
Thinking of his own Gods, a Greek
In pity and mournful awe might stand
Before some fallen Runic stone—
For both were faiths, and both are gone.
Wandering between two worlds, one dead,
The other powerless to be born,
With nowhere yet to rest my head,
Like these, on earth I wait forlorn.

Oedipus Rex is, in a sense, Sophocles' own meditation "on some far northern strand," his own "Dover Beach." Like Sophocles, Arnold could only bear witness to the loss and "wait forlorn" for the pattern to become clear. Such an act is in itself no small achievement for it keeps the memory of man's true nature alive and promises that there will be those who eventually recognize and embrace the new world.

Since Arnold's time the sweeping away of the old world has all the more become an accomplished fact. As he stated in his Preface to *Poems* in 1853, "the calm . . . the disinterested objectivity have disappeared: the dialogue of the mind with itself has commenced," a dialogue to which he himself contributed. And all through literature and criticism from the romantics to the postmodernists, I readily detect an ever-increasing subjectivity that has reached proportions that would have horrified Arnold, as many are horrified today. To see this subjectivity, one need only consider Sophocles' "calm . . . disinterested objectivity," what Arnold calls in Culture and Anarchy his "noble serenity," compared with Samuel Beckett's play that "waits forlorn": *Waiting for Godot*. In contrast with the healthy, objective action of Oedipus, Beckett's characters suffer pointlessly in a subjective void of squalor and restlessness. There is, as Estragon repeatedly says, "Nothing to be done." Like Euripides or Nietzsche, Beckett in the early 1950s revealed what was to come: the great truth of existence, the great postmodern "breakthrough," that there is no truth—all is nihilism, alienation, relativity, subjectivity, boredom, specious discourse, brute domination of man by man (as Lucky by Pozzo). Such waiting has nothing in common with Sophocles who perceives the historical reasons for the pervasiveness of the plague. It was as a young undergraduate that I first heard from an academician that no intelligent person could believe in God.

Modern literature merely builds, so to speak, on the interior void, which Arnold perceived long ago and which every subsequent movement in literature and criticism, including Arnold's own work, has tried to fill with one substitute or another. In poetry, Eliot's nostalgia for the dead world, Yeats's puerile system, and Auden's frequent Augustan pose are all marked by their extreme efforts to fill the public void, while most postmodern poets merely try to circumvent the issue by retreating into little subjective worlds of make-believe, nihilism, or pseudo-spirituality. In criticism, there has been the New Critical retreat into the text itself, which ushered in subsequent critical movements, all of which progressively announce the isolation of literature from mimetic, referential language and meaning, as if writers and critics have always been plagued with solipsism. Sophocles focused on the world outside his skull.

Only by turning to the public domain can writers hope to begin to find a standard of understanding that confronts the historical confusion of the modern age and that provides, to whatever limited degree, a new critical perspective from which to view the mass banality and horror of our time. For to reflect accurately the social milieu requires a sober confrontation with the immense anonymity of the slaughter of millions upon millions of people in World War I, World War II, and the many regional and civil wars of the most brutal and transformative century in history. And within these very horrors, within these nationalistic sins, must reside a new world now struggling to be born from the gore of man's old defilement and blasphemy before the reality of his own nature. Though the soul prefers to reel away from the public sacrifice of innumerable scapegoats, though it prefers a seemingly safe little solipsistic world, it must perforce strive to learn and understand its relationship to these incalculable facts, which have found, perhaps, their most terrifying modern referent in the dread specter of complete and absolute annihilation of the entire species of man, an image haunting the imagination of both the ancient and modern worlds:

Men of all nations: look upon these horrors.

Let every one of you reflect upon what you
Have done, and what you have left undone.
Let every one of you consider your limitations,
And what may very well be your last day.

Czeslaw Milosz's Mythic Catholicism

After Czeslaw Milosz received the Nobel Prize for Literature in 1980, American poets and critics often failed to know what to make of him. Many claimed, as one academician wrote in 1984 in *The New Yorker*, "There are no direct lessons that American poets can learn from Milosz." American poets, such critics claimed, have not witnessed the war atrocities of the modern era, had the experience of a highly unified European provincial culture, or benefited from the tutelage of a rural, traditional Roman Catholicism that Milosz himself testified no longer exists. I believe all such objections obscure the real issue. Milosz was often neglected or patronized because his work contravened much of the aesthetic dogma of the last fifty years, if not of the century.

In *Unattainable Earth* Milosz evinces all those characteristics that have given postmodern devotees intimations of mortality. In his Preface Milosz underscores that the "servant of the Muses" lives "among people," feeling, thinking, trying to understand others, "trying to capture the surrounding world by any means," which includes, but is not limited to, poetry itself. This is by way of explaining his weaving together prose jottings, fragments of letters from friends, excerpts from Baudelaire, Simone Weil, Pascal, as well as from others, and several poems from D. H. Lawrence and Walt Whitman—all of which resonate suggestively with his own work. The result serves "one purpose": his "attempt to approach the inexpressible sense of being." From such an attempt a "deeper unity" becomes discernible. This attempt "to capture the surrounding world" strikingly contrasts with the work of so many postmodern poets and critics who are quite content to withdraw from the world and write only about themselves.

In "Consciousness" Milosz writes, "Now, not any time, here, in America / I try to isolate what matters to me most," while preening as a Polish exile writing in America, a role he played to the hilt, decade after decade, measuring the new world with his Catholic rod, closing his soul to modern and American history and culture. To relegate Milosz to the Polish equivalent of what Robert Hayden bitterly called "a literary ghetto" would be to deny him too the laurel of American poet, a laurel he rejected and would have apparently loathed. Yet nothing is more American than the emigré who out of the suffering of exile "approaches," to some degree, the perception of the "inexpressible sense of being," though in the end Milosz as foreigner, who never could appreciate the fullness of American experience, fled back to Krakow and his mythic Catholicism, analogous to Yeats's use of Celtic faery tales. As the first American citizen to have received the Nobel Prize for poetry, he writes with knowledge of both worlds, Eastern Europe and the West, in his limited sense, and creates out of his disparate experience poems that span time and space and forge into the mystery of what it means to be a human being in our time. In the poem "Winter" he meditates on the death of a fellow poet he knew years ago in Poland, but from his home in California:

The pungent smells of a California winter,
Grayness and rosiness, an almost transparent full moon.
I add logs to the fire, I drink and I ponder.

His pondering turns to reflections on his having outlived so many, on "the clearness of the view": "And so I am here, approaching the end / Of the century and of my life." In this poem, as throughout his work, Milosz's authority comes precisely from his confronting so much of the history of the twentieth century, instead of avoiding it. After meditating on his friend and "The ashes of inconceivable arts" that have come and gone, he reflects on the evanescence of literary achievement, "a name lasts but an instant." Unlike so many who are anxious for their paltry name to endure, instead of seeking something greater than the individual self, the speaker suggests that what was important was the "chase with the hounds for the unattainable meaning of the world" and already sees a "heavenly forest" where a "new essence waits." Such humility and submission before the inexpressible stands all the more as an achievement at a time when the work of so many American poets is marked by the stultifying fad of nihilism.

Yet Milosz is aware of the claims of the prevailing intellectual fad. In his Nobel Lecture he openly acknowledges its "temptation":

> Like all my contemporaries, I have felt the pull of despair, of impending doom, and reproached myself for succumbing to a nihilistic temptation. Yet, on a deeper level, I believe, my poetry remained sane and in a dark age expressed a longing for the Kingdom of Peace and Justice.

Such temptation receives its due throughout his books, as does the striving and "longing for the Kingdom of Peace and Justice," the inexpressible essence. On the title page of *Unattainable Earth* Milosz alludes to the duality of human nature with a juxtaposition of two globes, one of the celestial sphere and one of the terrestrial globe. In one jotting he writes, "our duality will find its form in" "the poetry of the future" and "without renouncing one zone or the other." At a time when much of the planet has renounced one entire zone, Milosz brilliantly succeeds in acknowledging both.

Many of the poems or entries of *Unattainable Earth* are concerned with human sexuality, as in the opening poem on Hieronymus Bosch's *The Garden of Earthly Delights*. Unlike the sadomasochistic poems of Sylvia Plath and Robert Lowell, Milosz's poems have an uncommonly erotic yet unusually wholesome quality. In "After Paradise," transforming love is marvelously handled, as in the first half of the poem:

> Don't run any more. Quiet. How softly it rains
> On the roofs of the city. How perfect
> All things are. Now, for the two of you
> Waking up in a royal bed by a garret window.
> For a man and a woman. For one plant divided
> Into masculine and feminine which longed for each other.
> Yes, this is my gift to you. Above ashes
> On a bitter, bitter earth.

Here, as in poems on entirely different subjects, the antinomies are never gainsaid. And yet what other poet of the last fifty years could have written "How perfect / All things are"; or "we could have been united only by what we have in common: the same nakedness in a garden beyond time"? Such a view of sexuality reaches back to Plato's *Symposium* but has not been seriously entertained for a century, perhaps since Emerson's essay "Love." Juxtaposed with this view are such candid lines as "I was not a spiritual man but flesh-enraptured, / Called to celebrate Dionysian dances."

Though much can be learned from Milosz's desiring to go beyond time, there is just as much to be learned from his confrontation with time. In *Bells in Winter, Selected Poems, The Separate Notebooks, The Collected Poems, Provinces, Facing the River,* and *Second Space,* much of his work registers the overwhelming pressure of history on his consciousness. In *Unattainable Earth,* "Preparation" ranks foremost among such poems of memory. It begins "Still one more year of preparation" for the writing of a book in which the century "will appear as it really was":

> armies
> Running across frozen plains, shouting a curse
> In a many-voiced chorus; the cannon of a tank
> Growing immense at the corner of a street; the ride at dusk
> Into a camp with watchtowers and barbed wire.
>
> No, it won't happen tomorrow. In five or ten years.
> I still think too much about the mothers
> And ask what is man born of woman.
> He curls himself up and protects his head
> While he is kicked by heavy boots; on fire and running,
> He burns with bright flame; a bulldozer sweeps him into a clay
>   pit.
> Her child. Embracing a teddy bear. Conceived in ecstasy.
>
> I haven't learned yet to speak as I should, calmly.

These lines constitute what Milosz calls in *The Witness of Poetry* a "longing for perfect mimesis." Their power comes from the intersection of the individual with time and space, with history, with evil. Far from withdrawing into solipsism, he dares to contemplate the meaning of barbarous events, of which so many complacent poets choose to remain ignorant, clutching their "teddy bears." For him, as he says elsewhere, the "recovery of memory is a weapon against nihilism." This poem is followed by a pensée in which he asks, "How do we live on the surface pretending not to feel the terror?" This terror, the essence of barbarous events, held in memory, haunts all of Milosz's work, as in his *Captive Mind* of 1953, wherein he states, "it is not impossible that Russia will manage to impose her insanity upon the whole world and that the return to reason will occur only after two or three hundred years." Fortunately, such terror and prophecies are behind us. Milosz toughens his recognition of them as possibilities by allowing, for example in *Native Realm*, that both East and West are spiritually enervated.

Whatever becomes of what used to be the Soviet Union and other formerly communist countries, as Milosz says in the poem "Revolutionaries," in *The Collected Poems*, the man-god "leaves aside the irrelevant and aims at the goal / Which is power":

> . . . There, in their capitals,
> Let the torpid animals sleep, unaware
> Of what is prepared already. Compassion is not his hobby.
> They, dull and languid, will be exercised
> Till, in dread, obedience and fearful hope,
> They will lose the human nature in which they take refuge,
> Though it does not exist. Till their mask falls off
> And they enter the heights, transformed by agony.

Wallowing in the crude distractions of hedonistic materialism, the shortcomings of which Milosz fully perceives, the masses of the West lived at times unaware of the true proportion of the threat to their very lives and civilization, indeed, all too unaware of the dialectical grasp for "All the continents and seas." Deluded by their own good intentions, they attempted to take refuge in "human nature," which the worship of the cult of the man-god long ago repudiated as a bourgeois fantasy. Far from indulging in sentimental hope that they will be aroused in time, this poem suggests "the torpid animals" might sleep until it is too late, until the mask of complacent society falls off, or is torn off, and they enter the horrible heights of those who were devoured by the Gulag Archipelago, the Ukrainian famine, the Russian Civil War, the killing fields of Cambodia, all those crushed by the tread of tanks, as in Czechoslovakia, Hungary, and Tiananmen Square, all the pitiless evils of communism. Often reading Milosz I have thought, to live and write in defense of freedom, religious conscience, and democracy, even at times in the most dire poverty, is a blessing and a duty, especially after having read and heard in lecture rooms the violent sophistries of radicals at the University of Michigan and elsewhere.

For the victims of violence, "Lecture IV" raises a beautifully elegiac song that memorializes the priceless individual existence of "A little hunchback, librarian by profession," covered by the rubble of a destroyed apartment building that "no one was able to dig through" and "Though knocking and voices were heard for many days." Cutting through the abstractions and sophistries of communism, "so-called History" and "generalization," the true enemies of man, Milosz remembers and extols the sacred human nature of "The little skeleton of Miss Jadwiga, the spot / Where her heart was pulsating. This only / I set against necessity, law, theory." As sacred as the individual skulls that filled the ditches of Cambodia.

In his Nobel Lecture Milosz mentions the duty of the poet "to see and to describe." This makes poetry a crucial witness of what we human beings are and do. All too often postmodern aesthetics confuse "to see and to describe," that is, mimesis, with some intellectually cheap reportage. In *The Captive Mind* Milosz proclaims the high and noble seriousness of the poet's calling as witness of the horrors of the twentieth century:

The war years taught me that a man should not take a pen in his hands merely to communicate to others his own despair and defeat. This is too cheap a commodity; it takes too little effort to produce it for a man to pride himself on having done so. Whoever saw, as many did, a whole city reduced to rubble—kilometers of streets on which there remained no trace of life, not even a cat, not even a homeless dog—emerged with a rather ironic attitude toward descriptions of the hell of the big city by contemporary poets, descriptions of the hell in their own souls. A real "wasteland" is much more terrible than any imaginary one. Whoever has not dwelt in the midst of horror and dread cannot know how strongly a witness and participant protests against himself, against his own neglect and egoism. Destruction and suffering are the school of social thought.

This passage contains the much needed lesson that can aid poets to advance beyond the neglect of the social world, the stultifying obsession with the ego, the immense trivialities of postmodernism. For in the earlier excerpt from his Nobel Lecture, Milosz emphasizes "'To see and to describe' may also mean to reconstruct in imagination . . . so that every event, every date becomes expressive and persists as an eternal reminder of human depravity and human greatness." The ambition and difficulty behind "eternal reminder" stand out starkly from the little diversions of the age of solipsism. And of course "to reconstruct in the imagination" does not mean that one must experience or observe firsthand the horrors of concentration camps, total war, and all the brutalities the twentieth century proved so capable of producing. Distance may be an advantage. Only a philistine would contend Shakespeare had to witness the actual horrors of his plays to write about them. In *Beginning with my Streets*, Milosz states simply, "The century is largely untold."

Today, in place of a "longing for perfect mimesis," Milosz observes, again in his Nobel Lecture, the common conception of literature is one of "écriture, of speech feeding on itself." Such a theory holds that language cannot refer to anything other than itself, has, despite its claim to the contrary, "a hidden link" with totalitarianism, and is suffused with nihilism. Milosz rejects literature as *écriture* and throughout *Unattainable Earth* probes specifically the nature of language. He writes in one entry "I learned early that language does not adhere to what we really are," cannot, that is, express the "inexpressible sense of being." One of the major intellectual characteristics of the modern period has been man's misguided attempt to comprehend his own mind. The main tool used for the attempt has been language, which has merely resulted in ever-increasingly sophistic constructs that encircle and encircle and encircle what cannot be known or contained. By declaring in *Unattainable Earth* that the attempt is impossible, "My essence escapes me," Milosz honors transcendence and suggests man can at best humbly strive "to approach" what he cannot grasp. Therefore, in the closing entry of the book, he repudiates language as enchantment, *écriture* and propaganda, and invokes "an unnamed need for order, for rhythm, for form, which three words are opposed to chaos and nothingness." Much of what he suggests about language is perhaps more lucidly stated in *The Land of Ulro*: "Only one language can do justice to the highest claims of the human imagination—that of Holy Writ." Similarly, against "speech feeding on itself," at a *Partisan Review* conference in 1992, he refers to the "enormous erosion of the religious imagination" and mentions further the remedy: "For me personally, it is very important to give a spiritual dimension to poetry." In *A Year of the Hunter*, he unequivocally writes, "Poetry's separation from religion has always strengthened my conviction that the erosion of the cosmic-religious imagination is not an illusion and that the vast expanses of the planet that are falling away from Christianity are the external correlative of this erosion." Interested only in Christianity, he fails to perceive that vast expanses of the planet have also left behind the Islamic, Hindu, Taoist, Confucian, and Buddhist religions.

In an interview reprinted in *Beginning with my Streets*, Milosz assigns much of the blame for the obsession of American poets with themselves to "the extreme subjectivization of literature in the twentieth century, especially in the West." He goes on to say he has "always looked for a more spacious form" and emphasizes, as he has so often and in so many ways, "poetry seems to me a little narrow today." Given his historical and cultural memory and the scope of his intellectual ambition, it makes sense for him to bemoan that "epic poetry . . . has been largely abandoned." If any modern poet gets close to having a truly epic vision of life, it is Czeslaw Milosz. Yet what he lacks is the gift of the blessing of Calliope, though Clio, Erato, and Polyhymnia have shown no restraint in pouring out for him their copious blessings.

Like his contemporaries, Milosz is a child of dualities and contradictions, as he discloses in *Unattainable Earth*: "Sometimes believing, sometimes not believing, / With others like myself I unite in worship." Though "loyal and disloyal," he performs what is in itself an act of affirmation. One reason for such tensions must be his recognition that we are "In an intermediary phase, after the end of one era and before the beginning of a new one." In another entry he writes, "There is only one theme: an era is coming to an end which lasted nearly two thousand years, when religion had primacy of place in relation to philosophy, science and art. . . ." Milosz recognizes the validity of his own honest doubts and the abyss of evil and historical calamity that is swallowing everything before it, yet he does so while continuing to "unite in worship." Similarly, in "Lecture V" of *The Collected Poems*, the persona affirms "We plod on with hope," and then allows, "And now let everyone / Confess to himself. 'Has he risen?' 'I don't know.'" It was perhaps these lines that led Pope John Paul II to say to Milosz, "You always take one step forward and one step back." Milosz, kissing the hand of the Pope, revealingly responded: "Holy father, how in this century can I do otherwise?" In an essay in *New Perspectives Quarterly*, Milosz describes himself as a believer, while in *A Year of the Hunter* he refers to an experience in church on Palm Sunday as an "intuitive understanding that Christ exists." These contradictions achieve their fullest expression in "Two Poems" in *Provinces*: The first poem celebrates earthly life and its values, while the second poem, "A Poem for the End of the Century," bitterly, ironically recalls the religious past:

Don't think, don't remember
The death on the cross,
Though everyday He dies,
The only one, all-loving,
Who without any need
Consented and allowed
To exist all that is,
Including nails of torture.

Of these two contrasting poems, Milosz writes in a headnote that "taken together" they "testify to my contradictions, since the opinions voiced in one and the other are equally mine." To highlight either side over the other would be a distortion of his psyche. Milosz conveyed his complexity, as well as rhetorical method, to the Pope when he confessed, "Can one write religious poetry in any other way today?" In *Second Space*, in a "Treatise on Theology," Milosz allows "Wandering on the outskirts of heresy is about right for me," and then goes on to say, "One day I believe, another I disbelieve," finding consolation in the ancient rite resonating with his "skeptical philosophy." The propagation of the Church requires the subtlest of methods, addressing the pagans in a language they can understand, and the influence of the Catholic press shouldn't be underestimated. I have often thought of Virginia Woolf's Mr. Ramsay in *To The Lighthouse*, ascending the island rocks, in one of the most poignant settings of modern literature, "There is no God."

Perhaps because Milosz perceives our age as an intermediary one, he finds it more possible than most poets to hold out hope for the future. His hope, though, as we have seen, is not naive, foolish, or unaware of the incessant disintegration. It is that of one tried by experience, who yet believes there are reasons for such a poem as "Thankfulness":

You gave me gifts, God-Enchanter.
I give you thanks for good and ill.
Eternal light in everything on earth.
As now, so on the day after my death.

To give "thanks for good and ill" manifests a trust that transcends our usual human self-centeredness and that submits to the power of the mystery of being, a trust that acknowledges in another poem "They are incomprehensible, the things of this earth." Such trust is also the prerequisite to finding "Eternal light in everything on earth." Although from the viewpoint of traditional Catholic belief some might think such lines are suffused with gnosticism, of "willing belief," as he says of himself in *The Land of Ulro*, one must recognize the honest complexity of his commitment if one wishes to confront, as he has, the undeniable damage that has been visited upon all organized forms of religion and government during the modern era.

In reference to religion, while recognizing the undeniable damage, Milosz has often, nevertheless, expressed his skepticism and uneasiness with Catholicism. Although he seems to favor at times reversion to Catholicism, suggests he himself is a heretic, harbors the conceit of possessing the true truth among the great religions, he also writes of going "forward, but on a different track," of a "new vision," "a new awareness," "new perspectives," as in *A Year of the Hunter*:

> Why should we shut our eyes and pretend, rejecting the obvious, that Ancient Rome is again in decline, and this time it's not pagan Rome under the blows of Christianity, but the Rome of the monotheists' God? Since this, and nothing else, is the undeclared theme of contemporary poetry in various languages, obviously this conflict has already crossed the threshold of universal consciousness. . . . Perhaps . . . new perspectives will open up. . . .

Though never confronting the Catholic realities Paul Collins documents in *The Modern Inquisition*, Milosz has worked more deeply with the spiritual dislocations of modern life than any other poet of the twentieth century since T. S. Eliot.

In regard to government, Milosz's experience prepared him to understand where we have been and where we are going in a manner unique among modern poets. As a child he stared out on the miserable scene of refugees of World War I; as an adult, he witnessed all the horrors of World War II at first hand; as a communist, he was deluded by the major political delusion of the century; as an immigrant to the West, he felt the smothering of the individual human soul under an avalanche of materialism, relativism, hedonism, and decadence. All the more eloquently rings his plea in his Nobel Lecture for sanity eventually to prevail among the nations of the earth:

> We realize that the unification of our planet is in the making, and we attach importance to the notion of international community. The days when the League of Nations and the United Nations were founded deserve to be remembered.

This realization of the importance of international community can be found throughout his writings. Its source, beyond his own experience, was, by his own testimony, his uncle, Oscar Milosz, poet and seer, who predicted the "triumph of the Roman Catholic Church." Narrow Catholic hopes aside, history, lower case, moves toward the vindication of both of them, as well as of all those who have stood throughout this century for the further development of international institutions through which the nations might cooperate for the protection of the weak and vulnerable, for the protection of the little ones.

If "There are no direct lessons that American poets can learn from Milosz," the fault lies entirely with us and the age of academic criticism that has almost strangled the life out of poetry. They who claim Milosz has little to offer poets are precisely those American academics for whom, in his 1969 *Visions from San Francisco Bay*, far beyond the confines of Poland, supposedly about the New World, he displays scathing contempt for conforming to "the dominant spiritual climate" of nihilism, which he suggests invariably results in violence. More than any other poet, he has confronted the historical evils that totalitarian ideologies have perpetrated on millions of human beings and the decadent aesthetic dogmas of modern times, while most writers in England, Europe, and America have either withdrawn into isolated little worlds of nihilism and human treason or seek themselves to impose Marxist totalitarianism of one type or another on their fellow citizens. Far from being merely a "political poet," his poetry clearly reveals that his various concerns, undergirded by a wise and unusually perceptive understanding of the forces of the century, have always been the "attempt to approach the inexpressible sense of being," the nature of language, consciousness, belief, evil, sexuality, hope for the future, human freedom and dignity, and all that is embraced by that resonating verse "what is man born of woman." Instead of writing in an intellectual vacuum, Milosz has always struggled with history, with particular time and space, "Now, not any time, here, in America." Today he alone among poets proffers the inestimable lesson that there is indeed a way out of the stultifying clichés of postmodernism.

Saul Bellow's Soul

. . . for each one knows
A day is drawing to a close.
W. H. Auden

I do not presume to poke into the recesses of Saul Bellow's soul. What transpires there is between him and God. Rather I propose to discuss what Bellow has called the soul throughout much of his fiction. I will, however, by way of approaching Bellow's understanding of the soul, reveal a little about my own soul. For it is the reverberations Bellow sets off in my deepest being that keeps me reading him and believing he has a more profound perception of contemporary experience than any other American novelist. Judging from my earliest recollection, I first became aware of my being a soul when I was eight years old. I had committed a childish sin, but a sin nonetheless, and have a vivid memory of my owning up to my transgression within the confessional of Saint Anne's, in a dreary working-class suburb of Detroit, where my family, on my mother's side, Croatian Catholics for generations, worshiped. Through the screen that separated us, the priest admonished me to recite the requisite number of Hail Marys at the altar. During their recitation, on my knees, I poured out my heart in penance and gazed in adoration at the crucifix, the icon of Mary, Mother of God, and the multicolored candles flickering at the side of the altar. The years went by. I grew up to read Stendhal and Nietzsche and to loathe the church. Often, though, I have wondered, especially as society continues to break down, so strangely reminiscent of the collapse of the Roman Empire, whether there might not be something in the old religions still much needed by civilization. Such reflections can also be found in Saul Bellow's books. For Bellow is one of the few writers to remember man is a soul, not a mere conglomeration of social conditioning. Bellow's soul is the modern soul—the soul set free from its traditional Christian and Judaic past, I should add even from its Buddhist, Islamic, or Hindu past, yet hungry, seeking, longing for its rightful home.

In Bellow's introduction to Allan Bloom's *Closing of the American Mind* (1987), he admits that, while still a young man reading widely, he was "quickly carried away from the ancient religion." There is, then, no suggestion in his work that we ought to go back in that direction—back to Judaism or Christianity. Mutability has swept all that away forever. Having left that behind, as so many have, Bellow reveals in his Nobel Lecture what remains, though most are afraid to say so: "'There is a spirit,' and that is taboo." From this spirit come "true impressions," "persistent intuitions," "hints" of another reality. The value of literature itself lies in such "hints." Bellow increasingly repudiated the taboo against the spirit. It is from the "glimpses" of the "essence of our real condition" that the sense of our "real powers" comes—"powers we seem to derive from the universe itself." I cannot help recalling how men and women, as the late Roman Empire collapsed, turned fervently toward mysticism. The brutality, barbarism, confusion, and relativism of that thoroughly corrupt society drove thoughtful, sensitive people ever more toward transcendent understanding of the awful spectacle that surrounded them. Bellow never answered convincingly how his soul differs from Mithraism, Manicheism, Neoplatonism, and other vaguely pantheistic mystery cults, such as Emerson's oversoul.

As one who has lived in Japan beyond the initial *gaijin* or foreigner stage, I know the spectacle of this upheaval extends to other than Western shores. We are witnessing not merely the decline of Western society but of all the traditional religions and the societies they supported. Though largely focused on Western society, Bellow realizes the worldwide scope of the crisis. In *More Die of Heartbreak* (1987), Uncle Benn and Kenneth Trachtenberg flee to Japan to escape their sordid sexual affairs only to be taken to a strip show in Kyoto, "one of the holy cities of Asia," by Uncle Benn's colleagues in the botany department of Kyoto University. Similarly, Kenneth Trachtenberg, a specialist in Russian literature, observes the resemblance of St. Petersburg in 1913 to the Chicago of today: "By and by it became evident that the metaphysics that had long supported the ethical order had crumbled away." Whether

Russia, Europe, America, or the Far East, an unrelenting tidal wave
of change has inundated and is obliterating all vestiges of the past.
While the East, in the sense of the Soviet Union, "has the ordeal of
privation, the West has the ordeal of desire," or sexual anarchy.
Though in different ways, both ordeals are destroying the memory
of the soul. Having a global view of sexual anarchy, Bellow writes,
"whatever it is that snatches souls away by the hundred of millions
has to be reckoned with." We are left, then, with the soul or spirit
stripped of all orthodox accoutrements, encircled by a raging chaos,
of which Beirut offers the "authentically contemporary" model.

In *Mr. Sammler's Planet* (1970), perhaps Bellow's greatest novel,
Mr. Sammler states, "very often, and almost daily, I have strong
impressions of eternity" and calls them "God adumbrations."
Against the background of the collapsing of Western civilization in
New York, Sammler remembers the cultural and religious past of
Europe, his own Polish past in the Austro-Hungarian Empire, and
his days in Bloomsbury, England, when it was at its cultural zenith.
Thoroughly read in Freud, Marx, Weber, such "worthless fellows"
as Adorno, Marcuse, and Norman O. Brown, Sammler has reached
the point where he wishes "to read only certain religious writers of
the thirteenth century—Suso, Tauler, and Meister Eckhart."
Sammler's character is firmly "on the side of the spiritual, Platonic,
Augustinian." Early in the book Sammler emphasizes that "the best
and purest human beings, from the beginning of time, have
understood that life is sacred." It is not so much that Sammler
"literally believed" in Meister Eckhart, but "that he cared to read
nothing" else, finding there, by implication, food for the soul. The
violence of Raskolnikov, which he finds all around him in New
York, inside as well as outside the university, appalls him and
causes him to seek answers from deeper sources than fashionable,
shallow intellectuals. Unsurprisingly, Sammler simply tells Walter
Bruch, who comes to him seeking sophisticated rationalizations, by
way of sincerely offering him the help he truly needs, "I'll pray for
you." With the same purity of heart, Sammler admires Elya Gruner
for his virtuous human qualities that reflect the best, the highest in
human nature. For despite all the misery and despair brought on by

the malady of modern individualism, Sammler maintains "the spirit knows that its growth is the real aim of existence," which can be achieved only "by willing as God wills." And in this sense "the soul of Elya Gruner" meets "the terms of his contract," as each man knows his own contract in his inmost soul. For that, Sammler quietly counsels at the end of the book, is the truth each man inescapably knows.

Sammler observes that because "the sense of God persists," his "God adumbrations," the corresponding sense of the chaotic elements of modern life is heightened. The contradictions to his faith become all the more painful. His meditations on the mass murder of the Jews by the Nazis; his own killing of a Polish soldier during World War II; his perception of the increasing moral corruption of intellectuals; his recognition of the penchant for violence among New Left radicals; his awareness of the breakdown of civilized life in New York, "which makes one think about the collapse of civilization, about Sodom and Gomorrah, the end of the world"; the licentious sexuality of Gruner's daughter Angela and her brother Wallace's shiftless irresponsibility; the dire condition of many inner city blacks, as portrayed by the pickpocket; all these contradict Sammler's sense that God persists, for what truly merciful God, Sammler suggests, could permit such depravity and violence? Ultimately though, Sammler holds that "inability to explain is no ground for disbelief" and "all is not flatly knowable." One of the most common characteristics of the intellectuals Bellow so often loathes is that they imagine everything should indeed be "flatly knowable."

Instead of ignoring such contradictions, Bellow weaves them into the dialectical tapestry of his fiction. He juxtaposes them, as in *Herzog* (1964), with the "potato love" of Moses, with all the weak, dreamy, and idealistic emotions to which so many of his characters are inclined. Herzog's wandering mind sums up well this type of contradictory material in Bellow's work when he reflects

History is the history of cruelty, not love, as soft men think.... If the old God exists he must be a murderer. But the one true god is Death. This is how it is—without cowardly illusions.

Like Sammler, though, Moses Herzog dialectically dispenses with this view as merely accusing God of murder—putting him on trial for what we ourselves are guilty of. At the end of *Herzog*, God in a sense also persists. Herzog writes "'Thou movest me.' Something produces intensity, a holy feeling." He is satisfied "to be just as it is willed." Herzog returns to what Bellow calls Square One, to the "primordial person" that "precedes social shaping," "to some primal point of balance." To "resume your first self" is qualitatively different from "potato love" that remains dialectically undeveloped. And it has a maturity of vision and, therefore, an affirmation far above the quotidian. At the end of his Nobel Lecture, Bellow points out it is the "true impressions" from "that other world" "which moves us to believe that the good we hang on to so tenaciously—in the face of evil so obstinately—is no illusion." Far from living in a vacuum, Bellow fully faces the evil, contradictory material, boldly sees it for the reality that it is, and rightly values the good as having transcendent importance.

In an interview in *U.S. News and World Report*, after the publication of *The Dean's December* (1982), Bellow discusses the pervasiveness of such contradictory material and locates its origin in the soul. Talking of the hundreds of millions of people who have been murdered in the twentieth century, Bellow laments, "We have become used to brutality and savagery":

As a writer, I struggle with these facts. I'm preoccupied with the way in which value is—or is not—assigned to human life. A writer comes to feel that there is a way of grasping these horrors that is peculiar to poetry, drama and fiction. I don't admit the defeat of the humane tradition.

Far from turning away from these horrors, or buckling before them, as so many writers of the last fifty years have done, Bellow's choice to grapple with the reality of what Emerson called the "odious facts" exemplifies the best in the humane tradition. Today the work of very few writers shows, as does Bellow's, how much strength is still left in that tradition and how much ground can be reclaimed for it by assiduous labor and self-sacrifice. Bellow goes on to say that in the modern world "we are divested of the deeper human meaning that has traditionally been attached to human life." Emphatically, he states, "There's no sacred space around human beings anymore." In a November, 1990, interview on NBC, Bellow remarked that we are losing the sense of what it means to be a human being and to have a soul. "Our humanity is at risk," he warns, "because the feeling that life is sacred has died away in this century." In 1993 he writes, "everything worth living for has melted away."

In *The Dean's December*, Albert Corde specifically confronts the breakdown of American democracy and Soviet totalitarianism and fathoms the nihilism of East and West. During a long December visit to Rumania, where his wife's mother is dying, he learns at first hand what life is like in a communist country. While there, he reflects on his involvement in a murder trial back in Chicago and on two controversial articles of his in *Harper's* that attack the corruption of American society. Whether Corde meditates on the East, the West, or the developing world, he invariably discovers social oppression and decay. Bellow makes particularly brilliant use of Vico to bring out the decline of "human customs":

Children born outside the law and abandoned by parents can be eaten by dogs. It must be happening in places like Uganda now. The army of liberators who chased out Idi made plenty of babies. Eaten by dogs. Or brought up without humanity. Nobody teaching the young language, human usages or religion, they will go back to the great ancient forest and be like the wild beasts of Orpheus. None of the great compacts of the human race respected. Bestial venery, feral wanderings, incest, and the dead left unburied.

By implication this critique applies to the black ghetto in Chicago and elsewhere in America, though it is surely just as applicable in ways to white America. Reading this book made me recall my own experience living in Detroit and its suburbs where our failure to hand on human customs to the next generation is so apparent. I remember too studying with Robert Hayden and his confession that he had considered moving back to Detroit but the fear of violence eventually dissuaded him. I can still hear his bemoaning to me, "Blacks aren't any safer there than anybody else, you know." As Corde puts it earlier, "advanced modern consciousness" is "a reduced consciousness inasmuch as it contained only the minimum of the furniture that civilization was able to install." Bellow's deepest insight resides in his recognition that the collapse of civilization itself constitutes the most eloquent argument for the reality of truly positive values—spiritual values, if you will. Like Vico, who emphasizes the role the transcendent plays in maintaining the customs of civilization, Bellow dramatizes throughout *The Dean's December* that the progressive breakdown of society in Chicago and in the Soviet Union is largely the result of the loss of the knowledge of the soul.

Corde's purpose is "to recover the world that is buried under the debris of false description or nonexistence." By passing "Chicago through his own soul," Corde attempts to find the "underlying truth" of reality. The false descriptions of psychology, sociology, economics, and journalism merely exacerbate our plight. Corde's boyhood friend Dewey Spangler, now a journalist with an international reputation, fails to convey anything of real substance in his writing. He is basically a media hack pandering to the lowest common denominator. Corde, on the other hand, has "the high intention to prevent the American idea from being pounded into dust altogether." He has the inspired moral vision of the artist that penetrates the layers of deception to look at what is actually happening in America. In an interview in *Contemporary Literature*, Bellow succinctly states his position: "the first step is to display the facts. But, the facts, unless the imagination perceives them, are not facts." Bellow goes on to say that "without art, it is impossible to interpret reality." Because the technicians, experts, journalistic media hacks and pseudo-intellectuals lack the "musical pitch" of the humanistic tradition, they merely add to the cacophony of the "Great Noise." Spanning the modern world, both East and West, *The Dean's December* meditates profoundly on the state of the contemporary soul and concludes, "Something deadly is happening."

This "something" is more honest than an ostensibly precise word. In *Summations* (1987) Bellow mentions what writers should now pursue: "something lying behind the 'concepts' and the appearances." Earlier, in *Humboldt's Gift* (1975), Charlie Citrine brooded on a similar "something," fundamentally on the soul:

> I'm not a mystic. Anyway I don't know why mystic should be such a bad word. It doesn't mean much more than the word religion, which some people still speak of with respect. What does religion say? It says that there's something in human beings beyond the body and brain and that we have ways of knowing that go beyond the organism and its senses. I've always believed that. My misery comes, maybe, from ignoring my own metaphysical hunches. I've been to college so I know the educated answers. Test me on the scientific world-view and I'd score high. But it's just head stuff.

No one who has read much of Saul Bellow's work can doubt that he is a writer who in some hard to define way still regards mysticism and religion with respect. The way he attempts to restore such respect can clearly be seen in an exchange Citrine has with a collaborator on a proposed journal, the comically avant-garde Pierre Thaxter, who objects to Citrine, "For God's sake, we can't come out with all this stuff about the soul." Citrine observes, "Why not? People talk about the psyche, why not the soul?" Thaxter, submerged in all the dreck of modernism, all the "head stuff," retorts, "Psyche is scientific," adding "You have to accustom people gradually to these terms of yours." Wielding the knife of humor, Bellow undercuts the privileged position of modernism and exposes its unmitigated banality. Out of such play, he manages to bring truly serious reflections on the state of modern society and on the soul.

After observing "the ideas of the last few centuries are used up," Charlie says,

> I am serious. The greatest things, the things most necessary for life, have recoiled and retreated. People are actually dying of this, losing all personal life, and the inner being of millions, many many millions, is missing. One can understand that in many parts of the world there is no hope for it because of famine or police dictatorships, but here in the free world what excuse have we? Under pressure of public crisis the private sphere is being surrendered. I admit this private sphere has become so repulsive that we are glad to get away from it. But we accept the disgrace ascribed to it and people have filled their lives with so-called "public questions." What do we hear when these public questions are discussed? The failed ideas of three centuries. . . . Mankind must recover its imaginative powers, recover living thought and real being, no longer accept these insults to the soul, and do it soon. Or else! And this is where a man like Humboldt, faithful to failed ideas, lost his poetry and missed the boat.

Humboldt, Bellow's composite of Delmore Schwartz and Robert Lowell, remained faithful to the wornout ideas of symbolist poetry. Instead of "real being," Humboldt settled for the clichés of the prevailing modernist mentality. As Charlie Citrine writes early in the book, modern poets, unlike Homer or Dante, "didn't have a sane and steady idealization. To be Christian was impossible, to be pagan also. That left you know what"—the nihilism of the twentieth century. Hence, the soul receives nothing but insults, the failed ideas of disordered being. Like Sammler, Citrine has "incessant hints of immortality," and he is sickened that, for all our numerous, relativistic epistemologies, not one "speaks straight to the soul." With the demise of all the old ideas and the spread of disorder, Citrine argues that Humboldt's *poète maudit* "performance was conclusive" and "can't be continued." In a manner similar to Sammler, Herzog, Corde, and other characters in Bellow, Citrine has experienced all the vicissitudes of life, heard and studied all the rationalistic explanations, and has come to believe "Now we must listen in secret to the sound of the truth that God puts into us."

Despite the obviously insincere use of Rudolf Steiner's anthroposophy, a use which indicates a spiritual failure of imagination on the part of Bellow, essentially still the modern failure to find a true and satisfying way out of the predicament, Bellow argues broadly for the reality of the soul and opposes what he calls "the ruling premises":

> The question is this: why should we assume that the series ends with us? The fact is, I suspect, that we occupy a point within a great hierarchy that goes far far beyond ourselves. The ruling premises deny this. We feel suffocated and don't know why. The existence of a soul is beyond proof under the ruling premises, but people go on behaving as though they had souls, nevertheless. They behave as if they came from another place, another life, and they have impulses and desires that nothing in this world, none of our present premises, can account for. On the ruling premises the fate of humankind is a sporting event, most ingenious. Fascinating. When it doesn't become boring. The specter of boredom is haunting this sporting conception of history.

"The ruling premises," what Czeslaw Milosz calls the "fad of nihilism," have dogmatically repudiated any spiritual interpretation of reality throughout this century. Bellow's fiction increasingly opposes this dogmatism and asserts the reality of man's transcendent nature. "The ruling premises" are basically a catalog of failed ideas—three centuries' worth. Of intellectuals, Charlie earlier says, "I always said they were wasting their time and ours, and that I wanted to trample and clobber them." Citrine reflects that should the prevailing premise that nothing awaits us after death prove to be true, he would be astonished, "for the prevailing beliefs seldom satisfy my need for truth." He is unable to take stock in "respectable empiricism" because "Too many fools subscribe to it." "Besides," Citrine argues, "people were not really surprised when you spoke to them about the soul and the spirit." In an interview in *TriQuarterly*, Bellow states, "To have a soul, to be one—that today is a revolutionary defiance of received opinion."

In *The Theft* (1989), Clara, a country girl who becomes a successful executive in New York, has yet to be informed that "no more mystical sacredness remained in the world." She can therefore say sincerely to Ithiel Regler, "I love you with my soul." Ithiel, a political operator in Washington, refers to her as "a strange case—a woman who hasn't been corrupted." When he suffers abandonment by his wife, Clara hastens to Washington, "for a human purpose," to console him in his time of grief. Many years earlier when their relationship was more promising, Ithiel had given her an emerald ring that becomes for her a "major symbol," "a life support," not only of their love but of much more. The novella revolves around the theft of this ring and the necessity of its recovery. At a time when all universals have been mechanically banished from the human realm, Clara holds to this ring as a symbol of the existence of love, however far "down in the catacombs" it might be. In fact, Clara knows "a lot and at first hand about decadence." Rather tired of the "collapsing culture bit," she prefers "to see it instead as the conduct of life without input from your soul" though she cannot give specific details. The ring becomes for her symbolic of all that is "the real thing," clear, perfect.

At the end of the novella Clara describes Ithiel as a truthful, realistic observer who knows the big picture. One of Bellow's tough-minded characters, "He likes to look at the human family as it is." Ithiel concedes, though, that his idea of "what is real" is not as deep as hers. She possesses an understanding of the soul that goes beyond his worldly perception. Nevertheless, his realism gives him the advantage in his political world of international negotiations and intrigues. He cynically remarks to her that "Neither the Russians nor the Americans can manage the world. Not capable of organizing the future." Of the "new Soviet regime" under Gorbachev, Bellow puts into his mouth words that surely reflected, at the time, Bellow's own assessment of Gorbachev and that to some extent proved their prescience:

> Some of the smartest migrs are saying that the Russians didn't announce liberalization until they had crushed the dissidents. Then they co-opted the dissidents' ideas. After you've gotten rid of your enemies, you're ready to abolish capital punishment—that's how Alexander Zinoviev puts it. And it wasn't only the KGB that destroyed the dissident movement but the whole party organization, and the party was supported by the Soviet people. They strangled the opposition, and now they're pretending to be it. You have the Soviet leaders themselves criticizing Soviet society. When it has to be done, they take over. And the West is thrilled by all the reforms.

To this evaluation of East and West, Clara answers, "So we're going to be bamboozled again." This passage demonstrates that, unlike many writers, Bellow does not live in a vacuum of Marxist clichés. His criticism of communism is one fully informed of the dialectical theories, actual history, and brutal reality of Soviet totalitarianism. Equally scathing is his critique of Western society, sunk in its own brand of decadence and, as Ithiel says later, craving "to be sold, deceived, if you prefer." Only Milosz and Solzhenitsyn have achieved such penetrating insight into the reality of East and West. Bellow's achievement may actually rank higher than theirs since it has not been forced upon him by catastrophe and exile but has resulted from the sheer struggle of his soul to resist the nihilism of modernity and to speak for what is noble and enduring.

In *The Bellarosa* Connection (1989), Bellow confronts in particular the condition of the Jewish soul. Sorella Fonstein says to the unnamed narrator of the novella, the founder of the Mnemosyne Institute:

> The Jews could survive everything that Europe threw at them. I mean the lucky remnant. But now comes the next

test—America. Can they hold their ground, or will the U.S.A. be too much for them?

Harry Fonstein escapes the Nazis with the help of Billy Rose, a famous American Jew in the entertainment business. Fonstein wants to thank Rose in person for his help, but Rose, thoroughly Americanized and largely assimilated, wants nothing to do with him. The USA has proven too much for him. Fonstein resists assimilation and clings to the old world, to Mitteleuropa. Though the Fonsteins make a fortune in the thermostat business, they increasingly isolate themselves as a way of dealing with life in America. At the end of the novella, the narrator, "a Jew of an entirely different breed" from the Fonsteins, closer to Rose, attempts to reestablish contact with the Fonsteins after many years of having lost touch with them. He finally succeeds in reaching a Jewish friend of the Fonstein's son Gilbert. This friend, who is house sitting, reveals that they died six months earlier in an automobile accident. The narrator continues to talk to Gilbert's friend and discovers that Gilbert has become a professional gambler "more in the Billy Rose vein than in the Harry Fonstein vein" and is at that moment a pilgrim to America's holy city, Las Vegas. Although it occurs to the narrator the Fonsteins avoided him for years to hide the truth about their son, it is the "low-grade cheap-shot nihilism" of Gilbert's young Jewish friend that disturbs him the most. Since even the narrator's own son has grown up to become "all administrator and executive," he ultimately learns that America has proven "too much" for everyone concerned. In a dream his soul brings him the truth that he himself has become "half Jewish, half waspish." Yet he holds to "the roots of memory in feeling" and to the disclosure of his dream that he has "made a mistake, a lifelong mistake." His deepest answer to the nihilism of Gilbert's friend, who is thoroughly lost to the clichés of modernism, becomes his written "mnemosyne flourish," his account of the entire Bellarosa connection; in a sense, the novella itself, Bellow's own account of the Jewish soul in the modern world and in America. Holding to his dictum "Memory is life," the narrator establishes "at the very least that I am still able to keep up my struggle for existence."

It is this "struggle for existence" that is at the heart of Bellow's work. In his Nobel Lecture he states that neither science nor art is any longer at the center of human concern, but rather confusion and the individual struggling "with dehumanization for the possession of his soul." We seem to be in the "early stages of universal history" and are being "lavishly poured together," experiencing the "anguish of new states of consciousness." As Bellow remarks in an interview in *Salmagundi*, "we're in some sort of ideological or moral interregnum," "we're between epochs." The "central energies of man," as he states in his Nobel Lecture, are consumed with this crisis: "The decline and fall of everything is our daily bread." The Great Noise drowns out the small still voice of the soul. Leaving aside all nostalgia, all longing for a restoration of the Judaic or Christian past, Bellow asserts in *TriQuarterly*, "The modern age is our given, our crushing *donnée*." For a writer in the realist tradition, one who chooses to look at the facts, one capable of recognizing the novel is "a sort of latter-day lean-to" for the shelter of the spirit, on a decidedly lower level than the epic, there is no escape into the kind of puerile fantasies of the self that have consumed the time of so many writers during the last fifty years or so. The only other American novel that approaches Bellow's confrontation with the modern soul is Isaac Bashevis Singer's *The Penitent*.

In 1987 in "The Civilized Barbarian Reader," an adaptation, published in *The New York Times Book Review*, of his introduction to Allan Bloom, Bellow identifies some important benefits of decline not mentioned in the version in the book itself:

What no one was able to foresee was that all civilized countries were destined to descend to an inferior common cosmopolitanism, but that the lamentable weakening of the older, traditional branches of civilization might open fresh opportunities, force us to reassess the judgments of traditional culture and that we might be compelled—a concealed benefit of decline—to be independent. To interpret our circumstances as deeply as we can—isn't that what we human beings are here for? Quite simply, when the center does not hold and great structures fall down, one has an opportunity to see some of the truths that they obstructed. Longstanding premises then come in for revision and old books are read by a new light.

My own experience leads me to believe Bellow is quite right about "this concealed benefit of decline." The descent into "an inferior common cosmopolitanism," an emerging world culture constructed largely on the popular mass culture of the West, has indisputably weakened the traditional foundations of every country around the globe. For more than a century, Westernizing, essentially modernizing intellectuals have been at the forefront of social change in Russia, the Middle East, Japan, and elsewhere. The civilization of Western Europe and North America has spread over the entire earth. Much good has resulted from this long historical process, but much harm has also occurred to humane ways of life and thought.

The decline has reached such prodigious proportions, I cannot avoid believing there might be something in the past still much needed, in an appropriate form to our changed condition. This reassessment of modernism is made possible by the very decline of modernism itself—its failure to produce a society worthy of its highest claims. All around us now, in the West as well as in the East, "great structures" are falling down, opening the way for a clear view of how bankrupt they have been all along. While we stand among their ruins, we know we cannot go backwards after having enjoyed their many benefits. We are forever changed. We need a "revision" of "longstanding premises," surely not a simple-minded return to the past, which we can all be glad is gone forever. As Bellow writes, "in the end a man must master his own experience," and we require a new mastery of our new circumstances, of our global, multicultural experience; a mastery that nevertheless does justice to the past—what our experience has been—and that yet rises above what Herzog calls "knee-jerk nihilism." Though we stand free of all traditional accoutrements, ever more free of all the clichés of modernism, we can find in the midst of such confusion, "an open channel to the soul," an open channel "to the deepest part of ourselves."

The Dialectic of Chinese Literature

I walk slowly into the cave. A Mogao grotto on the old Silk Road in the Gobi Desert. T'ang dynasty. Alone. The light from the entrance barely lights my way. The air seems old, old as the twelve hundred year old cave, but dry, dry as the desert air of Arizona. The farther I go the more I am enwrapped by the darkness until I stand before the altar and strain to make out the figures of the statues. At the center Buddha sits in lotus position, his right arm raised, preaching the Law. To each side stands a disciple, one, his companion Ananda, aged and suffering. Bare-chested servants bow their heads toward the Buddha in servitude and obeisance. The guardians stand at the flank attired for battle, ready to defend and protect. As my eyes adjust, I begin to see more than just the dim outlines of the images. Bodhisattvas adorn either side of the wall murals; behind the Buddha, in glorious T'ang dynasty detail of flames and flowers, a heavenly nimbus signifies his transcendent nature. The old cave builders knew how to touch the human soul, how to clothe human consciousness with something other than itself, how to raise it to a higher level. I want to bow, I want to pray, I want to beg the Buddha for compassion. As the cave itself was painstakingly carved into the mountainside, I am driven into the interior of my own being and on toward its center. Suddenly the door is thrown wide open, a group of noisy tourists tramps in behind me, laughing and flicking their flashlights everywhere. I am back in the late twentieth century.

No pilgrims here. We are out to see the sights. Buddhism, a lovely, true, beautiful way of understanding human experience, is gone, gone forever, gone as much as Christianity, Judaism, Islam, Hinduism, or any other transcendent conception of human existence. We're here for business, copulation, and scholarship. Walmart and Madonna. One way or another, play is the thing, and lots of it. No time for perfection of the soul. There have been and are those who want to go backwards to one great religion or another. Of them, whether Christian or Buddhist, I think always of what Nietzsche had to say in *Twilight of the Idols*:

Whispered to the conservatives. What was not known formerly, what is known, or might be known, today: a reversion, a return in any sense or degree is simply not possible. . . . Nothing avails: one must go forward—step by step further into decadence (that is my definition of modern "progress").

(tr. Walter Kaufman)

If this is true of conservatives who have wanted to go backwards, perhaps to the thirteenth century, what should be said of liberals who have wanted progress, which Nietzsche called decadence? In particular, I think of the theories of Marx, the acceptance of them by Chinese communists, and Mao's lamentable implementation. Buddha never encouraged his disciples to perpetrate appalling violence and social upheaval.

For that matter, Confucius too had a more profound vision of life than Karl Marx and Mao Zedong. In his dissertation, Marx repudiated the moral and metaphysical tradition of Western philosophy in favor of doing something for the progress of the world, while Mao repeatedly rejected Confucian ethics and called for revolutionary deeds of terror. I think of Mao telling the young Dalai Lama to forget about religion. In *The Analects*, Confucius emphasizes a moral perspective:

Govern the people by regulations, keep order among them by chastisements, and they will flee from you, and lose all self-respect. Govern them by moral force (*Te*), keep order among them by ritual (*Li*), and they will keep their self-respect and come to you of their own accord.

(tr. Arthur Waley)

Although there is wisdom in such ethical Confucian teachings about eliciting individual and social order, modern Chinese experience, by definition, has been an irrevocable movement away from the Buddhist, Confucian, and Taoist past.

In the *Tao Te Ching*, Lao Tzu, the philosopher-founder of Taoism, states, "The Way that can be spoken of is not the constant way; the name that can be named is not the constant name." Essentially, an affirmation of mysticism, the Tao is transcendent to human understanding. Experience, not words about the Tao, is important. Man and the universe share the same *chi*, "breath" or "spirit," and the goal of human existence is to harmonize the two. Chuang Tzu's famous maxim makes the same point: "If you've gotten the meaning, you can forget the word." Although Taoism emphasizes individual mystical states of mind, it also had a social vision that in some ways is similar to Confucianism and that had resonance for some emperors. Chapter thirty-seven of the *Tao Te Ching*:

> The way never acts yet nothing is left undone. Should lords and princes be able to hold fast to it, the myriad creatures will be transformed of their own accord. After they are transformed, should desire raise its head, I shall press it down with the weight of the nameless uncarved block. The nameless uncarved block is but freedom from desire, and if I cease to desire and remain still, the empire will be at peace of its own accord.
>
> (tr. D.C. Lau)

Wu-wei, "active passivity," can be seen here as a form of royal self-restraint that calls forth from the people what is highest in them, "the nameless uncarved block." In his study of the classical philosophers and poets, Mao, a modern student of Marx, failed to understand and respect both the value of *Wu-wei* and the mysticism of the Chinese soul.

From at least the time of Nietzsche, many observers of Western culture, such as Max Weber, Robert Bellah, Allan Bloom, and others, have perceived an analogous change of values. To understand both the East and the West, it is essential to understand there has been a parting of ways, often for the better, at times for the worse, but definitely never to be reversed. We know in our inmost hearts and in our most common everyday experience that we live in a post-Judeo-Christian world. As Saul Bellow in 1993 wrote, "everything worth living for has melted away." Amusingly enough, even to many Chinese and Japanese, some in America are increasingly looking with nostalgia to Asia for a spirituality they find lacking in our own culture. But, alas, the mystic East is mystic no more. As spiritually dead as Europe. In terms of China, this psychomachia or dialectic between the traditional and the modern runs throughout its twentieth century literature, which is as profound, in its own context, as anything written in the West.

To understand this dialectic we must first look at the traditional background of Chinese sensibility as reflected in the best classical poets. T'ao Ch'ien (AD 365-427), a Taoist recluse, in the "home and gardens" school of poetry, who lived, as he writes, "in a time of decadence," represents an expression of the early Chinese sense of life before Buddhism becomes firmly established. He was, however, a friend of monks who belonged to the White Lotus Society, which later evolved into Ch'an, the Zen form of Chinese Buddhism. His poems demonstrate a profound knowledge of Taoism, Buddhism, and Confucianism, a gentle openness to each tradition, and a willingness to permit his consciousness to perceive life, where appropriate, through each one. This openness is evident in the poem "Substance, Shadow, and Spirit," a dialectical discussion that takes place between different points of view within the poet's soul. Substance, slightly tinged with the Buddhist sense of illusion, introduces the inevitability of death and change. Shadow offers Confucian solace: "Do good, and your love will outlive you; / Surely this is worth your every effort." Spirit attempts to resolve the dilemma from a Taoist perspective:

> Doing good is always a joyous thing
> But no one has to praise you for it.
> Too much thinking harms my life;
> Just surrender to the cycle of things,
> Give yourself to the waves of the Great Change. . . .
> (tr. James Robert Hightower)

Going with the flow of things, with each great tradition a part of his inner being, T'ao Ch'ien presents a richly dialectical tension that, although tending a little more toward Taoism, allows each one to register its place within his consciousness. How different from the exclusivity of Western Christian belief that holds only one religion can be true, and all others are pagan, or the modern belief, Western as well as Eastern, grounded in historicism, that all religions are the same and categorically false.

While T'ao Ch'ien tends to Taoism, Tu Fu (712-770) perceives life predominantly through Confucianism. His own family had a long and deep heritage of Confucian service and literary achievement. Tu Fu's attempts to emulate his family's example were marked by dire vicissitudes. He repeatedly took and failed the required examinations for civil service and suffered peripatetic exile. His struggle to serve the emperor plays a central role in his poetry and becomes a backdrop against which he dramatizes the historical upheavals of the day. Although it is commonly said that China never developed the epic genre, Tu Fu's lyric poetry, when taken together, has epic breadth and reach. His great poem "Journey North," while only about one hundred and forty lines, attempts to sum up, with compassion, tragedy, and pathos, like true epic, the whole vision of life during his time. The poem begins with Tu Fu, a few years after the An Lu-Shan rebellion, "These times have brought us hardship, sorrow," serving the exiled emperor who has just issued an order allowing Tu Fu to return home to his family. Though he feels shame at the special favor, though worry about the still raging rebellion makes him reluctant to leave, he bows and accepts, thinking, in a Confucian way, "the Ruler truly is lord of our rising again, / about state affairs certainly diligent."

As Tu Fu travels homeward, he writes,

> Slow, slow   we cross paddy paths
> men, smoke   sparse in the desolation
> those we meet   most of them wounded
> groaning, sobbing   and even bleeding
> (tr. Hugh M. Stimson)

No longer in the court, he experiences everywhere the individual and social devastation of the rebellion. He counterpoints the suffering with the beauty and timelessness of chrysanthemums and mountain berries. Lingering briefly on his own personal circumstances, he thinks,

> My longing thoughts   are by Peach Spring
> more sighing   for the clumsiness of my life's course

"Peach Spring" is the title of a Taoist essay by T'ao Ch'ien about a fisherman happening upon a grove of peach trees on each side of a stream blossoming for hundreds of yards. The fisherman follows the grove along until it ends at a spring flowing into the stream through an entrance at the base of a hill. Inside he discovers an idyllic world of men and women secluded from the troubles of the outside world. Later, after returning to his own village, neither he nor any one else can rediscover the peach spring and the visionary community. Tu Fu, like many Chinese painters and poets before and after him, alludes here to T'ao Ch'ien's *Peach Blossom Spring* as a vision of a more perfect world than the one that he is experiencing, a vision by which to measure his own individual shortcomings and failures, as well as the violent anarchy of his times.

The pathos deepens when Tu Fu arrives home after an absence of more than a year to find his wife and children impoverished, clothed in rags, and starving. Upon arrival, he himself is so "sick in mind and chest / vomiting, diarrhetic," it takes him "several days" to recover from his journey. In a long and detailed description of his family's suffering, he describes further the individual, personal consequences of social rebellion and wonders how long the emperor will train his troops before finally using them to subdue the rebels and thereby restore order. After celebrating the eventual counter-offensive and extolling the virtue of General Ch'en, who convinces the emperor to execute Yang Kuei-Fei, his courtesan who has led the emperor astray, no sentimentality in Tu Fu, the poet exclaims, "today, the nation still lives!" Tu Fu further reveals in the closing lines his Confucian devotion to moral social order as the emperor returns to the capital, Chang-an, where

> the parks and tombs   truly have their gods
> are swept, sprinkled often and without fail
> bright, bright   the Great Founder's deed
> his establishing   most broad and pervasive!

Returning to the seat of authority in Great Unity Hall, the emperor renews the Confucian rituals and reestablishes the imperial line of the Founder of the T'ang dynasty. The rebellion has been squelched, Chinese civilization itself preserved and set back on a "broad and pervasive" course leading forward into the future. An epic vision of an epic struggle for civilization.

Roughly contemporary with Tu Fu, Wang Wei (701-761), unlike Tu Fu who pays scant attention to Buddhism, devoted his life and work to the religion. He wrote little of the social world but spent many years studying Buddhism and at times living the life of a recluse in one mountain retreat or another south of Chang-an, present day Xian. In the same "field and gardens" tradition as T'ao Ch'ien, he wrote about the subtleties of country experience often using nature metaphorically for Buddhist meditation. One of his earliest poems is a ballad based on T'ao Ch'ien's *Peach Blossom Spring*, a vision his later life and work seem to try to capture. In the first stanza of his poem "Suffering from Heat," Wang Wei describes the hot sun searing the earth. Everything is scorched from the grass and trees to the rivers and swamps. His own clothes are so heavily saturated with sweat they must be "washed again and again." In the second stanza, he writes,

> I long to escape beyond space and time;
> In vast emptiness, dwell alone and apart.
> Then long winds from a myriad miles would come;
> Rivers and seas would cleanse me of trouble and dirt.
> Then would I find that my body causes suffering;
> Then would I know that my mind is still unawake.

I would suddenly enter the Gate of Pleasant Dew
And be at ease in the clear, cool joy.

                              (tr. Hugh M. Stimson)

Like T'ao Ch'ien's fisherman, the persona "longs" for an idyllic world, here "beyond space and time," in the full "emptiness" of Buddhism, alone like an eremite wrapped in meditation. The "long winds" are clearly metaphorical, as is all the natural description cleansing the speaker of "dirt." More obviously Buddhist ideas are presented in the notion that the "body causes suffering" when the "mind is still unawake." The lovely signature of Ch'an Buddhism comes in the word "suddenly"—suddenly the mind does awake and attain. In a classic of Buddhism, the "Gate of Pleasant Dew" is mentioned as the portal leading to nirvana. With the closing line, Wang Wei alludes again to nirvana in his choice of the word "cool." "Nirvana" can be found in Sanskrit as early as the Bhagavad-Gita where it means "to cool by blowing," "blown out," "extinguished." Metaphorically, Wang Wei, the Buddhist in general, longs for the heat or fire of the passions and desires to be cooled, extinguished, in the indescribable bliss of Mahayana Buddhism.

Also a student of Buddhism, though usually less given to mysticism, Po Chu-yi (772-846), more than any other T'ang poet, had the gifts of compassion and courage that inspired him to speak out against the social injustice of the ruling class of which he himself was a member. His genuine concern for the weak and vulnerable explains his unprecedented popularity which extended during his own lifetime all the way to Korea and Japan. He understood the power of poetry to confront the social landscape, to speak for those who had no voice, and stir those of authority to remember the impact of their actions on ordinary people. Given his study of Ch'an, his poetry at times meditates just as profoundly on the inner nature of the human being. His nickname "Lay Buddhist of the Fragrant Mountain" speaks of other than worldly concerns.

In the poem "An Old Charcoal Seller," Po Chu-yi concentrates on a humble, individual peasant who becomes the victim of imperial injustice. The subtitle of the poem is "To Complain of the Royal

Commissary System," essentially a system of forced requisition. In contrast to the honest intentions and hard labor of the old man clothed in rags, hungry, trying to earn his living, riding his cart of charcoal in the morning toward the market, hopeful the cold weather will result in a good price, Po Chu-yi writes

All of a sudden, two dashing riders appear;
An imperial envoy, garbed in yellow (his attendant in white),
Holding an official dispatch, he reads a proclamation.
Then turns the cart around, curses the ox, and leads it north.
(tr. Eugene Eoyang)

He in his threadbare rags, and they in their sumptuous robes, are obviously from different worlds. His fate is sealed: "No use appealing to the official spiriting the cart away." The official tosses on the ox a mere "length of red lace" in token payment for the loaded cart of charcoal. Many of Po Chu-yi's poems display his deep, sincere compassion for the weak and vulnerable.

As entry into a different world, I take the work of these classical poets and philosophers as sounding many of the quintessential emotions and beliefs of the Chinese people during the last twenty-five hundred years. With the advent of the twentieth century, new concerns and interests begin to shape the consciousness of modern China.

Lu Xun (1881-1936), better than any other writer, marks the turning away from the old Confucian order to modern life. As a young medical student in Japan he studied Western Enlightenment philosophy and the modern scientific worldview. Among others, he read Rousseau, Hegel, Tolstoy, Ibsen, Byron, Schopenhauer, and especially Nietzsche, whose theory of the superman seems to have impressed him. When in 1911 Sun Yat-sen established the republic, Lu Xun, like many Chinese, had initially high hopes, but, as the country fractured into regions of contending war lords, Lu Xun watched the first chance China had for modern civilization crumble into increasingly violent chaos. Many within the new government failed to understand the nature of their responsibilities and failed to live up to the high calling of their duties. Rightly disillusioned, Lu Xun himself, nevertheless, failed to understand the modest, balanced nature of democratic political philosophy and thereby eventually prostituted his literary ability to the revolutionary romanticism of Marx and Mao. In a manner similar to Ezra Pound, Lu Xun chose to use his formidable literary gifts, during at least his last several years, to serve a base, violent, dehumanizing vision of life.

Lu Xun wrote his best work long before he allowed himself to sink into the communist crevasse. Written in April of 1918, his story "A Madman's Diary" reflects his revulsion with the Confucian order of traditional village life. The persona, left nameless throughout the story, visits his old home in the country and stops to see two brothers he knew in high school, having heard that one of them was ill. It turns out the younger of the brothers has recovered but left behind his diary. The rest of the story consists of extracts from the diary, all written during the brother's illness. As the persona reads them, a complex picture of mental illness and accusation emerges. Set among "country folk," the diary reveals that cannibalism has just occurred in nearby "Wolf Cub Village," and the brother fears that "They eat human beings, so they may eat me." He reflects on many such incidents in Chinese history and legend:

> In ancient times, as I recollect, people often ate human beings, but I am rather hazy about it. I tried to look this up, but my history has no chronology, and scrawled all over each page are the words: "Virtue and morality."

This "virtue and morality" belong to the Confucian tradition but prove insufficient to prevent barbarism from surfacing. As he reads his book of history, the words "Eat people" begin to fill the spaces between the lines. He finds cannibalism everywhere he turns in the village and even within his own family, for his elder brother is an "eater of human flesh." On further reflection, the Confucian classics themselves contain such observations as "People exchange their sons to eat."

People leer at him in the street. Their deceitful smiles prove their rapacious designs. In vision half real, half nightmare, the diary records a young man suddenly entering the house and the brother informing him that "They are eating men now in Wolf Cub Village." The young man, at first taking it for madness and a joke, tries to brush it off. The diary then records: "His expression changed, and he grew ghastly pale. 'It may be so,' he said, staring at me. 'It has always been like that. . . .'" The brother leaps from bed "soaked with perspiration." The leering continues. The older brother refuses to listen to reason: "members of the same group can still eat each other." Villagers linger outside, laughing cynically. The older brother tries to drive them away while stigmatizing the younger one as a madman. In frenzied desperation, near the end, the younger brother addresses the people:

> "You should change, change from the bottom of your hearts!"
> I said. "You must know that in future there will be no place for man-eaters in the world."

How this change will happen the story does not say. Lu Xun had no idea, only vague hope, sentimentality at best: "Save the children." He knew, quite rightly, that the debased Confucian culture supported cannibalism, had become the main pillar. It needed to be left behind. The present was barbarism; the future dark with no visible path leading toward it.

A year later in 1919 Lu Xun wrote his story "Medicine" which seems to suggest the remedy for the debilitated traditional Confucian culture. Old Chuan, who runs a teahouse, has a son dying of consumption. One morning the old man wakes up early and waits in the street. Soldiers and people are out early too and gather just at the crossroads. "Then a sound was heard," the sound of a criminal's beheading, and people rushed past him. One stops and sells him, for a bag of silver, "a roll of steamed bread, from which crimson drops were dripping to the ground." Upon returning to his teahouse, Old Chuan and his wife bake the *mantou*, a common Chinese roll, and feed it to their ailing son who goes off to bed to rest. An old customer who has heard of Old Chuan's good luck reveals for the reader the folk superstition Lu Xun is attacking: "A guaranteed cure! Eaten warm like this. A roll dipped in human blood like this can cure any consumption!" Not Little Chuan, who dies shortly. Lu Xun had watched his own father die a slow death over four years and had been sent out by the so-called physician many times to collect all sorts of herbal remedies that would provide the magic cure. According to his own testimony, his bitter memories were the impetus behind his early study of modern medicine and science in search of a real cure that might have helped his father, as his writing was, in some ways, an attempt to find a cure for China's many maladies.

The next spring Old Chuan's wife visits the graveyard where she performs the traditional rites of grieving before the boy's grave. As she burns paper money, unexpectedly, on the other side of a path, the mother of the executed criminal mourns at her own son's grave. He had been described in the teahouse as a "young rogue" who had "even tried to incite the jailer to revolt" against the last imperial dynasty, the Qing. Here Lu Xun shows the average folk in the teashop failed to understand the struggle for a republic. Clinging to the old dynasty, the folk wrongly condemned the young man. On his grave both mothers now observe a wreath of red and white flowers left by an unknown supporter of the republican cause. His mother mourns:

> "Son, they all wronged you, and you do not forget. Is your grief still so great that today you worked this wonder to let me know?" She looked all around, but could see only a crow perched on a leafless bough. "I know," she continued. "They murdered you. But a day of reckoning will come, Heaven will see to it. Close your eyes in peace. . . . If you are really here, and can hear me, make that crow fly on to your grave as a sign."

The folk superstition proves futile. The day of reckoning is not yet. The crow stays in the tree. After some time, the two mothers give up waiting and begin to walk away:

> They had not gone thirty paces when they heard a loud caw behind them. Startled, they looked round and saw the crow stretch its wings, brace itself to take off, then fly like an arrow towards the far horizon.

The medicine here is republican. The flowers are not only red; they are also white. Although the young man has been executed, there are those who remember him and the cause he nobly gave his life for. That far horizon is farther than even Lu Xun realized. Like so many modern intellectuals who cut their teeth on Nietzsche, for Lu Xun, that horizon was increasingly nihilistic, as in his classical poems, *Wild Grass*. That he ended up involved with communism is actually quite common, marks a devolution that Dostoevsky had understood many decades earlier, and shows, as with Ezra Pound, a failure of spirit and imagination.

Lu Wenfu (1928-) suffered long and hard from the horrors of the communist regime and understands in his fiction, as in the writings of Fang Lizhi, Wei Jingsheng, and Harry Wu, that communism's most egregious crime is its stifling of the human spirit. As a young man, he fought in the Red army against the Koumintang and dreamed of the "happy society" socialism would usher in. Like so many writers, in 1957, he was denounced as a Rightist, during the Hundred Flowers purge and the Great Leap Forward, and sentenced to manual labor to reform his thinking. After three years of running a machine lathe, he was deemed reformed and allowed again to write. Then, in 1965, Mao took China down the violent path of the Great Proletarian Cultural Revolution, and Lu Wenfu was once more denounced and sentenced, this time, to the life of a mechanic. He later wrote of his experience during the Cultural Revolution:

> I was 'struggled against,' forced to confess my crimes and paraded through the streets with a placard around my neck. I

was already numb to the pain, and worried about when this disaster for my country would end.

Finally, in 1969, he was sent out to the countryside where he farmed for several years. For more than a decade, Lu Wenfu wrote nothing until after the Cultural Revolution ended with Mao's death in 1976. What little was left of the traditional culture had been trashed; the ruthless persecution of "stinking intellectuals" like Lu Wenfu had been encouraged by Mao himself; thousands of Taoist and Buddhist temples and relics had been destroyed; millions of lives ruined; perhaps as many as 400,000 individual human beings murdered.

In 1979, Lu Wenfu wrote his brilliant short story "The Man from a Peddler's Family." Into it he poured all the sufferings of his life. The story begins with the protagonist, Mr. Gao, reflecting on Zhu Yuanda, a seller of wonton. Thirty-two years ago, Mr. Gao had heard for the first time the sound of his bamboo clapper, announcing the advance down the lane of the little kitchen stove on its carrying pole, figuratively "calling or relating something." Zhu Yuanda came from a long line of street vendors, generation after generation, reaching back into the distant dynasties. Following in the footsteps of his father, he continues the family trade. At the time, apparently 1947, Mr. Gao is out of regular work and must sit up late at night, in an unheated room, grading student notebooks for a bare existence. After the Beijing Opera let out late, Zhu Yuanda would bring him "a little warmth," a hot bowl of wonton to his "main customer." Though formerly friends, after the liberation of 1949, Mr. Gao, now a cadre, considers Zhu beneath him. Occasionally, he would still hear the clapper, "calling, saying something." Gao remembers, as the Anti-Rightist campaign and Great Leap Forward raged, "I never bought anything from him and I wouldn't allow my wife or children to go. I believed that buying his things was aiding the spontaneous rise of capitalism." The Anti-Rightist struggles continue, disturbing Gao, until, in what may be an allusion to Buddhism, he ponders how "The world seemed out of joint." Lu Wenfu is clearly suggesting there is something more to the business of the clapper than just petty bourgeois capitalism.

Yet Mr. Gao goes through his own internal struggles and battles. For a time he attempts to correct or reform Zhu Yuanda, and later tries to ignore or forget him, hoping to save his own skin from the social upheavals. They had, though, formerly shared "a genuine affection," one that Gao cannot entirely forget despite his position within the communist order. Back and forth, he meditates on Zhu, finding him sometimes to be a capitalist, at others, one of the proletariat: "And then a thunderclap split the earth. The bugles of the Cultural Revolution were sounded, announcing the end of all capitalism." Gao himself becomes implicated in the madness and is "publicly criticized and denounced." He manages to avoid his own destruction but happens past Zhu Yuanda's house one day to find it and him in the midst of a horde of Red Guards smashing the "Evil Den of Capitalism." Gao, himself a cadre, knows better. He knows Zhu is a simple, decent man attempting only to feed his father, mother, wife, and four children, by, as he says, "my own efforts." In brilliant words, Lu Wenfu undercuts with scathing irony the pious, radical beliefs of decades of revolutionaries like Lu Xun, when Gao thinks, of the Red Guard's destruction of everything Zhu Yuanda owned, "How could a noble theory produce such piracy as this!" The worst offense is when the "wonton carrying-pole was dragged out," "a thing of exquisite workmanship," a thing redolent of the past, of the best of Chinese traditions, and shamelessly hacked into splinters. Zhu's family is reduced "to picking up garbage in the streets" in order to make ends meet. Lest the reader imagine Zhu was an exception, Lu Wenfu emphasizes that the seller of wonton was only one of many on the same street who suffered when he mentions the hot water boiler, the cobbler, the barber, and the flatbread seller as all meeting the same pitiless fate.

Like hundreds of thousands of real human beings, Zhu is sent to the countryside for reeducation. Eight years go by. Gao hears nothing of Zhu. Unexpectedly one day Gao hears that Zhu's sons are working in a local factory and later that Zhu himself is back. Before leaving, Zhu had given Gao the only thing that had somehow escaped destruction, the bamboo clapper. Gao, imagining he'll now want to return to his old business, begins to anticipate it. In a moment of fantasy, Gao remembers how as a young man he heard the sound of the clapper coming up the lane and thinks that now people will hear again Zhu Yuanda's approach: "Their lives, too, demand that there be others bringing them warmth and convenience. It had taken me more than twenty years to learn this elementary lesson." It had actually taken more than thirty years, and I wonder if Lu Wenfu is not hoping here that China itself has finally learnt the lesson after its "decade of disaster." I myself am not so sure. No longer interested in his clapper or selling wonton, Zhu longs only for an iron rice bowl for his children and himself. As Zhu leaves, Gao watches him walk down the street and poignantly thinks, "In these past years I and others had hurt him. We had stifled so much spirit." All the dreams and theories brought to naught by the broken stature of a ruined man. As in other modern Chinese writers, such pathos takes place against a social background intentionally drained of Confucian, Buddhist, and Taoist morality and transcendence.

The poems of Duoduo (1951-) are about the same upheavals and ruins. Cognizant of modern Western poetry, his own style came to be known in Chinese as "misty," an obscure, surrealist style of literature used by writers who were thought of as being "wounded" by the "decade of disaster." Later, as a journalist, he covered the June 4th, 1989, Tiananmen Square massacre. Since then, he has been living in exile in Europe and England. During the early 1970s while the Cultural Revolution was still wreaking its destruction, he began trying to understand the meaning of those cultural ruins. In 1973 in his poem "Era," he writes,

> An oppressive era has revived.
> The sound of a gun faintly shakes the earth.
> War is stubbornly reclaiming land.
> Livestock is requisitioned. Peasants return from fields,
> ploughs dripping with blood . . .   (tr. Gregory Lee)

His consciousness is overwhelmed by the violent, brutal nature of Chinese communist experience. Unable to ignore it or shut it out, he confronts the appalling reality, making out of it stark, restrained poetry of condemnation. Behind such words is an observing mind permeated, perhaps, with something like the *jen* or humaneness of Confucius and Po Chu-yi. Tragic vision is part of that consciousness, as in the closing lines of a poem written in 1973, "There Could Be":

No more storms, and no more revolutions,
wine offered up by the People to irrigate the soil.
There could be a life like this.
It could be so good, and it will be as good as you want it to be!

Instead of blood dripping from the ploughs and saturating the soil, wine, in libation, as it were, could be China's blessing, one that she once more lost in 1989. "No more storms, and no more revolutions" is Duoduo's desperate plea and visionary hope. Tempered with realism and historical memory, with a deep sense of personal, individual responsibility, the Chinese poet's traditional responsibility for society, he writes, in "Legacy," in 1987, "Trees are weary with mourning. Dead men / surround them. The command of the dead: / 'Continue mourning.'"

Similarly, the poet Bei Dao (1949-) has confronted and written about the upheavals of the Cultural Revolution. As an idealistic Red Guard for some time during the Cultural Revolution, he saw and at times participated in the madness which made his belated reaction against it all the more powerful when it finally came. He first began publishing in 1972 and was involved in the early demonstrations at Tiananmen Square in April of 1976. Written during those public protests, which began on the campus of Beijing University, his poem "The Answer" voices his determination to stand up and be counted:

Baseness is the password of the base,
Honour is the epitaph of the honourable.
Look how the gilded sky is covered
With the drifting, crooked shadows of the dead.

> The Ice Age is over now,
> Why is there still ice everywhere?
> The Cape of Good Hope has been discovered,
> Why do a thousand sails contest the Dead Sea?

The poet then vehemently proclaims his own opposition and "The voices of the judged": "I don't believe. . . ." In the last two stanzas, he accepts the consequences of his courageous defiance and looks forward to "A new juncture":

> If the sea is destined to breach the dikes,
> Let the brackish water pour into my heart;
> If the land is destined to rise,
> Let humanity choose anew a peak for our existence.

> A new juncture and glimmering stars
> Adorn the unobstructed sky,
> They are five thousand year old pictographs,
> The staring eyes of future generations.
>   (tr. Bonnie S. McDougall)

Here is the voice of an individual consciousness speaking for those who have no voice, speaking with the tragic burden of historical memory, boldly opposing the injustice of an oppressive theory of life that crushed millions upon millions of his people. Although I am not able to judge the language itself, I venture this poem to be the greatest, most heroic Chinese poem of the twentieth century. Bei Dao's one failure of sentimentality may be his description of the sky as "unobstructed." The summer of 1989 proved otherwise. Perhaps in fairness to Bei Dao, he summons up a much longer past, five thousand years of Chinese humanism, a tradition longer than, and superior to, communist barbarism, a past that somehow might win out in the end.

Bei Dao also summons that past in some of his other poems. While the end of "The Answer" has a Confucian flavor, the poem "Bodhisattva" shows Bei Dao meditating seriously on China's

Buddhist past. Poised in meditation, "the flowing folds of your robe / are your faint respiration." In the traditional position of Buddha, "you sit cross-legged on lotus / joy has its source in mud." The symbol of birth into the Pureland grows out of the muck and mire at the bottom of the common pool of life. Bei Dao emphasizes a pearl in the Bodhisattva's forehead that "stands for the sea's matchless power," clearly symbolic of a state of consciousness beyond the quotidian. In "The Old Temple" Bei Dao alludes, perhaps, more to Taoism and Confucianism. The temple is run down and dilapidated. Cobwebs cover everything; columns are splintered; weeds grow everywhere. "The dragons and strange birds flew off," perhaps the phoenix bird, *fenghuang*, and "the stele is chipped, the writing on its surface worn away." To this scene of decay and neglect, a scene indicative of changes in human consciousness, Bei Dao suggests

> yet perhaps
> with a glance from the living
> the tortoise might come back to life in the earth
> and crawl over the threshold, bearing its heavy secret

As a favorite symbol of emperors, the tortoise here has resonance for much of Chinese history and civilization. If resuscitated, it might just make it over the threshold. No better words than these could be found to adorn the stele on its back, words in memory of the murdered millions.

Li Ping's autobiographical novella *When Sunset Clouds Disappear* was published in 1981. It tells the story of a young communist, atheist cadre who visits Mount Taishan, the holiest of China's sacred five mountains, and meets there an old man whom he soon realizes is a "Taoist transcendent" and Buddhist monk. As they climb together up the ten thousand stairs toward the summit, they carry on a wide-ranging discussion of Western and Eastern philosophy, science, and religion. Through a brilliantly dialectical exchange of their views, Li Ping expresses the tensions that exist in the modern Chinese soul. The old man says at the climax of their discussion:

But you have forgotten that beyond beauty there is goodness. It is the search for truth, beauty, and goodness that constitutes the whole spiritual life of humanity. What seeks truth is science; what seeks beauty is art; and what seeks goodness is religion. While we were on our way here, you said to me that religion was not real. But now I can say to you: since art need not be real, why must religion be real? The significance of art does not lie in its truth but in its beauty. In the same way, the significance of religion does not lie in its truth but in its goodness. There are many religions in the world, from those of Jesus and Allah in the West to Buddhism and Daoism in the East, and their branches and sects are numberless. Do you mean to say that none of them really has anything of value? Even if their doctrines are contradictory and confused, their main point is simply to guide people, so that the powerful may be merciful and the fortunate benevolent, so that the sufferings of human life are comforted and the void of the spirit has some support. So long as goodness is spread throughout the world, whether my Buddha exists or not is secondary. As for the sutra banners and precious scrolls, they serve only to make the mind reverent; fasting and meditation are simply a way of nurturing life. Everything about religion is in essence created by the human mind. If you believe it, it exists; if you don't, it doesn't; it's entirely a matter of sincere faith. As the ancients said long ago, "my mind is my Buddha." It should be apparent from this that religion takes morality as its basis, and does not really conflict with science. But in recent times ignorant people have set about testing and overturning the existence of Heaven on the basis of their experience in this dusty world, and it is for this reason that we have had these endless contending theories and quarrels!

(tr. Daniel Bryant)

The monk is partly referring here to the "endless contending theories and quarrels" of communism. In the best tradition of art, Li Ping does not resolve the dialectic of the modern Chinese soul. Rather, he presents it in all its richness and lets it speak for itself. Far from being won over by the old monk, the young cadre says near the end to a European tourist whom they meet on Taishan and who speaks well of Western religion, "As you know, any kind of religion is alien to me." A modern person, he repeatedly says he cannot understand the old monk. Li Ping discloses his own character in this dilemma, dramatizes it through the cadre's struggle, calls his position into question by the cadre's involvement in the Cultural Revolution, his destruction of Nanshan's house, a young woman he falls in love with, his wasting of his own youth, and his loss of her companionship. Juxtaposed to the cadre, Li Ping also has Nanshan speaking favorably at times of religion, but she essentially believes in "the finest traditions of Chinese Confucianism," *t'ien* or "Heaven," and the memory of "our own ancestors." Lamenting partly the "decade of disaster," like Bei Dao looking ahead, the novella closes with the words, "Yes, what is past is gone; henceforth our field of vision should turn towards the broader future."

The British historian Arnold Toynbee wrote shortly before his death in 1973 in *Mankind and Mother Earth*,

> The underlying essence of religion is, no doubt, as constant as the essence of human nature itself. Religion is, in fact, an intrinsic and distinctive trait of human nature. It is a human being's necessary response to the challenge of the mysteriousness of the phenomena that he encounters in virtue of his uniquely human faculty of consciousness.

For more than two hundred years, the Western world and, indeed, the Eastern world, as in China and Japan, have been increasingly repudiating "the underlying essence of religion," denying that the human being is a moral and transcendent essence. The cultural and intellectual history is well documented and exists for those who care enough to read it. In the darkened cave of modernity, where Plato's light has been doused, few, however, seem to care, few are able to see through the intellectual clichés of modernism, repeated now decade after decade, by rote, mindlessly, reduced to nothing but received opinion, having lost the scent of the transcendent. The resources for finding a new vision of modern life are, as Toynbee affirms, within human nature itself. At times, postmodernism itself was an expression of dissatisfaction with the modern worldview and the beginning of a search for a vision beyond it. Within their own civilization and its place within modern world civilization, Chinese writers are either already aware of, or groping toward, this same understanding.

In the West, I believe we too stand in need of a broader future, a new vision. Our old visions of human existence, of the human spirit, are as exhausted as those of the East. Equally bankrupt are the modern ersatzes on which we have wasted so much time, energy, and even, in our own way, human lives. The Left has thoroughly proven itself incapable of fulfilling its early promises, while the Right dreams, in its retrograde way, of the past, ossified in the present. The many dispirited millions condemned to our violent ghettoes, reservations, jails, and, indeed, society are the appalling evidence of our own failure of vision. Without a vision of transcendence to inspire and call forth from our people the best that is in them, they live for frivolity, hedonism, and decadence, obsessed with the self and materialism. Instead of gloating at the seeming victory of capitalism over communism, we should take note of the failure of capitalism itself to create and preserve a civilization worthy of human habitation. Every bit as much of a modern ersatz as communism, unrestrained capitalism both dehumanizes the spirit and devalues the moral and the transcendent, as thoroughly and cynically as the efforts of any politburo. Like the ancient Hellenistic period around the Mediterranean lake, both the East and the West, around the globe, stand in need of, and in dialectical struggle for, a whole new vision of human existence. In the cave of our dark nihilism, we can, as human beings, endowed with the capacity, grope our way forward to the altar and find again that sweet bliss, so well etched on the faces of the statues of Dunhuang, that calms, sustains, and renews the stormy individual soul, cut loose from positive values and traditions, and bring back to contemporary society a vision of life worthy of the modern, international, global civilization we are now all struggling to create.

Japan's Floating Bridge of Dreams

In *The Tale of Genji*, after the death of his beloved Murasaki, Prince Genji grieves for an entire year while preparing himself to renounce the world. Alone, Genji understands at last what a rare woman Murasaki was and how deeply she loved him. Involved continually with other women, he gave her cause for much pain during her life and finds himself overcome with regret now that she is dead. The author Murasaki Shikibu (AD 978-1016) writes, "each little incident came back," depriving him of all peace of mind. Following his ablutions and prayers one snowy morning, he says to a few ladies of the court, "I have often wondered whether the Blessed One was not determined to make me see more than others what a useless, insubstantial world it is. I pretended that I did not see the point, and now as my life comes to a close I know the ultimate in sorrow" (Seidensticker). Genji's thoughts here are suffused with a Buddhist conception of human experience, of the illusory quality of life, of the evanescent, floating nature of the world, what the Japanese call *mujo*. He himself emphasizes he has, in the end, been lessoned by his experience. After visiting and merely reminiscing with the Akashi lady one evening, he returns alone to his quarters and continues "his devotions on through the night." In the morning he sends her the following poem: "I wept and wept as I made my slow way homewards. / It is a world in which nothing lasts forever." During his year of grieving he slowly leaves the world behind. Throughout Japanese literature, Shinto, Confucian, and Buddhist teachings form the contemporary society and shape the consciousness of the best writers.

As early as AD 604 with Prince Shotoku's Constitution, Buddhism had begun to influence life in Japan. The first great collection of Japanese poetry, the *Manyoshu*, comprises poems from this time to near the end of the eighth century. Of the many poets represented in it, Kakinomoto Hitomaro has always been recognized as the most outstanding. Although little is known about his life, he wrote many lyric poems during the Fujiwara Period (686-710). A minor bureaucrat, he was often required to travel from one part of Japan to another in order to fulfill his duties. His experience of traveling made possible some of his finest poems, such as "On Passing the Ruined Capital of Omi." Although all the early emperors ruled in Yamato, the Emperor Tenji, "a god," moved his court in 667 to Omi where it lasted for only about five years before being destroyed in war:

> . . . though I am told his royal palace towered here,
> And they say here rose its lofty halls,
> Only the spring sun is dimmed with mists.
> As I see these ruins of the mighty palace
> My heart is heavy with sorrows!

Reminiscent of Shelley's "Ode to Ozymandias," Hitomaro's sense of evanescence reflects the tenor of Japanese sensibility prior to Buddhism having made a full impact on it. Although some of his other poems show a slight Buddhist influence, most of them are panegyrics to the empress or members of the royal court, alluding frequently to traditional pre-Buddhist Shinto deities such as Amaterasu, Izanagi, and Izanami. In one poem, speaking of Empress Jito, he writes, "It is truly the reign of a divinity." In another, he refers to her as "our great Sovereign, a goddess." While passing islands near Kyushu, he finds, "they remind me of the mighty age of the gods."

Despite his apparent lack of interest in Buddhism, Hitomaro is the first truly great Japanese poet, harkening back to the older myths. In addition to historical evanescence, his poems about his separation from his wife, and later her death, reveal a similarly heightened awareness of the impermanence of life. From one of his posts, he thinks of his wife alone back near the sea of Iwami:

> Like the swaying sea-tangle,
> Unresisting would she lie beside me—
> My wife whom I love with a love
> Deep as the miru-growing ocean.

> But few are the nights
> We two have lain together.

In all of world literature, I believe this poem is one of the most genuine, beautiful, pristine expressions of the love of a man for his wife that can be found. After mentioning his aching heart, Hitomaro unabashedly says, "I thought myself a strong man, / But the sleeves of my garment / Are wetted through with tears."

During the Heian Period (794-1185) Buddhism was often confined to the aristocratic level of society, as at the court in Kyoto, depicted in *The Tale of Genji*. Late in the Heian Period, the poet Saigyo (1118-1190) left the military class to which he was born and became a monk at the age of twenty-three. Almost six hundred years had gone by since Buddhism first entered Japan in about AD 538, and the Heian Period of peace was in decline with the battles between the clans of the Taira and Minamoto looming on the historical horizon. During his life Saigyo took a number of journeys around Japan to visit temples or places associated with poets or other renowned figures. Often he would write his poems while on the road, meditating along the way:

> Limitations gone:
> Since my mind fixed on the moon,
> Clarity and serenity
> Make something for which
> There's no end in sight.
>
> (tr. William R. LaFleur)

The limitations of the world are here transcended. The moon, a symbol of enlightenment, opens infinite possibilities for the contemplation of Saigyo. The "clarity and serenity" are the repose and peace of mind that Saigyo has discovered do not exist in the hectic capital of Kyoto, worldly and increasingly deteriorating into violence.

Saigyo lived, in fact, long enough to witness the social destruction of the Minamoto and Taira clans. At times he would add headnotes to his short waka poems to set the context. In one such note he writes, "In the world of men it came to be a time of warfare. Throughout the country—west, east, north, and south—there was no place where the war was not fought. The count of those dying because of it climbed continually and reached an enormous number. It was beyond belief! And for what on earth was this struggle taking place? A most tragic state of affairs":

> There's no gap or break
> In the ranks of those marching
> Under the hill:
> An endless line of dying men,
> Moving on and on and on. . . .

To appreciate fully this poem, one must realize there had been over three hundred years of relative peace for the Heian capital before this time in Japanese history. Even a solitary, wandering monk like Saigyo could not live entirely oblivious of the mayhem, escape its awful reality, *aware* or *lacrimae rerum*.

In 1185 the Minamoto clan, after more than thirty years of intrigue and warfare, finally defeated the Taira at Ichinotani, the largest battle up to that time in Japanese history, and moved the capital to Kamakura. *The Tales of the Heike* recount many of the incidents of the war throughout the period. Like Saigyo, others tried to withdraw from the chaos into private contemplation. One such recluse was Kamo no Chomei, author in 1212 of *The Ten Foot Square Hut*. Although merely a very short essay of twenty pages, it has had a profound influence on Japanese writers and culture. Its allusions to the Chinese Taoist tradition of mountain recluses, reaching back even to India, indicates Chomei knew what he was writing and how deep its roots ran in the Asian psyche. Initially a city dweller in Kyoto, he became disaffected with the social turmoil of the period, which he chronicles in some detail, and progressively withdrew until he was living alone by his fiftieth year in a small hut in the mountains. Far from a prison cell of loneliness and despair, the "little impermanent hut" frees him from worldly society and permits him, as one who "thinks deeply," the "calm," "quiet," and peace of mind necessary to escape the "fleeting evanescent nature of man." As *The Tales of Heike* put it, "for men of sensitive soul, the world now seemed a hopeless place." Chomei withdrew, encouraging others to do the same in his allusions to the Buddhist and Taoist recluse traditions, and sought what Saigyo sought, embellished so often in Saigyo's symbol of the moon, nowhere more clearly than in this poem:

> fukaki yama ni
> kokoro no tsuki shi
> suminureba
> kagami ni yomo no
> satori o zo miru

> In the mountains' deep
> Places, the moon of the mind
> Resides in light serene:
> Moon mirrors all things everywhere,
> Mind mirrors moon . . . in satori now.

Satori or enlightenment, the goal of Japanese Mahayana Buddhism, was open to all who sought its radiance. The medieval Japanese poets, story tellers, and thinkers all agreed. The very purpose of life was the fulfillment of being in contemplation, "in light serene," "in satori now."

After the upheavals of the late Heian Period and early Kamakura Period (1185-1333), Buddhism, formerly often an aristocratic religion, spread much more extensively among the common people. Similarly, Zen Buddhism, evolved from Chinese Ch'an, was taken up by the new military rulers and helped to knead the spiritual ideals of Buddhism all the more deeply into the culture. Early in the Ashikaga Period (1338-1573), Zeami Motokiyo (1363-1443), the greatest of Japanese playwrights, gave dramatic form to Zen and Amitabha Buddhism. The very essence of Zeami's art is the sense of transcendent mystery or *yugen* that he tried to evoke through his plays. Often drawing from *The Tales of Heike* and other chronicles or legends, he recreates, in his play *Atsumori*, one of the most stirring incidents at the battle of Ichinotani, the death of a young warrior. Having seen this play performed in Japan by the National No Theater, I believe it to be one of the most profound pieces of dramatic art in the world. The slow stylization of movement and acting evokes a realm of detachment from the everyday world, lifting the audience to a rare and higher level of human experience.

Atsumori, a handsome sixteen or seventeen year old *bushi* or warrior, a member of the Taira or Heike clan, flees in defeat the battlefield at Ichinotani shortly behind the retreating nobles and other soldiers. Unfortunately, by the time he reaches the seaside, the boats have already pulled out too far from shore to allow him to board. At just that moment Kumagai, a warrior of the Minamoto or Genji clan, rides up and, though hesitating because of the youth's beauty, calling to mind Kumagai's own son, beheads Atsumori. Kumagai discovers a flute on Atsumori's person, realizing he must have been the young man he heard playing beautifully inside the enemy encampment just that morning. Stricken with grief by the tragedy, he "turned toward the religious life and he eventually became a recluse." Zeami takes this tale and transforms it into a meeting between the wandering soul of Atsumori and Kumagai, now turned priest, "going down to Ichinotani to pray for the salvation of Atsumori's soul." Atsumori at first appears as a reaper cutting grain in the fields but soon reveals himself as a ghost:

Atsumori: Would you know who I am. . . .
Listen . . . I am Atsumori.
Priest: How strange! All this while I have never
stopped beating my gong and performing the rites of the
Law. I cannot for a moment have dozed, yet I thought
that Atsumori was standing before me. Surely it was a
dream.
Atsumori: Why need it be a dream? It is to clear the
karma of my waking life that I am come here in visible
form before you.   (tr. Arthur Waley)

The priest chants, "Namu Amidabu," "Hail Amida Buddha," and reflects, "After such prayers what evil can be left?" In highly stylized lines, reminiscent of the effect of stichomythia, they recall how they were once enemies, but now "friends in Buddha's Law," reflecting on the decadence of the Taira clan and its precipitous fall from power culminating in destruction at Ichinotani. At the end of the play, the ghost of Atsumori approaches the priest to strike him with his sword,

> But the other is grown gentle
> And calling on Buddha's name
> Has obtained salvation for his foe;
> So that they shall be reborn together
> On one lotus-seat.

Putting his sword aside, in the closing line of the play, Atsumori sublimely chants, "pray for me again, oh pray for me again." The former enemies, united by a shared vision of life, transcend their worldly loyalties and meet, as it were, in the Pure Land.

Writing two centuries later, in the early Edo Period (1600-1868), Matsuo Basho (1644-1694), like Saigyo, began life under the tutelage of a military family. His father was a samurai for the *daimyo* or local ruler of Ueno castle, where Basho became in time a servant and friend of the ruler's son with whom he grew up and was educated in poetry. At the age of twenty-two, Basho went to Kyoto where he studied, including Chinese literature, for the next five years, assiduously devoting himself to Zen, especially after moving to Tokyo in 1672. When his Banana Tree Hermitage burnt down in 1682, he began traveling frequently with one or two disciples to different parts of Japan. Clearly with the exiled poets of China and the wandering poet Saigyo in mind, Basho set out in 1689 on his greatest journey, which he later recounted in *The Narrow Road to a Far Province*, an epic of world stature. A mixture of prose and poetry, it narrates his journey from Tokyo to the Northern provinces of the island of Honshu and then down along the Sea of Japan ending near Lake Biwa.

In the Prologue, Basho tells his reader that "Life itself is a journey." The metaphor is clearly one of spiritual pilgrimage, and he evokes the "poets of old" who died during their travels. Setting out in May, he and his disciple Sora travel north past a number of sights, including Nikko, a famous Shinto shrine, and then, before long, the Buddhist temple Ungan where his Zen teacher Butcho once had a hut. After viewing the master's old hut, they push on, seeing, among other noteworthy historical and literary landmarks, a famous weeping willow tree at Ashino that Saigyo had written about. Wandering from one place to another, "resigned from the beginning to the evanescence of human existence," Basho reaches the Tsubo Stone: "over six feet high and about three feet wide. It was covered with moss, and the inscription was difficult to read" (tr. Dorothy Britton). In a passage that suggests how all things in life are mutable, with perhaps little remaining from the castle that once occupied the site, he emphasizes that "This monument was made a thousand years ago and is a very real and vivid link with the past." Representing the very essence of *sabi*, Basho calls the stone "one of the things that has made my trip worthwhile" and writes that he "wept for sheer joy."

As they continue traveling they pass Sendai, Matsushima, and many other places of note. The high point of the book comes, I believe, if the book can be said to have a climax, at the hilltop temple of Ryushaku. Having first passed it by, Basho and Sora decide to backtrack a little to see it since many people tell them it is worth the effort and "situated in a particularly pure and tranquil spot." Basho painstakingly describes this hill to set the scene for the haiku poem he makes the summit of the passage. As pilgrims, they first arrange to stay the night with priests at the bottom of the hill before beginning the climb past "massive boulders" piled all over with "luxuriant pines and cypresses of great age, and the ancient earth and rocks were green with velvety moss." Suffused with the atmosphere of sabi, they clamber up the rocks of the hill, past the peripheral sanctuaries, and reach the "main Buddhist sanctum" where they at last are able to say their prayers. Basho's own sentence is the best introduction to his haiku. "In the profound tranquillity and beauty of the place, our hearts felt deeply purified":

Shizukasa ya
iwa ni shimi-iru
semi no koe

In the silence,
a cicada's voice
penetrates the rocks.

Satori and poetry become one in a transcendent vision of life that conveys itself best through metaphor. Man and nature commune in harmony piercing the same adamantine mysteries.

The next day, they travel on, eventually watching craftsman make swords at Gassan where Basho observes, "I realized then that to excel in anything requires much more than ordinary effort." Basho finally ends his journey in October near Lake Biwa at Ogaki which he soon leaves to observe the rededication of Amaterasu's shrine at Ise. His poetry is the last pure expression of Japanese spirituality before the culture begins to turn to a secular outlook during the eighteenth century.

The Meiji Period of modernization begins in 1868. By the end of the nineteenth century, several anthologies of Western literature had been translated and published introducing Japanese writers to a variety of new literary styles and genres. After a long and natural period of imitation and derivative writing, as a result of the fresh exposure to the outside world, Japan, deeply affected by its centuries of *sakoku* or forced isolation, produced its first truly modern poet in Hagiwara Sakutaro (1886-1942). Born northwest of Tokyo in Maebashi, "in front of the bridge," at the center of Japan, Hagiwara made himself into a Japanese Baudelaire, writing in an at times obscure symbolist free verse, in the colloquial tongue, about alcoholics, bars, squalid love, and sin. He also acknowledged Poe, Schopenhauer, Nietzsche, and Dostoevsky as Western writers important to him, while an heir of the lyrics of Saigyo and Basho.

Hagiwara has been commonly recognized by Japanese critics as the most important modern Japanese poet since the publication of his first book of poems in 1917, *Howling at the Moon*, which he wrote in provincial Maebashi, often longing for life in Tokyo where he did at times live. In "Sad Moonlit Night," Hagiwara gives voice to his sense of life in modern Japan, after hearing a dog howling on a wharf:

> A damned thief dog
> is howling at the moon above the rotting wharf.
> A soul listens,
> and in gloomy voices,
> yellow daughters are singing in chorus,
> singing in chorus,
> on the wharf's dark stonework.
>
> Always,
> why am I like this,
> dog,
> pale unhappy dog?   (tr. Hiroaki Sato)

The symbolic moon of Saigyo no longer reflects transcendence but misery, alienation, self-pity, and despair, a psyche as distressed as the "damned" dog. Hagiwara is painfully conscious that something is lacking in or has gone wrong with "the rotting wharf" of modern life. At the end of the poem, identifying not with the moon but with the howling dog, he further projects his own feelings of loneliness and unhappiness and ponders the nature of the modern self, lost and restlessly struggling in the same malaise as the West.

In 1925 Hagiwara published a collection of poems that includes "Owatari Bridge," which I quote in full. The Japanese poet and critic Miyoshi Tatsuji wrote about this poem that "It is not only the jewel among Hagiwara Sakutaro's poems, but a masterpiece that occupies a prominent place among the countless poems written since *shintaishi* [new style poetry] became free verse":

The long bridge they've erected here
No doubt goes from lonely Sosha village straight to
    Maebashi town.
Crossing the bridge I sense desolation pass through me.
Carts go by loaded with goods, men leading the horses.
And restless, nagging bicycles.
When I cross this long bridge
Twilight hunger stabs me.

Ahh—to be in your native place and not go home!
I've suffered to the full griefs that sting like salt.
I grow old in solitude.
How to describe the fierce anger today over bitter
    memories?
I will tear up my miserable writings
And throw every scrap into the onrushing Tone River.
I am famished as a wolf.
Again and again I clutch at the railing, grind my
        teeth,
But it does no good: something like tears spills out,
Flows down my cheeks, unstanched.
Ahh—how contemptible I have been all along!
Past me go carts loaded with goods, men leading the
    horses.
This day, when everything is cold, the sky darkens over
    the plain.   (tr. Donald Keene)

Having lived for a year and a half in Maebashi, where I taught at
Gunma University, I cannot read this poem without stirring up my
deepest emotions. While it is true that Maebashi is a provincial
town, since everything of cultural importance to most Japanese takes
place in Tokyo, I can't share Hagiwara's bitter feelings. I have
many warm memories of Maebashi which is now surely less isolated
than during Hagiwara's lifetime, or even when I was there. Almost
daily I saw the cemetery of the Buddhist Shojun temple where
Hagiwara's remains are buried. It was while I was living in

Maebashi that I first forced myself to read Baudelaire and recall reading him on the express train from nearby Takasaki to Tokyo. Crossing the Tone River on its bridges at least a couple of times a week, I enjoyed the sight of fishermen in rubber waders fly casting, the bridge crowded with bicycles, often children on their way to school. Hagiwara's poem "Owatari Bridge" impresses deeply upon me how the state of the consciousness of the individual poet affects perception. Accepting the decadent clichés of the *poète maudit* of modern Western literature, Hagiwara chose to view life through tainted, distorting lenses. Standing between express cars, rocking along between Maebashi and Tokyo, I knew Baudelaire's vision of life, though true in terms of social change and loss, was essentially unhealthy, the product of a sick mind and soul. Modern life in Maebashi helped me to understand that. Unfortunately, Hagiwara never learnt that lesson but ended his ever-darkening life, as he put it, "in the shadow of the hazy landscape of Nihilism," writing poems heavily influenced by Nietzsche, while militarism took over his country.

For Japan and its writers, the modern darkness deepens during the period of military fascism and World War II. With the defeat and unconditional surrender, immense shock waves rocked the entire culture calling into question the pseudo-Shinto and Confucian values Japan had based its society on for almost a century. As writers returned from one front or another of the war, they found a Japan devastated by the Allied bombing. Maebashi, for instance, was reduced to rubble along with its bridges. Before long, the entire country was restructured by the Occupation. Japanese writers now understood much more deeply the experience of the Western World War I generation. Better than any other postwar poet, Tamura Ryuichi (1923-1998) registers, since his own hometown in the suburbs of Tokyo no longer existed, the shock and disorientation of the modern Japanese psyche. Briefly a student of Hagiwara Sakutaro, Tamura had little interest in classical Japanese poetry, which emphasized the unity of man and nature, but read widely in Western literature and was especially influenced by T. S. Eliot, Steven Spender, C. Day Lewis, and W. H. Auden, whom Tamura eventually met in New York in 1971. In a literary magazine called *Arechi* or "wasteland," Tamura and other postwar poets gave voice to the despair and horror they felt, unequivocally stating, in an early manifesto, "The present is a wasteland." The first poem in which Tamura finds his true voice and distance from his material is the prose poem "Etching," published in 1956:

Now he sees a landscape he saw in a German etching it appears to be an aerial view of an ancient city between twilight and darkness or a realistic drawing of a modern-day cliff being taken from midnight toward dawn This man the one I began to describe killed his father when he was young that autumn his mother went beautifully insane

(tr. Christopher Drake)

The critic Ikuko Atsumi has said of this poem that it aims at a universal vision of East and West, ancient and modern. The extreme nationalism of the Japanese fascists now defeated, the "he" can view the fullness or "landscape" of Western culture, specifically German, declining into "darkness" or rising as "a modern-day cliff," ominous, dehumanized, marked by loss and angst. Atsumi suggests the father "possibly refers to the emperor system in Japan, and the mother he made beautifully insane to Japan's aesthetic consciousness." The East too descended into a wasteland of madness and violence, the ancient now discredited and rendered nugatory. This is the "Etching" come to light, etched into Tamura's consciousness and all postwar Japanese writers of worth. Blending together the perspective of the subjective "I" and objective "he," aware of the horror, Tamura introduces into Japanese poetry a voice of detachment, observing life outside his own personal existence with meditative restraint, seeking a deeper understanding of modern human experience.

Having known and read Tamura's work for more than fifteen years, I have often thought of him as akin somehow to Robert Lowell. He has a memory of Japan's past that he never idealizes, but works with and probes it, pondering always without sentimentality the modern and by-gone days. Like Lowell and so many postmodern

Western poets, Tamura also goes through a time of fairly formalistic writing, but he seems to outgrow it and returns to engaging universal experience outside his own little personal consciousness. Many other Japanese poets, as in the United States, are still stuck in such solipsism. Saigyo and Basho both believed poetry must consider the transcendent and involve conceptual knowledge outside the self, not merely aesthetic formalism. As late as 1982, in what is one of his greatest poems, "Spiral Cliff," Tamura looks soberly at modern world history. After the speaker reflects on a photograph of a deer "falling off a cliff" and wonders "what's after it," he says,

> Our century ends without decadence
> after the night and fog of Nazi gas chambers
> after Soviet forced labor camps
> after two U.S. atomic bombs on Japan
> there's no thrill left in killing,
> no fear of the soul, no crime in adultery. . . .

In "our century," the values requisite for perceiving and defining "decadence" have disappeared, "crime and evil disconnected," all restraining sense of the soul lost. As a result, unimaginable horror has been perpetrated in every region of the globe on an appalling scale affecting both the social and individual realms. Like a roller coaster, "our century ends on pure speed." Recalling the photo of the deer, he thinks,

> I'm afraid of high places
> the cliff in me
> am I the hunter
> or the prey?

The "high places" are both those of earlier mentioned "boardrooms / of huge corporations," East and West, in a manner reminiscent of Kaneko Mitsuharu's *Book of Mud,* and the "modern-day cliff" of confusion, now "the cliff in me." The ambiguity of the question "am I the hunter / or the prey?" acknowledges the complexity of modern life where all are somehow complicitous in human tragedy. Terrified by "blank paper," by "what dreams will live and die there," Tamura accepts the writer's obligation to struggle for values worthy of all human beings, not just Japanese.

Next in dream half nightmare, he sees his own inner cliff protruding "between dreams / spiraling" down. Waking in the dawn, lying horizontally across the bed, he reads the morning newspaper full of massacre and civil war:

> Vanishing
> cliff dream
> vertical dream
> elementally
> Gone

All the dreams have vanished as off the edge of a cliff. Vertical dreams have been replaced by the horizontal, exactly the information that fills the newspaper. Like the best of modern writers, Auden or Lowell, Tamura has the honesty and strength of intellect and spirit to recognize it is all "gone." I believe his vision of modern life and Japan is true, for it has been my own experience, lived not only in Japan but also in the United States, where "without decadence" the culture sinks to ever more dehumanized levels of violence, depravity, and social fragmentation. The importance of Tamura's poetry has not been sufficiently recognized in the West and, perhaps, even in Japan.

Shortly after the Meiji Restoration of 1868 narrative writing also becomes heavily influenced by Western literature. Although there are many excellent early fiction writers and those who, like Junichiro Tanizaki and Yasunari Kawabata, tend to reflect more traditional aesthetics, or those of the "I-novel," Kobo Abe (1924-1993), a Marxist, is the first significantly modern Japanese novelist. His childhood in Manchuria helped him to look harder and more objectively than other writers at modern Japanese life, particularly in Tokyo, where Abe lived the rest of his life, while his growing up in Manchuria surely added to the sense of alienation that pervades his work. His early stories following World War II already express a profoundly existentialist angst and absurdity that has often led to his being compared to Kafka, Camus, Sartre, or Samuel Beckett. To my mind, though, it is precisely the fact that Abe is Japanese that is important and to view him as a mere imitator of the West would be a mistake. Rather than casting his experience into Kafkaesque terms, he is responding to his own experience of modern Japanese life. I believe Westerners need to think deeply about what that means for modern Japan, especially those dreamy Westerners who romantically idealize the traditional image of medieval Japan, as though it still exists.

In "Magic Chalk" (1950), Abe tells the story of "a poor artist named Argon." Flat broke and starving, Argon discovers in his shabby apartment a piece of red chalk with which he mindlessly draws pictures of food and dishes on the wall. Falling asleep, he groans, "I've got to eat!" Suddenly, he is awakened by the sound of food and crockery crashing to the floor: "The pictures he had chalked on the wall had vanished." Seeing food all around, he eats his fill and reflects, "the laws of the universe have changed." He then draws a bed, since he lacks one, as well as other furniture and food. The realization hits him that he can create an entirely new world and spends four weeks contemplating just how to do it. Driven to despair by the burdensome responsibility, he finally decides merely to draw a door to the new world, but upon opening it finds, "an awesome wasteland glaring in the noonday sun." He would have "to draw the world all over again" and begins with Eve, "stark naked," to whom he identifies himself as Adam and "also an artist, and a world planner." Eve, however, borrows his chalk, draws a gun, and shoots him. Other people in the building hear the gunshot: "By the time they ran in, Argon had been completely absorbed into the wall and had become a picture":

After everyone left, there came a murmuring from the wall. "it isn't chalk that will remake the world . . ." A single drop welled out of the wall. It fell from just below the eye of the pictorial Argon.   (tr. Alison Kibrick)

Writing shortly after World War II, Abe understands modern Japan has lost something of immense value, and a mere artist can not replace it.

In Kobo Abe's masterpiece *The Woman in the Dune* (1962), the protagonist Niki Jumpei, an amateur entomologist, travels to the seaside to collect specimens. He happens on a village built in the midst of the dunes with houses at the bottom of huge craters or cavities of sand. Peering down into one of the cavities at a small house "submerged in silence," he muses, "no matter what they did . . . there was no escaping the law of the sand." This "law" soon becomes clear when village men trick him into going sixty feet down in a cavity to spend the night at an old woman's house. Before long, he realizes that there is probably no way to get back out. The "ceaselessly flowing sand," "this shapeless, destructive power," which "had no form" of its own, was continually pouring down on the little house threatening to destroy it and bury its occupants alive. Every night the woman shovels sand into baskets which the village men haul up by rope and carry away, just enough to prevent their suffocation. Watching her, Niki Jumpei remarks, "you'll never finish, no matter how long you work at it." Later, the narrator explains, "the only certain factor was its movement; sand was the antithesis of all form." Despite his many appeals for help from the village men, the village benefits from the sand being fought back and they refuse to permit him to leave.

The men, however, are careful to provide the woman and man with the necessities of life as long as they continue to perform the nightly work of clearing back the everdrifting sand of reality, for the sand is manifestly symbolic. Upon his request, they even give Jumpei a newspaper. Reading the usual headlines of political, business, and domestic crimes and intrigues, Jumpei thinks,

There wasn't a single item of importance. A tower of illusion, all of it, made of illusory bricks and full of holes. . . And so everybody, knowing the meaninglessness of existence, sets the center of his compass at his own home.

This "illusion" is not the illusion of Buddhism, the floating world of Genji symbolizing a world of spiritual import. It is the illusion of everyday life through which the nihilist sees "the meaningless of existence," at last confronted, the real truth of human experience. "The world," Abe has Jumpei say in a simile, "is like sand." Modern Japanese writers have found the transition easy to make from the illusion of *samsara* to the illusion of nihilism which is quotidian reality. Similarly, the old woman turns out not to be so old after all, and Jumpei learns social customs are merely illusions too, as he rapes her brutally and repeatedly while she at times enjoys or submits to it. When the opportunity for escape finally comes, drained of all inner meaning, strength, and purpose, he no longer has the will to leave.

In "Beyond the Curve" (1966), Abe writes about a man who, while climbing up a hill, comes to a halt before a curve in the road:

> For the life of me, I couldn't visualize what lay
> beyond the curve. . . .
> I knew perfectly well that beyond the curve was the
> town on the hilltop where I lived. My temporary lapse
> of memory in no way altered the fact of its existence.

He stands there agonizing in his mind about what might or ought to be around the curve until he is overcome by anxiety, fearing "the town's very existence would fade away and then vanish." He considers, "I myself was no longer myself, but some mysterious other." Nausea overtakes him. He manages to turn around and walk back down the hill. His "old confidence was gone." Taking refuge in a coffee shop, he wonders, no longer sure, who he is since he has forgotten his name and where he works. Frantically fumbling with the contents of his wallet and pockets, looking for clues, he realizes, "I had mislaid . . . myself." Abe expresses here not only the universally modern sense of existential void but especially the Japanese fear of the loss of traditional identity under the onslaught of modernity. Abe's persona significantly and desperately says, "Until I found that town beyond the curve, there could be no resolution." And so it is for modern Japan. He takes a taxi up the hill, beyond the curve:

> Spatially, the town had a solid physical existence, but temporally, it was a vacuum. It existed—yet horribly, it had no existence whatever . . . the town I knew was gone.

Though seeking answers from others, he "alone was lost, uncomprehending." Physically, materially, like the West, Japan exists; in terms of social or psychological time, the "vacuum," quintessentially the same as in the West, has swallowed everything: "The town I knew was gone." What lies beyond the curve, if anything, remains to be seen.

Instead of wanting to go forward around the curves of the future, Yukio Mishima, like some writers in the West, attempted to go backwards to the supposedly safe and happy days. No other Japanese writer has seen as deeply into Mishima's suicide and the "vacuum" of modern Japanese life as has the 1994 Nobel laureate in literature, Kenzaburo Oe:

> His death was a performance for the foreign audience, a very spectacular performance. The relationship between Mishima and the emperor system was rather dubious; the Japanese knew that. But from foreigners' point of view—say, an American reader's point of view—the Japanese emperor system is something inexplicable. Therefore, that final act by Mishima, tied in with the emperor system, appeared to be a kind of mystical thing. In actuality, he did it in order to entertain foreign readers.

As in this excerpt from a 1986 interview, Oe, also influenced early on by Marxism and existentialism, especially Sartre, has had the vision and strength to confront in his writing not only the nostalgia of Mishima but also the past and present implications of the emperor system for Japan. In 1971 his novella "The Day He Himself Shall Wipe Away My Tears," written just after Mishima's suicide, courageously explores the nature and meaning of emperor worship. Having known Japanese students and friends who fiercely supported the emperor, loathed him, or were simply indifferent, with most falling into the last category, I believe it may be difficult for Americans to appreciate fully the scope of Oe's achievement in this novella. Oe tried to convey the challenge of his theme when he wrote in an essay, "A man who criticises Mishima and his works must have the determination to criticise the total culture that orients itself toward the Imperial hierarchy." Far from falling short of this determination, Oe creatively confronts the Japanese fascist and wartime past in "The Day He Himself Shall Wipe Away My Tears" and thereby truly serves the Japanese people and, I would argue, the emperor as well.

Oe grew up in a small village on the island of Shikoku where the events of the story take place. While in a Tokyo hospital dying of cancer, the persona narrates the densely complicated events of his father's fervent devotion to the emperor, filtered through his own consciousness as a child and a mentally unbalanced adult recalling his "happy days." His Japanese mother, who grew up in China, and whose own father was involved in the Daigaku Incident of 1910-11, an attempt to assassinate the emperor, believes her son has never been mentally stable since the age of three. Lying in his hospital bed, he recalls "hate-filled exchanges" between his mother and father about the role of his grandfather. Later in his life, she had always refused to discuss anything with her son about his father, a military official who returned from Manchuria a few years before the end of the war and who died attempting to lead an uprising in support of the emperor after his 1945 announcement of surrender on the radio. Respected by the village people, the father, suffering from cancer, secludes himself in the family storehouse. For the boy observing his father, he becomes a "kind of idol," obedient to the emperor. After his older brother deserts in Manchuria, the boy shouts in defiance at his mother, "I don't have no traitor's blood in my veins":

Even now he could recall, with extreme vividness and reality... wanting to shout Long live the emperor! so that [his father] would acknowledge that it was his young son who was the true heir to his blood.

Oe slowly leads the reader to the realization that the young boy has grown up to repeat the obsessions of the father, destroying himself in the process. When the mother, "a simple old country woman," visits him as a thirty-five year old adult in the hospital, she struggles to no avail to get him to recognize what an absurd, cowardly figure his father actually was, while cancer literally and symbolically continues to eat him up. Near the end she says to the persona's wife, whose own marriage and life have been ruined, "Sooner or later the Japanese are going to change their attitude about what happened, and I intend to live to see it, yessir! THIS IS THE DREAM. THIS MUST BE THE DREAM!" This is clearly the dream of Oe and many Japanese. He more than any other modern Japanese writer has had the courage to write fiction that might help Japan to accomplish it.

Also set mostly in Shikoku, as many of Oe's stories are, *The Silent Cry* (1967), presents two brothers who return to their country village nestled in a valley. Although a dialectical struggle takes place between them, reminiscent of Dostoevsky's *Brothers Karamazov*, the older brother Mitsusaboro is the central figure of the novel, which is told from his point of view. In the opening paragraph, Mitsusaboro thinks to himself,

Awakening in the predawn darkness, I grope among the anguished remnants of dreams that linger in my consciousness, in search of some ardent sense of expectation. Seeking in the tremulous hope of finding eager expectancy reviving in the innermost recesses of my being
. . . still I find an endless nothing.

He crawls into a hole dug for a septic tank and claws at the sides with his bare fingers trying to get the walls to cave in on himself. At the end of the summer his best friend, who had been injured in front of the Diet demonstrating against the Japan-US Mutual Security Treaty, had painted his head red, stuck a raw cucumber up the anus of his naked body, and hung himself. Mitsusaboro reflects, "And I too have the seeds of that same, incurable madness. . . ." Beginning in the hole, haunted by despair, madness, and nihilism, he gropes and searches throughout the novel for something worth living for. At dawn sticking his head up "two inches above the ground," he notices,

> the backs of the dogwood leaves were a burning red... a red that reminded me of the flames in the picture of hell that I'd seen in our village temple every year on the Buddha's Birthday. . . . The dogwood was a sign to me, its meaning only imperfectly clear, that produced a sudden resolve.

Not only has his friend hung himself, but Mitsusaboro and his whiskey-drinking wife have placed their brain-damaged infant in an institution. With a resolve born of hell, he climbs out of the pit.

The picture of hell in his village temple appears a couple of times in the novel, especially at the end. Meanwhile, many a bleak event occurs. His brother Takashi, who also demonstrated against the Security Treaty but enjoyed the violence, returns from America where he contracted VD in a ghetto and "completely lost his faith in life"; they escape from Tokyo back to their little village in Shikoku; Takashi incites a strange revolt in imitation of their great-grandfather's brother who had led a farmers uprising in 1860; his wife and Takashi commit adultery; Takashi confesses to incest with their half-wit sister, rapes a young village girl, smashes her head to a pulp, and then kills himself in a gruesome manner that leaves his corpse covered in blood; Mitsusaboro himself realizes he has "lost all true identity," no longer belongs in the village, and can not start there a "new life" or build a "thatched hut." The life of the village too has changed under the impact of modern life, and the Buddhist priest points out to Mitsusaboro numerous ways in which "The one thing that's certain is that the valley's decadent."

Viewing the picture of hell again after Takashi's suicide, Mitsusaboro experiences a "profound sense of peace." "Tenderness" radiates from the depiction of "the sufferings of the dead and the cruelty of the demons." When they had first seen the picture after arriving in the village, Mitsusaboro's wife had remarked, "the dead seem so used to the demons that they're not scared any more." He now describes this same quality that gave him "mental release" earlier as a "mild, comforting kind of torment." After spending the night in a hidden cellar in which his great-grandfather's brother had lived out his life following the uprising of 1860, he stands with his head thrust up through the floor boards, looking at the fiery red dawn, paralleling his similar position gazing out of the septic pit:

> The "tender" red of the painting was essentially the color of self-consolation, the color of people who strove to go on quietly living their murkier, less stable, and vaguer everyday lives rather than face the threat of those terrifying souls who tackled their own hell head-on.

In what Oe intends as an ending of "self-consolation" and tenderness, barely escaping sentimentality, he and his wife, who is now pregnant with Takashi's child, decide to attempt a "new start" by keeping the child as well as getting back the one in the institution. Yet the silent, modern cries of desperation, madness, and nihilism, heard throughout the novel, are not gone. They linger in the forest and the night and overwhelm Oe's *deus ex machina* ending of Mitsusaboro quixotically running off to Africa, lighting out for the frontier like Huck Finn. The perceptive reader can only say with Takashi, about the friend hanging himself, "OK, message received." Oe understands his Buddhist painting represents a trace from the past, one he no longer takes seriously as signifying transcendence, like the *nembutsu* dance the villagers try to revive, but serves as a source of aesthetic imagery, evidence of cultural change.

This same evanescence comes through in the short story "The Way of Eating Fried Sausage" (1993), wherein Oe's persona is staying at the University of California in Berkeley preparing to speak at a symposium. Living in the faculty club, he remembers his Uncle Hyoei back in Shikoku who was a Buddhist priest at the local temple. Variously perceived by the family as a "great man" and a "misfit," he attempted to combine the study of Buddhism with the modern natural sciences at Waseda University in Tokyo but gave up, returned to the village for twenty-five years of independent study of Buddhism, as well as the Bible and the Quran. The persona, never named, except as K-chan as a child, has with him in Berkeley Uncle Hyoei's copy of *The Buddha's Last Journey* and recalls Uncle Hyoei's last journey in the early sixties to Tokyo, announced in a national newspaper: "Pulled by five sheep, an old Buddhist philosopher heads toward Tokyo from the depths of the Shikoku forests." The newspaper and village people anticipate his "preaching to the public," his "elucidating the teachings of Buddha to the people, especially to confused youth." Before long though, he has begun to live the life of a vagrant in Shinjuku Station. Injured during massive demonstrations against the Security Treaty, by students who are infuriated when he "challenged" them, Hyoei tells the persona who visits him in the subway station,

> the students had no knowledge of Buddhism. They were headstrong and unwilling to listen to other people; the windows of the five senses, which should be open to the wisdom of truth, were closed.

Rejected by the very people he is hoping to help, Hyoei later tells the persona's wife, alluding to *The Buddha's Last Journey*, "It's all the same: everything will pass away." Essentially handing on the torch, he urges her to tell her husband to "keep on with his ascetic training," meaning his writing novels.

Some time later, the persona is passing through Shinjuku Station and observes Uncle Hyoei sitting in lotus position eating a piece of fried sausage on a stick: "he ate slowly, savoring the taste ever so slowly with his mouth and tongue," "as if in meditation," like a "yogi," in "vast loneliness," "reverently." Struck by the sight, he realizes it is now time to help Hyoei return to Shikoku, where he shortly "died without suffering much." Thinking back on all the events of Uncle Hyoei's life, from his room at the University of California, the persona is profoundly moved by his memories. At times a skeptical modern man, university educated to know better, he suggests Uncle Hyoei was impractical and not all there. He recalls at one point how Hyoei, a brilliant misfit in the village, would shout at his sheep, "Hey, you, hey! No matter how time passes, you're still a fool, aren't you? Around here everybody's a fool!" This memory blends with the vision of him in the station eating his sausage, and the persona at times finds himself eating his own food like Hyoei, tasting, savoring each bite: "There are times when the gestures of this middle-aged body and soul still repeat those of Uncle Hyoei. Then I say, in a muffled voice, 'Hey? Hey!'" Naturally drawn to what has been his experience, remembering and even imitating the Buddhist piety of his Uncle whom he grew up admiring, the modern persona tries to shake off the past, to resist his own foolishness, yet wondering, doubting, questioning just how foolish Uncle Hyoei was, from an older and wiser perspective, embracing both contemporary Japan and the United States.

In a 1991 interview Oe remarks, "What I've been trying to do in my work is recover the human habits and customs of this village, to recall them from the past, to breathe life into all those things that have passed away." Elaborating further, he admits what so many modern writers, East and West, if they have any integrity at all, must admit: "this notion of a small village in Shikoku is itself already a kind of fiction, a product of a personal mythology, and so I think I'm skating on somewhat thin ice." I believe Oe's "personal mythology" is also something Westerners who wish to understand modern Japan should think soberly about. For in his later work, Oe has deepened into a writer capable of confronting, in Japanese terms, the "thin ice" of the modern world, sifting through its clichés, including his own, and has begun to look back at the Buddhist past with more searching eyes, while understanding it was and is gone forever. In terms of fiction, Oe has come to the profoundly prescient realization that Ienaga Saburo articulated in *Shin Nihonshi*:

Modern culture which had its source in Europe and America does not simply belong to Westerners only, now it is the world's culture and no one can overlook that. Pre-modern oriental

culture does not have the power to replace this modern culture.
. . . Now the Japanese together with the other peoples of the
world are facing the great task of overcoming the contradictions
and lacks of modern culture. Today may be said to be the age of
the labor pains of giving birth to a new future.

Infinitely more arduous than a quixotic return to an idyllic Eastern
or Western medieval village, Ienaga Saburo rightly perceives that
modern culture has become, in a sense, one universal international
culture, rife with contradictions and shortcomings affecting us all.
As we continue together to grope our way forward beyond modern
culture, Kenzaburo Oe has proven himself, by plunging deep into
the nature of contemporary Japan, one of the most subtle and
insightful writers of the twentieth century.

Unlike modern Japanese writers, Murasaki Shikibu, the author of
The Tale of Genji, believed with every fiber of her being in the
Buddhist vision of life. It suffused and sustained her consciousness.
She viewed and filtered her characters and their actions through its
Law, finding, as other classical Japanese writers found, the
sustenance of life in its teachings. Japanese society itself was shaped
and formed and elevated through Buddhist worship that taught
moderation and respect for all life, abhorred violence and social
disunity, upheld exquisite images of compassion and mercy, as in
Kannon and *Miroku Bosatsu*, thereby chastening the ruthless and
the selfish who had no vision of the future. Complemented by Shinto
and Confucian values, Buddhism ennobled the Japanese mind.
Together the three great traditions gave young and old the necessary
guidance through life any culture needs in order to maintain social
order and a sense of justice, for the high and mighty could at times
be held to account before the *kami*, the great teachings of the sages,
and the transcendent sutras. Like the Western world, Japan has lost
the sustaining influences a religious vision of life gave its culture,
and nowhere has the loss been registered with more sensitivity and
poignancy than by the best of its modern writers, for a culture that
has loved a Murasaki can never truly forget her, though the
universal *tsunami* of skepticism, materialism, and nihilism that has

swept over the entire globe has likewise rolled across Japan, especially since its debacle of World War II. Murasaki Shikibu writes, "the shining Genji was dead, and there was no one quite like him." His son Kaoru, who is not truly his own son, "did not shine with the same radiance." Yet the Kaoru of modern Japanese literature has in a sense continued Genji's "devotions on through the night" of modernity, remembering through negation, if nothing else, what once existed, even as it acknowledges, "It is a world in which nothing lasts forever."

India's Kali Yuga

But how many gods are there really, Yajnavalkya?
One.

Brhadaranyaka Upanishad 3.9.1

When I think of my earliest recollection of India, I think of my Great-uncle Bill's service in her Majesty's Royal Army. While placing flowers on his grave with my family on Memorial Day, I recalled hearing he would give alms to the poor. I wasn't quite sure what "alms" were but it sounded good. And then somewhere in early adolescence I recited in class Alfred Tennyson's "Charge of the Light Brigade" and fell in love with Rudyard Kipling's "You're a better man than I am, Gunga Din" and "East is East, and West is West, and never the twain shall meet." In high school and college I took classes in world religions and non-Western history and literature and began to appreciate much more the diversity of human experience and consciousness. Reading Rumi, Attar, and Tagore in the 1970s, I first encountered the spirituality of Islam and Hinduism reflected in literature. They helped me understand more deeply not only the religious experience of their own regions of the world but also what was distinctive in the Western sensibility of George Herbert, Emerson, Whitman, and other British and American writers. With time, I learned to respect the truth of all the great religions, the universal experience of transcendence, the affirmation of humane morality. With time and experience living in Japan, on an American Indian reservation, and many international friends, I came to understand that people around the world, like many in the West, were torn between the traditional worldview of their culture and the largely secular worldview of modern civilization. The struggle for understanding inherent in this tumultuous process constitutes an attempt to define a whole new human civilization, evolving, as it were, into global civilization, a common heritage, ever-increasingly shared and contributed to by all the peoples of humankind.

The traditional worldview of India begins to find expression in the *Vedas*, the *Upanishads*, and the great epic poems the *Mahabharata* and *Ramayana*, as well as in other sacred texts, variously dated from 1400 to 100 B.C. Within the *Mahabharata*, the *Bhagavad Gita* recounts the meeting between the warrior Arjuna and Krishna, initially as his charioteer, on the field of battle, poised between the opposing armies of the Pandavas and Kauravas. As the son of Pandu, adopted and raised by King Dhritarastra, Arjuna sees "fathers-in-law, and friends, in both armies," which causes him to put down his weapons in anguish. Unwilling to slay his own kinsmen, emphasizing the violation of *dharma* or law, Arjuna tells Krishna he cannot commit violence against his own family members, led by Dhritarastra's oldest son Duryodhana. Krishna urges him to perform the duty of his *ksatriya* or warrior caste and fight:

He who thinks of him as slayer, he who deems him slain—these both are void of judgement; he doth not slay, nor is he slain. Never is he born or dies; he came not into being, nor shall come hereafter; unborn, abiding, eternal, ancient, he is not slain when the body is slain.   (tr. W. D. P. Hill)

Here Krishna speaks in the poem for the transcendence of *atman* or the individual human self or soul and its indestructible nature: "therefore for no being shouldst thou grieve," again urging him to perform his duty proper to his warrior caste. As their discussion unfolds between the armies, Krishna voices another theme: "Hold equal pleasure and pain, gain and loss, victory and defeat." Counseling detachment from the fruit of one's actions, Krishna extols "viewing with balanced mind success and failure" and "without attachment ever perform the work that thou must do." Upholding the castes and the four stages of life of Hinduism, Krishna bestows on Arjuna the unifying vision or *darsana* of his all-encompassing form as Brahman, the Absolute or Eternal, Vishnu, the creator, and Shiva, the destroyer of the universe. Having once attained to a higher plane of understanding of *bhakti* or devotion, Arjuna shoulders the burden of his dharma, returns to his chariot, and engages in battle.

The *Ramayana* focuses on the incarnation of Vishnu as Rama, instead of as Krishna in the *Bhagavad Gita*. Written by the poet

Valmiki, the poem recounts the story of Rama's devotion to his father and his love for Sita, incarnation of the goddess Lakshmi. The *Ramayana* exists in many different versions throughout India and South East Asia. In the novelist R. K. Narayan's modern prose version, based on Kamban's Tamil *Ramayana*, Rama's life mission is to destroy the *asuras* or evil demons of the world. As a young man he undergoes various trials in the forest in preparation for his ultimate battle with Ravana, the leader of the demons. Viswamithra, a sage and advisor, tells Rama, upon the completion of these trials, "O great one, you are born to restore righteousness and virtue to mankind and eliminate all evil." Soon Rama falls in love with Sita as the young princess and daughter of neighboring King Janaka and, in a passage reminiscent of Odysseus in Homer, wins her hand through a test of his strength when he manages to bend Shiva's great bow. Following the pageantry of their marriage, King Dasaratha of Ayodhya, Rama's father, decides the time has come to pass his throne to Rama. His intention, however, is frustrated by the resentment of Rama's childhood nurse, whom he insulted once. She plays on the jealousy of one of Dasaratha's wives Kaikeiyi, who insists her son Bharatha be given the throne and Rama be banished to the forests for fourteen years after which the throne may pass back to Rama. Dasaratha rages against her but submits in the end since he had once granted her many years ago two wishes for her having saved his life. To the dismay of everyone, Rama joyously, piously renounces his claim to the throne, accepts the decision of his father, recalls his profiting from his earlier tests in the forest, and leaves with Sita and his brother Lakshmana for the wandering life of ascetics.

In exile Rama eventually destroys several other local *asuras* who disturb the spiritual retreat of sages in their *ashrams* or hermitages. At this point emphasizing the spiritual nature of Rama's mission, the narrator reiterates, "Rama's whole purpose of incarnation was ultimately to destroy Ravana, the chief of the *asuras*, abolish fear from the hearts of men and gods, and establish peace, gentleness, and justice in the world." One *asura* escapes, Ravana's sister, and flees to inform him of Rama. Falling in love with his sister's description of Sita, Ravana kidnaps her and carries her off to his island kingdom of Lanka. Before long the monkey Hanuman joins Rama and burns Ravana's capital to the ground, as a result of Ravana's own trick of setting his tail on fire. Throughout these episodes, as throughout the *Ramayana*, the poet's vision is one that extols moral strength and virtue, as in Rama's advice to the monkey ruler Sugreeva: "Gather around yourself those that have integrity, courage, and judgement; and with their help govern your subjects. Whatever you do, let it be based on the sanctioned codes of conduct." Following Rama's journey to, and the siege of, the island, and Rama's cutting off Ravana's ten heads and arms, Rama uses a special weapon made by the Creator Brahma to finish off Ravana, while invoking its power "with prayers and worship." As Ravana finally dies, the narrator describes

Ravana's face aglow with a new quality. Rama's arrows had burnt off the layers of dross, the anger, conceit, cruelty, lust, and egotism which had encrusted his real self, and now his personality came through in its pristine form—of one who was devout and capable of tremendous attainments. His constant meditation on Rama, although as an adversary, now seemed to bear fruit, as his face shone with serenity and peace.

Similar to other passages in the *Ramayana* the vision is one of human qualities obscured by more ruthless, rapacious traits. As the reader is often told, it was for the destruction of Ravana and the establishment of peace, "to honour our ancestor's codes and values," that Rama was manifested.

Once Sita is tested through an ordeal of *sati* or fire and proves her faithfulness and integrity, Rama accepts her back, and she sits next to him on his throne in Ayodhya. In pleasant courtly circumstances, from time to time, Rama begins to forget his origin:

Now Brahma, the Creator, came forward to speak and addressed Rama thus: "Of the Trinity, I am the Creator. Shiva is the Destroyer and Vishnu is the Protector. All three of us derive our existence from the Supreme God [Brahman] and we are subject to dissolution and rebirth. But the Supreme God who creates us is without a beginning or an end. There is neither birth nor growth nor death for the Supreme God. He is the origin of everything and in him everything is assimilated at the end. That God is yourself, and Sita at your side now is a part of that Divinity. Please remember that this is your real identity...."

In this one passage R. K. Narayan highlights through his version of the *Ramayana* the three major traditional Hindu deities or forms of the Supreme God and their unity in Brahman. A similar traditional expression of unity is "Atman and Brahman are one." Sharing a religious vision comparable to that of the *Bhagavad Gita*, the *Ramayana* upholds a high and demanding conception of the spiritual nature of the individual human being, the necessity of a moral ethic, and their intimate relation to social order.

Islam entered India within a generation of Muhammad's death in AD 632. By the founding of the Mughal empire in 1526, Islam had already been in India for several hundred years. Before looking at poems by Kabir (1440-1518), I believe it is necessary to have some understanding of Sufism which, as a development within Islam, began to enter India in earnest in the twelfth century. The Persian poet Farid Ud-Din Attar's *Conference of the Birds* (1120-1200) is suffused with a Sufi sensibility. Attar constructs the allegory of the poem around the journey or pilgrimage of an assembly of various kinds of birds in search of the king of the birds, the Simorgh. The Hoopoe serves as their guide, opening the conference and welcoming each one. Before long each bird makes excuses why it cannot set off in quest of the Simorgh. Much of the poem is given over to these excuses and the Hoopoe's attempts to inspire them to set off across the seven valleys at the end of which resides the Simorgh. Symbolically, these valleys are stages on the mystic Sufi Way towards *tawhid* or unity with God. Sufis as early as the ninth century Al-Junayd of Baghdad had emphasized *tawhid* and similar notions of *fana* or oblivion of one's self, along with sobriety or obligation to society creating a continual strain of homesickness for the individual. When the birds finally arrive at the Simorgh, Attar writes,

> There in the Simorgh's radiant face they saw
> Themselves, the Simorgh of the world—with awe
> They gazed, and dared at last to comprehend
> They were the Simorgh and the journey's end.
> (trs. Afkham Darbandi and Dick Davis)

The essential pun here is of course that "simorgh" means thirty birds in Farsi, the final number, out of many thousands, to persevere and attain the goal. The central paradox of Sufism and the source of its conflict with orthodox Islam results from this unity being at odds with the transcendence of God. Nevertheless, Attar expresses the Sufi experience of human consciousness in his uniquely beautiful and metaphorical poem—an epic of the human spirit, culminating in a vision analogous to Dante's cosmic rose. The unifying mysticism of the Sufis explains a significant part of the influence of Islam in India.

More than any other poet, Kabir represents the confluence of Sufism with Indian forms of spirituality. Born into a low-caste Hindu family, he worked as a weaver and drew on the *sant* or holy man tradition of devotional poetry in the *bhakti* tradition. Influenced by both Saiva and Vaisnava Hinduism, his conception of the transcendent tends to be in the universal terms of *nirguna*, "without attributes." Just as often his poems evince a highly Sufi sensibility of universality, while rejecting both Hindu and Muslim orthodox forms:

> I have no disputes,
> For I have renounced the path of both the Pandit and the
>   Mullah.
> I weave and weave, to make my own way,
> And I sing of the Supreme Being to empty the self.
> All the codes inscribed by the Pandit and the Mullah,
> Those I absolutely renounce and will not imbibe.

> Those pure of heart shall find the Supreme Being within,
> Kabir says in knowing the self, one realizes the Supreme Being.

Having abandoned the doctrines of the Hindu and Islamic religious leaders, Kabir, perhaps like Emerson, makes his "own way." As were many poems by Kabir, this one was collected in the central text of the Sikh religion, the *Adi Granth*, and reflects as well that strand in the Indian religious psyche. Like the Sufi or *bhakti* poets, direct experiential knowledge of the Supreme Being or Brahman resides foremost in the consciousness of Kabir and leads him to identify the self in some way with the transcendent. Many Hindus, Muslims, Sikhs, and people of various persuasions in India shared Kabir's perception of unity, such as the Baul poets and those who worshiped such Hindu-Muslim saints as Satya Pir. The universality of the Baul singers and holy men, who rejected orthodox Hinduism and Islam in a manner reminiscent of Kabir, can be judged from these lines from the nineteenth-century wandering Baul poet Lalan Fakir:

> Everyone asks: "Lalan, what's your religion in this
>   world?"
> Lalan answers: "How does religion look?"
> I've never laid eyes on it.
> Some wear Hindu rosaries around their necks,
> some Muslim rosaries, and so people say
> they've got different religions.
> But do you bear the sign of your religion
> when you come or when you go?
>   (tr. Carol Salomon)

Far from highlighting difference and exacerbating inter-religious conflict, such as at modern day Ayodhya, Kabir and the Bauls, or perhaps rather people attracted to their ideas, preferred, for the sake of social stability and order, if nothing else, what was held in common, mollified the passions, and brought people together.

During the nineteenth century, many individuals and such movements as Rammohun Roy's Brahmo Samaj or "Society of

Worshipers of the One God" and the Arya Samaj sought to revive
or redefine Hinduism in progressive and monotheistic terms. The
family of the Bengali poet Rabindranath Tagore (1861-1941)
participated in this process of reevaluation. As he once wrote, "life
for our family has been a confluence of three cultures, Hindu,
Mohammedan and British," and in his writings Tagore draws on
these diverse sources. In regard to Hinduism, he studied and used the
bhakti and Baul traditions in his poetry, especially in the *Gitanjali*,
the collection of poems which led to his receiving in 1913 the Nobel
Prize. Many of these poems were written at his *ashram* Santiniketan
after his early morning meditations with students and teachers in the
prayer hall or during a summer spent in retreat in the Himalayas.
Poem "38" conveys well the spirit of the book:

THAT I want thee, only thee—let my heart repeat
without end. All desires that distract me, day and
night, are false and empty to the core.
As the night keeps hidden in its gloom the petition
for light, even thus in the depth of my unconsciousness
rings the cry—I want thee, only thee.
As the storm still seeks its end in peace when it
strikes against peace with all its might, even thus my
rebellion strikes against thy love and still its cry
is—I want thee, only thee.

The universality of this "thee" is intentional though grounded within
the entire book in terminology more clearly Hindu in origin,
reference, and nuance. Along these lines, Tagore once described his
religion to Albert Einstein in 1930 as "the reconciliation of the
Super-Personal Man, the Universal human spirit, in my own
individual being." The fervor of this poem seems akin to the Baul
poet Lalan's "When will I be united with the Man of my Heart?"
Tagore surely understood he was writing or rewriting and translating
his poems so that an English-speaking, Western, Christian audience
could find in them comprehensible expressions of parallel religious
sensibility or experience. The intensity of longing for the divine in

the parallel structure of "I want thee, only thee" evokes not only the intensity of the Vaisnava *bhakti* reformer Caitanya (1486-1533), Indian Sufi poets, and Kabir, but it also speaks in terms sufficiently consonant with such Western mystics as St. John of the Cross to allow a world-embracing range of response and interpretation.

The role of Hindu poet-saint was the basis on which Tagore's reputation rested in India as well as in the West. He genuinely believed in the veracity of Hindu spirituality and its saving grace. After receiving the Nobel Prize he increasingly found himself in possession of an international audience. Speaking in India in 1924, after his trip to Japan and China, where he had told one group "gradually world ideals will grow in strength until at last they have fulfilled their highest mission—the unification of mankind," he conceived of Asia as in opposition to the West:

> I feel that Asia must find her own voice. Simply because she has remained silent so long the whole world is suffering. The West has got no voice. She has given us nothing that could save us—that which gives immortality. She has given us science—a great gift no doubt—which has its special value, but nothing that can give us life beyond death. Her cult of power is based on pride and greed and the deliberate cultivation of contempt for other races. . . . I do feel that if Asia does not find her own voice, humanity will not be saved. That was my message to China and Japan and they listened to me. . . .

Far from having listened to Tagore, the polite response of the Chinese and Japanese to his dominant message of reaffirmation of the mystic East against the materialistic West constituted an unequivocal repudiation. The radical writer Qu Qiubai, later revered by Mao, wrote, indicative of China's accelerating collapse into communism, "India has already become modern India, but Tagore still seems to want to return to the abode of Brahma. No wonder he and India are moving in opposite directions—he has already retrogressed several hundred years!" Lu Xun and other prominent modernist radicals, engaged in clearing away the Confucian past, regarded Tagore as a dreamy, quixotic voice. The response was much the same in Japan. The modern world had arrived long ago in India and East Asia, but Tagore, clinging to the past, failed to comprehend.

In *Crisis in Civilization* in 1941, the year of his death, while recognizing some aspects of what he calls the greatness of English literature, individuals, and Western civilization, Tagore had an even more sober evaluation of modernity than in 1924:

> There came a time when perforce I had to snatch myself away from the mere appreciation of literature. As I emerged into the stark light of bare facts, the sight of the dire poverty of the Indian masses rent my heart. Rudely shaken out of my dreams, I began to realize that perhaps in no other modern state was there such hopeless dearth of the most elementary needs of existence.

Embittered in tone and acknowledging to a greater depth the "indifference of a so-called civilized race," namely the British, to the penury of the Indian people, Tagore describes the modernizing of the Soviet Union, China, Iran, and Japan in highly unrealistic, uninformed, and idealized terms. With the specter of international "cataclysm" and war spreading around the globe, he closes his last brief address to the world:

> Today I live in the hope that the Saviour is coming—that he will be born in our midst in this poverty-shamed hovel which is India. I shall wait to hear the divine message of civilization which he will bring with him, the supreme word of promise that he will speak unto man from this very eastern horizon to give faith and strength to all who hear. . . . Perhaps . . . dawn will come from this horizon, from the East where the sun rises.

This passage presupposes modern loss and renewal. Full of hope to the end, though severely chastened, Tagore looked out on the exploitation of India and on the world's second plunge into worldwide carnage in terms highly characteristic of his Hindu religious sensibility and looked forward to a whole new stage of evolving human civilization based on a spiritual ideal.

The novelist R. K. Narayan (1906-2001) was born into a Tamil-speaking, Brahmin family. For several years he attended Christian schools in Madras, where he was raised by his grandmother, a devout Hindu who taught him the traditional songs and prayers. His fiction often presents a persona who undergoes a crisis that drives him back in some way to a resolution suffused with an evocation of the Hindu past. Often portrayed as a simple pious Hindu, R. M. Varma, of the University of Jodhpur, more insightfully observes, "Cultural ambivalence is a marked characteristic of Narayan's fictional technique and he hovers between his Hindu faith and lack of it. He merely uses it as a landscape in his fiction." In *The Vendor of Sweets* (1967), Narayan presents a character named Jagan who owns a small shop that sells sweetmeats. Presented as somewhat of a religious crank, he is a follower of Gandhi who still works his spinning wheel and sits in his shop reading the *Bhagavad Gita* in between customers. In order to spare any animal from slaughter for shoe leather, he seeks out dying cows and cures their hide himself through a smelly process that revolts his wife and family. The narrator further highlights his eccentricity when he is portrayed as gazing at the stars one night thinking "Who lives in those? . . . Probably all our ancient sages are looking down at us." As the author of a book on "Nature Cure and Natural Diet," on which the publisher at Truth Printing obviously has no desire to waste resources, Jagan often appears to live in an idealized traditional India of long ago incongruously conflated with the modern present.

Jagan's only son Mali fully lives in the modern world, not only of India but of America as well. Dropping out of college, as Jagan had as a young man out of misconstrued loyalty to Gandhi, Mali, without consulting with his father, enrolls in a creative writing program in Michigan and helps himself to Jagan's attic stash of rupees in order to pay his expenses. Mali rarely says anything directly to Jagan so that he has to acquire his information on Mali's activities from a sycophantic cousin who periodically drops in at his shop for handouts:

> "Going there to learn storytelling! He should rather go to a village granny," he said, all his patriotic sentiments surging.
> "Exactly what I told him," echoed the cousin.
> "Did Valmiki go to America or Germany in order to learn to write his Ramayana?" asked Jagan . . . .

The cousin and Jagan trade further ethnocentric, provincial clichés about modern America: Americans eat beef and pork, take intoxicating drinks, and the women are "free" basking "in the sun without clothes." Narayan consistently portrays Mali as a son who has lost all the traditional Hindu virtues while Jagan spoils him and makes excuses for him.

After three years in America Jagan abruptly receives a cable announcing Mali's return with "another person" whom upon arrival at the train station he introduces as his wife, Grace. Jagan suffers a severe shock. His son has not only gone to America, where he in fact does begin to eat beef, but married there without informing his family. Further disoriented because the girl is a Korean-American, Jagan thinks she is Chinese and reflects, "Don't you know that one can't marry a Chinese nowadays? They have invaded our borders." Having stopped reading the *Bhagavad Gita* while receiving letters he believed were from Mali in America, but were actually from Grace, Jagan starts reading it "becoming mentally disturbed once again." Narayan subtly dramatizes his reading of the Gita as linked to his disturbed relationship with his son and thereby with modern India. Before long Grace, his new daughter-in-law, begins to take charge of the house and care for Jagan, his wife having died while Mali was in America. Soon she transforms the part of the nineteenth-century house in which she and Mali live with modern Western paintings and furnishings. Mali, though, in terms of communicating with his father, has changed little and continues to drain his father of money, launching an absurd scheme to manufacture "story writing machines," the prototype of which he shows Jagan, who closely inspects the knobs and settings:

> Characters: good, bad, neutral.
> Emotions: love, hate, revenge, devotion, pity.
> Complexities: characters, incidents, accidents.
> Climax: placement and disposal, and conclusion.

Narayan dramatizes Jagan reeling away from the artificial and worthless machine telling Grace, in the room in his own house that now "looked like an office in a foreign country," "our ancestors" "composed the epics and recited them, and the great books lived thus from generation to generation in the breath of the people." In one of the few revealing statements by Mali, "with a gesture of disgust," he interjects, "Oh, these are not the days of your ancestors. Today we have to compete with advanced countries not only in economics and industry, but also in culture." Satirizing what creative writing programs churn out in America, Narayan underscores simultaneously the gulf between father and son, traditional and modern.

As their relations continue to worsen, Jagan one day meets in his shop a bearded man, Chinna Dorai, who lives "in Kabir Lane." Formerly a stone cutter, he wants Jagan to support him while he finishes carving a statue of the goddess Gayatri begun by his master long ago. Jagan goes with him across the river to see the little dilapidated shrine in the primordial jungle:

> Watching him in this setting, it was difficult for Jagan . . . to believe that he was in the twentieth century. Sweetmeat-vending, money, and his son's problems seemed remote and unrelated to him. The edge of reality itself was beginning to blur; this man from the previous milliennium seemed to be the only object worthy of notice; he looked like one possessed.

Chinna Dorai, full of allusions to the gods of the *Bhagavad Gita*, *Upanishads*, and *Panchatantra*, a "man from the previous milliennium," sweeps Jagan into the mythical past. Calling up in his mind the *sannyasi* stage of life, Jagan reflects, "Am I on the verge of a new *janma*" or rebirth. Full of derision for the modern city, its crowds, buses, and businesses, Chinna Dorai, "intoxicated at the sight of" the half-finished statue, tells Jagan, "If I can devote my life to the completion of this task I will die in peace," while later adding, "It's only a man like you that can help me." Although Jagan is unwilling to invest in his son's impractical story-writing machine, Chinna Dorai perceptively judges his character in regard to his own designs which he stresses would provide Jagan with a garden "retreat." Wavering, Jagan broods, "Yes, yes, God knows I need a retreat." The narrator significantly refers to it as "an escape" from "his wife's death, son's growth and strange development, and how his ancient home . . . was beginning to resemble hell on earth."

Jagan returns home from the jungle retreat only to discover before long from Grace that she and Mali are not actually married:

> He stood looking at the girl. She looked so good and virtuous; he had relied on her so much, and yet here she was living in sin and talking casually about it all. What breed of creatures were these? he wondered. They had tainted his ancient home.

Shock upon modern shock rolls over Jagan. His son not only lived unmarried with a foreign woman of mixed descent in his ancestral home but shamelessly concealed it from his father. As Jagan explains to the cousin, "Even my grandfather's brother, who was known to be immoral, never did this sort of thing." His "dirtied" home, "which had remained unsullied for generations, had this new taint to carry." Since all of Jagan's traditional, conventional relations have already "ostracized him" over the "beef-eating Christian girl for a daughter-in-law," Jagan realizes they would "remove themselves further" should they learn of the "latest development." In a significant moment of honesty, Jagan observes he "felt grateful for being an outcast, for it absolved him from obligations as a member of the family." Jagan sits in the dark by the Sir Frederick Lawley statue, a relic from the British past, and meditates on his own arranged marriage in a richly embellished chapter that brilliantly evokes the traditional marriage customs of the joint family system in India and devastatingly insinuates the decayed state of his own house and modern India.

Jagan awakens in the dawn from his night of memories, fantasizing again of entering "a new *janma*." In regard to the traditional ceremony marking a man turning sixty, the narrator honestly concedes again that Jagan himself "had had his fill of these festivals." In his own way, the narrator frequently intimates, Jagan has picked over and repudiated various customs from the past. So one relative is imagined as saying how could the son Mali be different with "a father like Jagan." Narayan suggests a subtle, logical, and culminating connection of decline between father and son:

> Mali had proved that there was no need for ceremonials, not even the business of knotting the thali around the bride's neck. Nothing, no bonds or links or responsibility. Come together, live together, and kick each other away when it suited them.

The values of the *Ramayana* and other sacred texts have no resonance for Mali. Complicitous himself yet appalled by his son's conduct, Jagan struggles to understand and decide what action to take. He suffers yet another blow when Mali is suddenly arrested and thrown in prison for drinking and driving. The event reveals fully the self-seeking, amoral calculation of the cousin who is willing to twist the truth in order to free Mali. Disgusted, Jagan, lost and faltering, unable to cope fully with the clash of his traditional values with the modern world, resolves absurdly to retreat across the river, taking his bank book with him, after agreeing to pay for a lawyer for Mali and offering an airline ticket for Grace to return to America: "It's a duty we owe her." V. S. Naipaul has remarked of Narayan's *The Vendor of Sweets* that it is "a novel in which his fictional world is cracked open, its fragility finally revealed, and the Hindu equilibrium . . . collapses into something like despair." In his "On Alternative Modernities," Dilip Parameshwar Gaonkar has similarly observed, "Everywhere, at every national or cultural site, the struggle with modernity is old and familiar." Narayan has so thoroughly undermined and complicated Jagan with the tensions of modernity, deep within the structure of the narrative voice itself, only the most shallow or tendentious reading can fail to perceive the scathing critique of both the antedated and bankrupt, traditional and modern, values of India and Western civilization.

Writing in English and Marathi, Dilip Chitre (1938-) has published several books and anthologies of poetry. At the Iowa International Writing Program from 1975-77, his 1980 book *Travelling in a Cage* includes the poem "My Father Travels." Set somewhere in India, the persona thinks of his father traveling home "on the late evening train / Standing among silent commuters in the yellow light." Bleak in atmosphere, summoning up almost the "Unreal City" of Baudelaire and T. S. Eliot's *Wasteland,* while more personal and postmodern in tone, Chitre describes the suburbs sliding by the father's "unseeing eyes." His raincoat and sandals are coated with mud as he moves "homeward through the humid monsoon night." Arriving home he drinks "weak tea" and eats "a stale chapati," contemplating "Man's estrangement from a man-made world." Invoking modern existentialist interpretations of twentieth century life, Chitre suggests his father "trembles at the sink," as much from "The cold water running over his brown hands" as from the prevailing, enervated vision of human existence:

His sullen children have often refused to share
Jokes and secrets with him. He will now go to sleep
Listening to the static on the radio, dreaming
Of his ancestors and grandchildren, thinking
Of nomads entering a subcontient through a narrow pass.

Clearly there is alienation between him and "his sullen children," their frequent rejection of a common world. Apparently more modern in his reading than Jagan's pouring over the *Bhagavad Gita,* the father still remembers the mythical past and dreams of his Aryan ancestors flooding into India "through a narrow pass," as he struggles to cling to some aspects of his own narrow traditional world, while his children reject it. Like Jagan's retreating or traveling into an imaginary world, his going to sleep carries the suggestion of stifling futility.

T. Ramachandran (1946-), writing in Malayalam in Kerala under the pen name Tiyyar, expresses even more poignantly his sense of loss of the past in his own translation of his 1981 story "A New Order," published in *Malayalam Short Stories*. Kerala is arguably the most cosmopolitan of Indian states due to its early trading relations with Syrian Christians, Muslims, and Chinese. During the 1930s and '40s socialists and communists opposed the appallingly oppressive caste system under the Brahmins and laid the political groundwork that resulted in the Progressive Literature Movement and Socialist Realism of modern Malayalam writers and in India's first communist state government in 1957. Writing in a surreal modernist style of stream-of-consciousness, redolent perhaps of Kafka and Robbe-Grillet, Ramachandran presents a persona who is losing his lover, rented room, and mind. He malingers about his room and sleeps and dreams for whole days and nights "like a corpse," "day-dreaming of the past and the future." Mrs. Thomas, his lover, whose husband is his landlord, sends him a seductive letter inviting him to stay with her and relax at her Keralan plantation in a country valley. Preferring to stay in his room, his grip on reality continues to break down until he receives from Mr. Thomas a new lease that throws him out and turns his room over to someone named Nanappan, whom he seems to know. The mental state of the nameless persona and the incoherent style of the story can be discerned from his reflections as he reads the lease:

The two signatures formed a line. Vadakkethil Nanappan Nanappan (sd) OM, Pothumpandathu Thomas Thomas (sd)+They grew clearer and closed . . . OM . . . . CROSS. . . . It was the union of opposites. Reconciliation of two conflicting civilizations. . . .

Misreading the legalese of the document into the Hindu mantra OM and the plus sign into the Christian cross, alluding perhaps to the first century AD mission of St. Thomas to Kerala, the persona intimates the conflict weighing upon his consciousness is that of two civilizations, East and West: "The union of the eternal man and his counterpart was revealed in OM+." This union he connects with Mrs. Thomas, perhaps a Christian, and cannot comprehend the "sudden rupture" of his life with hers and with his room, the place he prefers to live, though the tea man abuses him as "the shameless one." Nanappan moves in but does not throw him out. The persona reaches "the end of the journey" and gives up "the quest" of uniting the two opposites. The cry of a siren cuts through the night, the same cry, I would say, Oe Kenzaburo hears rising from Shikoku. He returns to his room, "the basis of my belief and the hub of a new cosmic dust wind," after frenetic wandering in the streets, and looks in only to discover "Bloodstains blossomed into red flames in the corners down the steps of history, our history." Failing to reconcile the "two conflicting civilizations," he has mistaken Nanappan for the cause of his displacement, lost his sanity, and murdered him. Using the ambiguous indefinite article, "A New Order" represents ironically the loss of individual and social order, East and West, "the flowering of a new civilization . . . And my mean self its very ideal." Unifying religious perspective collapses into immorality, madness, and violence, the obliterating, destructive blasts of "a new cosmic dust wind" sweeping over India as elsewhere on the globe.

In terms of Sufism and Islam, the Egyptian Nobel laureate Naguib Mahfouz (1911-2006) has subtly and accurately registered the impact of this whirlwind on the Muslim world in such a way that his work also illuminates the twelve-hundred-year history of Islam in India. His first novel to consider Sufism in the modern world was *The Thief and the Dogs* (1961). Shortly after release from prison the thief Said Mahran visits a Sufi Sheikh Ali Al-Junaydi, whose name evokes the classical Sufi saint and tradition, and asks him to permit him to stay with him for a while. The Sheikh realizes Said lacks genuine Sufi piety and seeks only a roof over his head. Since Said's father was a loyal follower of the Sheikh, often taking Said as a boy with him to pray with the Sheikh, he eventually relents. Before long Said attempts to rob again and to take revenge on his wife and former friend who have married during his absence. Accidentally killing two other men who get in the way, Said spends most of his time homeless and running from the dogs, until he is finally caught. An immoral, unprincipled, modern anti-hero and criminal, his conversations with the Sheikh mark significant stages in the conflict between modernity and the past, but Said cannot retreat into the extreme, isolated religious world of the Sheikh, nor can Sufism or the Sheikh understand and offer him a persuasive conception of life.

Similarly, in the following year, Mahfouz published the short story "Zaabalawi," about a young man suffering from an "illness for which no one possesses a remedy." Overcome one day by "despair," he determines to search for a Sufi Sheikh Zaabalawi who his father once told him could perform miracles. Either people have never heard of him or have no idea where to find him. Frantically, forgetting all else, he wanders from place to place hanging his hopes on the elusive Sheikh Zaabalawi. Mahfouz remarked once in a 1989 interview, "I reject any form of sufism achieved at the expense of man's concern with the world and the life of people."

In 1983 Mahfouz published *The Journey of Ibn Fattouma*, the story of Qindil Ibn Fattouma's travels through several countries in search of the land of Gebel or perfection, a sweeping vista and modern literary pilgrimage of the soul, reminiscent of Attar. As a boy he asks his devout Sheikh one day,

"If Islam is as you say it is, why are the streets packed with poor and ignorant people?"
"Islam today," he answered me sorrowfully, "skulks in the mosques and doesn't go beyond them to the outside world."

Believing "in the intellect and in freedom of choice," the Sheikh unknowingly fills him with a burning desire to seek out other lands in order to learn how to reform the land of Islam. As young manhood arrives he sets off to the land of Mashriq, a primitive land where people live in a state of nature, naked and worshiping the moon, "merging into universal lovemaking." In the land of Haira the king is worshiped and all dissenting voices are ruthlessly suppressed. Around the king's palace are human heads afixed to the top of poles:

> I went off, certain that they were martyrs to justice and liberty, deducing this from what usually occurs in the land of divine Revelation. This is a strange world replete with madness. . . .

This critical voice is the voice of Mahfouz himself. Ibn Fattouma is eventually thrown, unjustly, for twenty years, into prison, where he converses with other prisoners who had "questioned critically some of the anomalous actions pertaining to justice and human freedom." Cervantes' Muslim captivity resonates. Noticing everywhere he travels similar evils in his Islamic homeland, he begins to worry that the land of perfection does not exist in this world and is suddenly just as arbitrarily released.

The next land is Halba, the land of freedom, where "god is reason" and the poor are "several degrees better off than the poor of Haira and Mashriq." Despite murders and raucous demonstrations, Ibn Fattouma describes it as a land of plenty, free of despotism, and where "All religions are to be found," including "atheists and pagans." At one point Ibn Fattouma remarks, "The life of every people is generally revealed through some basic idea," reminding me of the historian Ibn Khaldun's emphasis on "group feeling." After Ibn Fattouma criticizes Halba as a land of irreligion and "anarchy," lacking "some moral basis," an assimilated Halba imam tells him,

> Your homeland is the land of Islam, and what do you find there? A tyrannical ruler who rules to please himself, so where is the moral basis? Men of religion who bring religion into subjection to serve the ruler, so where is the moral basis?

Mahfouz has the rare penetrating intellect and courage to confront issues of central and continuing importance to Islam, whether in Egypt, the Middle East, or India.

The land of Aman is one of "total justice" and "armed guards" spying on everyone, robbing people "of all spirit of adventure and freedom," while the state "owns everything." He is told "proudly, 'Our land is the only one in which you will not come across illusions and superstitions.'" Shortly, calvary parade by, their lances tipped with human heads. Quickly traveling on, the land of Ghuroub, patently India, proves "a paradise of people in a trance." In the forests men and women, recluses devoted to "communal singing," prepare "themselves for the journey to the land of Gebel," perfection at last. Finally ascending a mountain to Gebel, Ibn Fattouma writes "a journal of my travels," the book itself, as it were, sending it back to the land of Islam hoping it will do some good. Mahfouz has sent many messages. In January of 1994 he wrote a public statement, which he and dozens of prominent Egyptian writers and artists signed and which is just as applicable to Islam elsewhere, titled "Against Cultural Terrorism": "All of Egypt is desperately searching for the freedom of thought. . . . As a result of religion, we are suffering." Mahfouz, in October 1994, at the age of eighty-three, was stabbed in the neck by an Islamist fanatic, aided by over twenty accomplices, nearly killing him and severing a nerve impairing his control of his writing hand. Many writers and innocent people in India, Hindu and Muslim, have met with the same kind of terrorist violence or oppression, not the least of whom is Salman Rushdie.

Growing up in a Muslim family in Bombay, Pakistan, and London, Salman Rushdie asserts in his 1980 novel *Midnight's Children* the freedom and dignity of the human intellect. The narrator Saleem Sinai reflects on the magical, telepathic children born in 1947, the night of independence from Britain:

Midnight's children can be made to represent many things, according to your point of view; they can be seen as the last throw of everything antiquated and retrogressive in our myth-ridden nation, whose defeat was entirely desirable in the context of modernizing, twentieth-century economy; or as the true hope of freedom. . . .

Their lives become, as Jawaharlal Nehru congratulates Baby Saleem, "the mirror of our own." Rushdie weaves together the tensions and ambiguities of "antiquated" and modern India to form a myth of the new nation "in the Age of Darkness, Kali Yuga," identified by some Indian writers with T. S. Eliot's *Wasteland*. Qualifying and complicating "the disease of optimism" at every turn, Rushdie dramatizes the rare moment in history "when we step out from the old to the new; when an age ends." Even as Saleem's mind progressively deteriorates throughout the novel, the midnight children remain more than "the bizarre creation of a rambling, diseased mind. . . . illness is neither here nor there." The antinomies of his skeptical modern grandfather and religious grandmother, one with "a hole in him, a vacancy in a vital inner chamber," the other given to "credulity," connect him or sever him from the past, wrench him, deepen his perception of modern India, Pakistan, and Bengal. Cognizant of all the upheavals of twentieth century India, Rushdie posits a fragile hope for freedom passed on through Saleem's son to the next generation.

Reading Rushdie's novel *The Satanic Verses*, I often found myself recalling Thomas Jefferson's words, "It does me no harm whether a man says there are seventy gods or no God." Indeed, I cannot understand what all the fuss is about since the book is such a finely crafted work of art. Rushdie does for Islam no more than what Ernest Renan's *Life of Jesus* accomplished in 1863. To say with Nietzsche, upon looking around at this modern world, that God is existentially dead seems honest, apropos, and harmless enough. I believe it is one of the great achievements of Western civilization and the Enlightenment that a person should be allowed the sanctity of his or her own conscience. The fanatics who condemned Rushdie to death damaged and discredited Islam in the eyes of the world far more than he ever did in *The Satanic Verses*. Through ambiguous literary technique, Rushdie undermines and calls into question the dreams of Gibreel Farishta, including his treatment of the character

Mahound. When Gibreel succumbs to paranoia schizophrenia at the end of the novel, Rushdie unequivocally states, "he is moving through several stories at once," as many leading actors in India work simultaneously on several Bombay Talkies or popular movies. Similarly, Rushdie appears to leave space for religious faith when the dreamy radical poet Bhupen states, "We can't deny the ubiquity of faith. If we write in such a way as to prejudge such belief as in some way deluded or false, then are we not guilty of elitism, of imposing our worldview on the masses?" Rushdie, true to his own conscience, undercuts these words through the scorn of Swatilekha, a young radical woman: "Battle lines are being drawn up in India today . . . Better you choose which side you are on." This exchange confirms Rushdie's own intellectual position eloquently articulated in his essays and interviews that his is a secular rational mind, not that of a Muslim at all, let alone a traditional one.

Nor should Rushdie be condemned to death for his vaguely socialist, Marxist thinking. If the twentieth century has proven anything, it is that the democratic value of freedom of speech must allow the expression of even the most unpalatable notions, provided they do not incite acts of violence and social disorder. I often think of Milton's great words, "Let Truth and Falsehood grapple." That a man wishes to cling to a dead radical ideology, while hundreds of millions have awakened from the failed, murderous dream, must also be defended. At the end of *The Satanic Verses*, Rushdie seriously introduces Salahuddin's involvement with Bhupen and Swatilekha in

a remarkable political demonstration: the formation of a human chain, stretching from the Gateway of India to the outermost northern suburbs of the city, in support of "national integration." The Communist Party of India (Marxist) had recently organized just such a human chain in Kerala, with great success.

Though "political activity of a type that had always been abhorrent to him," Salahuddin participates, and the demonstration turns out "a pretty fair success." Salahuddin himself "could not deny the power of the image. Many people in the chain were in tears," proclaiming their "positive message," what Zeeny calls "a Communist show." Rushdie then indicts the "government-supporting" media for not covering such a display of outdated credulity and sentimentality. It will be interesting to see whether the several years and enormous resources the Western democratic government of Great Britain has spent protecting his gifted life will ever manage to penetrate Rushdie's leftist radical ideology and result in a more intelligent, nuanced political philosophy.

As a modern soul, I respect the transcendent spiritual truth of all the great religions. The classical texts that reflect India's religious sensibility demonstrate a multifarious, profound conception of human experience, purpose, and morality that elevates and enlightens the human consciousness of her peoples. Devotees of Vishnu, Shiva, Krishna, Rama, and the other innumerable deities found and find in their gods a multifaceted, unifying, visionary ideal of human possibility that enriched their lives and encouraged the individual and social cultivation of humane qualities. Similarly, to love Christ, Muhammad, Moses, Buddha, or any of the Founders of the other great religions, nurtured the individual's inner moral development and created unifying social order and coherence for entire regional civilizations. In the modern world, East and West, many have lost, during the last hundred years or so, all respect for, and understanding of, the religious dimension of the human psyche. Where once a despotic tyranny reigned that the Enlightenment thinkers rightly needed to challenge, other oppressive tyrannies and ideologies now flourish and prevail, fragmenting culture, coercing and isolating the individual, who yet remembers the vision of unity recorded in the artifacts of civilization. The modern literature of India, whether Hindu or Muslim, reflects the crisis of these same tensions for the individual and the social order. Whereas Kabir and other poets sought a deeper understanding and synthesis during the Mughal empire, India's modern writers attest to its decay and loss in terms highly consonant with the despairing, nihilistic tales of writers all around the globe. Given India's history and volatile diversity of religions, often erupting into communal violence and nationalism as reactionary forces attempt their flights into imaginary days gone by, retreating from the secular state and modern world, I find it doubtful that in the long run anything other than a new vision of religious unity, affirming the traditions of the past but fully living in the present, achieving a higher synthesis of humankind's religious experience, can ever hope to hold India together and mitigate the evil passions of Ravana. East and West meet in the tumultuous upheavals of modernity, a psychomachia of global proportions, struggling together to move beyond the received ideas of modernism and postmodernism to a more profound and worthy vision of human purpose and meaning.

Robert Hayden in the Morning Time

Voyage through death
to life upon these shores.
"Middle Passage"

Sitting in my study this morning, in the dark, I cannot find the words to pray. Outside, the darkness shadows the windows while I grope for words—words that do not come. It has been more than twenty-five years since I first met Robert Hayden. How can I write honestly about him? I shift in my armchair, feel the call to prayer slip away, turn on the light, move to my computer, and begin to write words I hope are true. For so many years, I have intentionally avoided any inclination to write on his work. Having edited his prose and poems, so that others might have a better understanding of the beauty and profundity of his work, I felt a debt was partly repaid, freeing me for a while. And now for months, strangely, I feel again compelled to think about him, read and reread his work, bringing back how very much I owe the man, older fellow poet, friend, father, brother, rare human being. He literally put food in my stomach and a roof over my head, making possible my education at the University of Michigan. So long ago now, it seems a dream.

Since then I have lived in Japan, on an American Indian reservation, been to China, had a NEH grant on India, grew repulsed by academia, written words that have painstakingly accumulated. I first began thinking of myself as a writer in high school and then spent years reading and writing on my own, outside the academic world, before I met Robert Hayden in 1979, the year before his death. I had transferred to the University of Michigan in hope of studying with Robert Hayden, and my hope came true more than I could have ever imagined. I had been reading his poetry for years. Living in Detroit, though I grew up in the white suburbs, I often went to the Detroit Public Library, read at times his books there, and became convinced that his vision of African-American history and experience was profound and superlative. As an undergraduate I once allowed my enthusiasm for his poetry public expression and confronted for the first time the sort of reverse racism with which my interest in his work has so often met. In a class in 1977 on interpretative reading, I read his marvelous poem "Frederick Douglass." The poem to me is inimitable not only in expression, as a grand old sonnet, conveying Douglass' tenacity, but also in its vision of future "lives grown out of his life, lives / fleshing his dream of the beautiful, needful thing." This dream was Hayden's dream as well, and it was and is my dream too. But black and white students were shocked at my reading this poem. Condemnation glared out at me, accusing me, a suburban white boy, for daring to read the words of a black man, as though I could understand them. Years later, when I met and told Hayden about this incident, he was horrified and perhaps understood more than I did how closely knit our lives were becoming. I have never been able to forget reading about William White, a Harvard graduate, who rescued Douglass from an angry mob of anti-abolitionists and paid dearly for his selflessness.

In the winter semester of 1979, I had my first class with Robert Hayden in contemporary poetry. During that semester, Hayden was told by his doctor that he had terminal cancer. By the end of the semester, he took me into his confidence, deigning to read a sheaf of my poems. Looking back, I believe my choosing to write essays for him on Countee Cullen and Pablo Neruda influenced his interest in my work though for reasons I did not yet again understand. By the fall he had asked me to work for him as a secretary, my apprenticeship, as he called it, helping him to put his papers in order, death an approaching reality. All semester, three afternoons or more a week, I walked out from my campus garret to his home to type letters, pack boxes, and, when lucky, sit and talk with him for hours in his tiny study burgeoning with books while the sun slowly sank in the west, marking another day.

They were difficult times for Robert Hayden, always wracked, as he so often said, between one struggle and another. I remember in perhaps late September he was especially distraught, believing his work amounted to nothing and that he could no longer write. Taking then a private tutorial from him in creative writing, I was scheduled to meet him in his office to look at some of my poems. I knew what he was going through and wanted somehow to convey to him the respect and admiration I felt for him as a poet. His own words seemed the best to me. We had already talked about his cancer, put all sentimentality aside, preferring the harsh truth, as much as possible, without being morbid and dwelling on it. Early in the morning, I walked over to the Farmers' Market on the other side of Ann Arbor and bought a large bouquet of zinnias, thinking of his poem by that name. Walking into his office, I could tell he was distressed as ever, struggling with his demons. Sitting quietly for a moment, I sheepishly offered him the gala bouquet of zinnias, from the old brown shopping bag at my feet, and recited his line, "More More More." To my surprise and worry, tears filled his eyes as he fought to hold back his emotions. Slightly fumbling he picked up a large empty coffee mug, signaling for the flowers, and walked down the hall for water, returning more composed, adjusting his bow tie.

It was not just Hayden's poems on African-American history that appealed to me. His interest in history stood out to me as remarkably different from other poets who tended to write only about themselves and their little stifling private worlds. Hayden has a way of blending the personal with the historical that fascinates me, as in the following lines, first published in 1955:

> From the corpse woodpiles, from the ashes
> and staring pits of Dachau,
> Buchenwald they come—
>
> O David, Hirschel, Eva,
> cops and robbers with me once,
> their faces are like yours—
>
> From Johannesburg, from Seoul.
> Their struggles are all horizons.
> Their deaths encircle me. . . .

This is not black poetry, which Hayden knew, in a sense, does not exist, but poetry about the global human condition, universal human evil all people are capable of committing, white Germans as well as black Rwandans. Here Hayden identifies the victims of Hitler with real people he knew as a child in the Detroit ghetto, mourning them not as abstractions but as particular individual Jews he once played with and cared about and still remembered with warmth. The personal concern and compassion of the poet for these victims suffuse the poem, intensify the urgency in which "they come" and "encircle" him, demanding he confront the meaning of their fate. And yet the observer in this poem views the horror with restraint and distance, an objectivity that also universalizes the experience. Here was a way of writing that I could respond to. He was the only post World War II poet who truly spoke to me in this manner. His poems were redolent of my own experience of life, what it felt like to be alive in the late twentieth century, without ignoring the victims or turning them into political abstractions.

His sequence of poems "Words in the Mourning Time," published in 1970, expresses the same intensity of vision but on a larger canvas. Beginning with the assassinations of Martin Luther King and Robert Kennedy, the poem meditates on the meaning of modern American history. A sense of profound tragedy permeates the poem, as in the second line, "destroyed by those they could not save," though clearly attempts were made. Throughout his poems, Hayden has a deeper, more profound sense of Greek-like tragedy, than any other poet since World War II. Victims, all, the persona mourns and grieves for them, as he grieves for the ruthless historical process, "whereby, / oh dreadfully, our humanness must be achieved." "Oh dreadfully," representative of Hayden's sensibility, apperceives a fathomless depth of pathos. The next three sections violate every convention of postmodern poetry, especially section III, wherein Hayden evokes another harsh image of horror as he sits eating dinner and watching the evening news about the day's events in Vietnam. A horrible nightmare victim "comes to my table," "The flamed-out eyes, / their sockets dripping." The poem is not intended merely to appall with horror but to stir imaginatively the complacent reader, who tunes out the news, continuing with his dinner. Embraced within the structure of the entire sequence of ten poems,

Hayden derives added dimensions of meaning from this poem of "major means," as well as others like it.

After two more poems about Vietnam, without naming it, in section IV, Hayden begins with "Vietnam bloodclotted name in my consciousness." The national nightmare becomes his nightmare, "recurring and recurring," like fear of his own death. Again, the historical victims in Vietnam and the personal blend as he reflects on his own students, individuals he knew and cared about, "brutalized killing / wasted by horror." All politics aside, the poet mourns and grieves the human loss and suffering, the madness of it. In section V, Hayden laments the tragedy not only of Vietnam but of human existence itself. His epigraph for this poem resonates with the tragic complexity of his mind and his penetrating moral judgment: "Oh, what a world we make, / oppressor and oppressed." Both oppressor and oppressed are condemned here, and human nature itself found irrevocably flawed. Now opening into the universal, the reference is wider than the particular horrors of Vietnam or black experience.

In section VI, Hayden focuses in on the oppressed and reveals they are no better than other human beings. "Lord Riot," in the midst of exacting havoc and mayhem and "terror," destroys: "sing burn baby burn." Far from defending and justifying violence, Hayden himself unequivocally condemns it among blacks, a courageous position to take when racist nationalists and separatists in the Black Arts Movement of the sixties and later the Black Action Movement (BAM) in 1970 at the University of Michigan denounced him as an Uncle Tom, an "Oreo." He scathingly described such radicals once to me as "fascists in superfly suits." Section VII rises above such banality and articulates a moral vision that all human beings, black and white, must strive to attain. The "voice in the wilderness" is that of Martin Luther King, Jr., calling black and white, to a commonly binding vision of love and brotherhood. Cheap sentimentality aside, the persona describes love as demanding "obedience to all / the rigorous laws of risk, / does not pamper, will not spare." Beyond coddling and the flaccidly maudlin building of self-esteem, white or black, the voice calls the reader to a long, hard, grueling discipline:

> Oh, master now love's instruments—
> complex and not for the fearful,
> simple and not for the foolish.
> Master now love's instruments.

Imminent danger and death are the tragic realities emphasizing the necessity of this arduous, universal duty. Hayden once said of this elegy for King, "I think it's much, much easier to hate than to love."

When I read this poem I often think of the following passage by Martin Luther King, in the last book he wrote, published in 1967, *Where Do We Go from Here: Chaos or Community?*

> Every nation must now develop an overriding loyalty to mankind as a whole in order to preserve the best in their individual societies. This call for a world-wide fellowship that lifts neighborly concern beyond one's tribe, race, class and nation is in reality a call for an all-embracing and unconditional love for all men. . . . When I speak of love, I am speaking of that force which all the great religions have seen as the supreme unifying principle of life. . . . This Hindu- Moslem- Christian- Jewish- Buddhist belief about ultimate reality is beautifully summed up in the First Epistle of Saint John.

Hayden admired in King this vision of love. After decades of many strident, irresponsible voices, on all sides, white and black, King's voice still rings clear in its sane moral and religious vision of universal human brotherhood before the Divine Essence, a voice we dearly need to remember. I find here too the African-American experience of slavery and white racism becoming emblematic for all people throughout the world, in the past, today, and the foreseeable future. I think too of Arthur Schlesinger's compelling words in *The Disuniting of America: Reflections on a Multicultural Society*: "The growing diversity of the American population makes the quest for unifying ideals and a common culture all the more urgent. In a world savagely rent by ethnic and racial antagonisms, the U.S. must continue as an example of how a highly differentiated society holds itself together." With roots reaching deep into the historical and religious past, King and Hayden both present a complex vision of humanity.

I cannot mention the complexity of King and Hayden without thinking of Ralph Ellison, who so often savored the word and also sought a "more human" vision than people on all sides usually settle for. I often ponder his profoundly complex vision of our national identity, as in his 1980 essay "Going to the Territory":

> . . . by ignoring such matters as the sharing of bloodlines and cultural traditions by groups of widely differing ethnic origins, and by overlooking the blending and metamorphosis of cultural forms which is so characteristic of our society, we misconceive our cultural identity. It is as though we dread to acknowledge the complex, pluralistic nature of our society. . . .

Artists and writers of any race who achieve this depth of insight are rare. Ellison may have had only one novel in him, but *Invisible Man* was a great one, wrought with real complexity, more than can be said for most writers, black or white, who crank out dozens of insipid, pretentious, formulaic books, especially under the cloying corruptions of affirmative action ideology: "America is woven of many strands; I would recognize them and let it so remain. . . . Our fate is to become one, and yet many—This is not prophecy, but description."

I am reminded too of Charles Johnson, author of *Middle Passage* and *Dreamer*, writing in *Being and Race: Black Writing Since 1970*, "Our lives, as blacks and whites, we come to realize, are a tissue of cross-cultural influences." Similarly, he remarked in 1996 in the *African American Review*,

> But I just never bought into black cultural nationalism. It always struck me as naive (all cultures we know about are synthetic, a tissue of contributions from others). The way its proponents portrayed other races—whites, for example—had

nothing to do with the supportive people I knew when I was growing up. In the end, black cultural nationalism only served to remind me of how thoroughly American my family and I have always been.

After so many hateful, shrieking voices, Ellison and Johnson's words continue to speak eloquently to our racial woes and possibilities, hold us all to account, and serve as an example for those writers capable of moving beyond racial rhetoric and cliché—a movement our society as a whole desperately needs to make. Ellison gave his book the rich tension of life, of actuality. No simplistic, utopian vision of love and brotherhood, he framed and packed his novel with the complexities he knew existed.

Unlike King, Ellison, Johnson, and Hayden, Malcolm X's vision was undeniably a vision of racist hatred and violence. In "El-Hajj Malik El-Shabazz," Hayden emphasizes Malcolm's transformation from a member of the racist Black Muslim movement to his pilgrimage to Mecca, "his final metamorphosis," where he embraces something closer to the orthodox Islamic vision of human brotherhood, found, as Martin Luther King pointed out, in all the great religions:

> He fell upon his face before
> Allah the raceless in whose blazing Oneness all
> were one. He rose renewed renamed, became
> much more than there was time for him to be.

Drawing from *The Autobiography of Malcolm X*, Hayden presents Malcolm as changing and evolving toward a more humane vision of God and humanity, beyond his earlier racist bitterness, bigotry, and resentment. I think of my being deeply moved by Hayden's son-in-law quoting to me the Bahai teaching that "the black man must 'forget the past,'" while the Bahai Writings also castigate the white man's condescending sense of superiority and state emphatically that "both races" must put forth a "tremendous effort" to resolve this "most challenging issue." In the "blazing Oneness" of prayer, Malcolm finally learned that "all were one." "Renewed renamed," "El-Hajj," meaning pilgrimage, stressing his nascent transformation, Malcolm tragically "became / much more than there was time for him to be." In Hayden's view, the popular interpretation of Malcolm X as violent, abrasive hero fails to acknowledge the complexity of his life. In *The Autobiography*, Malcolm writes from Mecca he was "praying to the same God—with fellow Muslims, whose eyes were the bluest of blue, whose hair was the blondest of blond, and whose skin was the whitest of white." Hayden remarked, in an interview, "Militants be damned, I believe Malcolm would have come to Bahai or something like that, close to that."

Similarly, in terms of violence, section VIII of "Words in the Mourning Time," after the "voice in the wilderness" has invoked the mastering of "love's instruments," Hayden soberly evokes and condemns again the disturbing image of riot, run wild, with anger and death, "harrowing havocking." Section IX also returns to destruction, once more in Vietnam. Setting historical violence and evil in the foreground, Hayden writes of the "gook woman" howling "for her boy in the smouldering, / as the expendable Clean-Cut Boys / From Decent American Homes / are slashing off enemy ears for keepsakes." These lines show Hayden poignantly aware of the contradictions and ironies of America's tragic debacle in Vietnam and echo the earlier line about his drafted students "brutalized" by war, by those who wanted to make the world safe for democracy and had no compunctions about ignominiously violating the UN Charter. Like several of his poems, between the horror and the vision, the poem breaks in half. Though I have often thought this a flaw in the poem, and still do to an extent, I now believe this stark contrast heightens and dramatizes the urgency of the last half:

> We must not be frightened nor cajoled
> into accepting evil as deliverance from evil.
> We must go on struggling to be human,
> though monsters of abstraction
> police and threaten us.

> Reclaim now, now renew the vision of
> a human world where godliness
> is possible and man
> is neither gook nigger honkey wop nor kike
>
> but man
>
>   permitted to be man.

With strength and clarity of moral vision, setting aside ideology, Hayden names evil as evil. Though briefly interested in the social program of Marxism during the late thirties, he fought that battle long ago with the "monsters of abstraction," allowing him here to reach the conclusion that the truly human must rise above the delusions of communism. His choice of the word "godliness" lends religious nuance to his fervent call for a renewal of "the vision of a human world." Through his brilliant subversion of the racist slurs, for whites as well as blacks, Jews, Italians, and Asians, he articulates resoundingly the finest expression of human oneness in American poetry. Technically, the elegant figure of chiasmus in the opening line of the last stanza intensifies and elevates the command form of the verbs, "Reclaim now, now renew." This theme of universality prepares the way for the last poem in the sequence.

In Section X, the epigraph "and all the atoms cry aloud" comes from the Bahai Writings, referring to the recognition by all creation of the new Manifestation of God. Against the detailed backdrop of twentieth-century historical horror, injustice, murder, bloodshed, and oppression, Hayden writes, "I bear Him witness now." Any Bahai would readily recognize that line as an allusion to one of the three most important prayers of Baha'u'llah, the founder of the Bahai Faith. Hayden has also packed almost every subsequent line in the poem with allusions to other passages of the Bahai Writings giving the poem a complexity of religious reference and subtlety unique in American poetry. After centuries of what Max Weber called the disenchanting of modern culture, from the Enlightenment on down to the sixties, Hayden understood a serious religious conviction violated the conventional, received wisdom of the educated, twentieth-century mind. In all truth, he himself found it difficult to accept and often struggled with the claims of the Bahai Faith. Anyone who knew Hayden well realized the depth to which, as he often confessed, "I still struggle with my faith."

Hayden once took me to have lunch with him at Bacchus' Gardens, a restaurant of his choosing just off the Diag of the campus of the University of Michigan, though now long out of business. During our conversation I quoted to him the closing stanza of the last poem in "Words for the Mourning Time":

> I bear Him witness now:
> toward Him our history in its disastrous quest
>   for meaning is impelled.

Without hesitating, derisively, he jabbed back at me, "Think that's true, do you?" I hailed the waiter to pour me another cup of coffee. I felt I understood Hayden's struggles, and said nothing. Often, when we were in his study, he would get up and shut the door, so that no one else in the house would hear. Many times I heard him say vehemently, "Why I continue to have anything to do with Bahais, I do not know! I do not know!" Appalled by their simple-minded piety, philistinism, banality, anti-intellectualism, censorship, and fanaticism, he truly regretted becoming a Bahai. On another occasion, he explained, referring to his wife, "It has always been important to Erma that I remain a Bahai." The demons were many for Robert Hayden, and, as he put it, faith did not come easy for him, a complexity much obscured and denied by Bahais who seek to exploit his reputation to acquire converts.

As Christopher Lasch pointed out, all too often our age imagines religious faith provides all-encompassing answers that render life easy and free from doubt. For many, it is perhaps true, but for those who are at all thoughtful and sensitive, religion becomes, as Hayden said in an interview, a hair shirt, endowing the individual with a conscience, stirring up his soul, and pricking him where he falls short. The Greek waiter sauntered back, leaving the bill, hair bulging from his open polo shirt, his skin-tight black knit pants accentuating his hips, as he wiggled off. Hayden howled with delight, "He's so queer it hurts!" Several of his poems confront this particular struggle, dramatize it, were his way of dealing with the pain, and broke unique ground, not yet sufficiently recognized, on this struggle of the human soul. For all his doubt and what he called The Problem, he said to me in exasperation once, shortly before he died, "Oh I hope I'm not a complete hypocrite." A complex man, with a complex vision. Torn in so many directions. As he once phrased it to me, "half in and half out of everything all my life." I often think readers on all sides, myself included, blacks, whites, and Bahais, want to reduce him, use him for some crude little ideological purpose, or dismiss him since he does not fit in smoothly with their agenda. The complexity of his poetic art and vision are much more demanding and challenging, not to mention aesthetically, intellectually, and spiritually rewarding.

In his poem "[American Journal]" he attempts to grasp the complexity of American culture in its fullness. Secure in his loyalty to his African-American heritage, a lifetime of poems behind him on every conceivable figure and dimension of African-American experience, Hayden chose to write a poem thoroughly universal in conception, subject, and scope. Filled with humor, the prose poem seriously explores the landscape of modern America, planet earth, and the nature of the universe. The persona Hayden puts on, in his inimitable fashion to don unique voices and characters, is a visitor from outer space exploring earth for his alien civilization. Told in the form of reports or journal entries, the visitor recounts for "The Counselors" back home what life is like for "the americans this baffling / multi people":

> disguise myself in order to study them unobserved
> adapting their varied pigmentations white black
> red brown yellow the imprecise and strangering
> distinctions by which they live by which they
> justify their cruelties to one another

Viewed, in a sense, *sub specie aeternitatis*, even from another planet, "imprecise" expresses the visitor's evaluation of the absurd "distinctions" affecting local life and manipulated by the inhabitants of all races to "justify their cruelties to one another." In that single phrase, we have one of the hallmarks of Hayden's talent as a poet, the ability to utter a piercing observation of moral or spiritual insight that resonates with fresh expression of a human truth dimly known but rarely acknowledged. There is another significant fact lying behind Hayden's use of "imprecise." How can I find the words to express it? It goes to the core of his vision as a poet. I grope for words untainted by our racist past but find there are none. "Mixed," "mulatto," "half breed," even "interracial," more sanitized and objective, contains derogatory nuances that do not exist when describing people of various European extractions. Hayden's natural mother, if not white, and I thought she looked a little like my own mother in the picture of her he showed me, was of at least more than African ancestry. And so what? What human being in America is not of more than one ancestry? So we might say now, but Hayden came of age in the 1930s, and had to live for years in Nashville, Tennessee, where Jim Crow laws still existed. Just as problematic, some blacks were and are as racist as some whites, and in a variety of ways. Hayden loved his mother deeply and often spoke of her. His love for her and struggle for his own identity prevented him from ever becoming a racist and forced him to grapple with complexity. I think of Ralph Ellison's frequently bold and courageous statements on race, despite censure from black nationalists and separatists. As evidenced in this poem, Hayden came to understand, from his own complex background, not only from the Bahai Faith, what Ellison once said: "Human beings are basically the same and differ mainly in life-style."

Similarly universalizing his belief in the oneness of religion, Hayden has the visitor observe, "many it appears worship the Unknowable / Essence the same for them as for us." Spiritual harmony, however, does not prevail in the poem, as in this world. The visitor records the Americans' "noise restlessness their almost frightening / energy" and describes them as "charming savages

enlightened primitives." Their apparent level of civilization is meant
to be lower than that of the alien who describes noisy, violent street
demonstrations clashing with the police, "pigs / I heard them called,"
beating the crowd with clubs. He flees "the brutal scene" to protect
his sensitive nature:

> a decadent people The Counselors believe I
> do not find them decadent a refutation not
> permitted me but for all their knowledge
> power and inventiveness not yet more than raw
> crude neophytes like earthlings everywhere

The space alien judges the Americans once more in universal terms,
pointedly finding them to be "raw / crude neophytes like earthlings
everywhere." On one level "The Counselors" represent oppressive
authority in any system of government, such as communism,
fascism, or even democracy gone awry, and function here like the
"brotherhood" in Ellison or "Big Brother" in George Orwell's *1984*.
In the distant world from which the visitor has traveled, they rule
with firm control and "would never permit such barbarous /
confusion." On another level, Hayden alludes to what Bahais call the
Continental Counselors and Auxiliary Board Members, appointed
administrative positions in the Bahai Faith. While the administrative
side of the Bahai Faith is too involved to discuss here, I think in
order to understand this poem it is necessary to realize Hayden
dissents from another aspect of his supposedly mindless religious
belief. Arnold Toynbee remarks in his *Mankind and Mother Earth*
that all forms of human organization, civil or religious, become
oppressive to the individual. The paradox is humankind cannot live
without some form of cooperative organization and government. In
private, Hayden often expressed pronounced disagreement, distrust,
and fear of the Bahai administration as oppressive, tyrannical,
coercive, and exploitative as any other group of human beings. Built
of inevitably flawed human beings, desiring perfection, it could not
be otherwise. If I honestly search my own soul, I must say that, in

over thirty years of membership in the Bahai Faith, I have often thought and experienced the same thing.

Like King and Ellison, who both grappled with the American Myth and Dream, Hayden, too, in his 1978 "[American Journal]," written during the American Bicentennial, wrestles with questions of national identity and destiny:

> america as much a problem in metaphysics as
> it is a nation earthly entity an iota in our
> galaxy an organism that changes even as I
> examine it fact and fantasy never twice the
> same so many variables

The crisis of modernity and America has long been recognized as tied to the rupture in the metaphysical universe, whether in political philosophy, literature, painting, or any other endeavor in the humanities or sciences. While qualifying carefully in an interview that he regarded "racial and national pride as a rather dubious value," Hayden went on emphatically to add, "I have a deep love for my country." Like King and Ellison, Hayden also shared the commitment of most blacks and whites to a democratic order dedicated to human dignity and freedom and genuinely shared the culture's most sacred dreams and myths:

> confess I am curiously drawn unmentionable to
> the americans doubt I could exist among them for
> long however psychic demands far too severe
> much violence much that repels I am attracted
> none the less their variousness their ingenuity
> their elan vital and that some thing essence
> quiddity I cannot penetrate or name

Every generation of Americans since St. Jean de Crevecoeur in 1782 has tried to define what it means to be an American. Hayden's persona delves into the same inner reaches of the national psyche, feels "curiously drawn" to the enigma that continues to evolve and unfold, apparently unlike his own extraterrestrial, ideal, static civilization out there in the heavens. Though he concedes there is "much that repels," the "essence / quiddity" fascinates him, even while he cannot precisely identify it, ending with the rich tension of life in America. "Unmentionable" appears for the same reason.

I believe Hayden's inner tensions are especially evident in his 1972 "Traveling through Fog." The persona mentions "Looking back, we cannot see." Everything is wrapped in fog, blurred by mist. "Behind us" as well as "beyond us now / is phantom territory." Our past or origin is as obscured as our ultimate destination:

> Between obscuring cloud
> and cloud, the cloudy dark
> ensphering us seems all we can
> be certain of. Is Plato's cave.

Between birth and death, man knows nothing of the world of the Ideas, the divine archetypes. Mere shadows, thrice removed from reality, constitute all we can dimly ascertain in "the cloudy dark" of human existence, "ensphering us," encasing us, entombing us in this world. Like the allegory of Plato's cave in *The Republic*, man sits in the dark, facing the wall, unable to discern the truth. The title implies direction and movement and salvages a chastened sense of epistemology, even as it indicts confinement. The circumspectly chosen "seems" reverberates from the walls of the cave. Untainted by maudlin sentimentality, the persona remains content to sketch the human condition.

Hayden expresses another part of that condition, its antinomy, in "The Night-Blooming Cereus," also published in 1972. The description of the cereus cactus bud as "heavy," pregnant with potential flower, creates anticipation. It is further described as packed with its miracle and swaying in the air, "as though impelled / by stirrings within itself." Later in the poem the plant is again partially personified as possessing a "focussed energy of will." The persona then states what may be the reaction of many, if not most, modern observers: "It repelled as much / as it fascinated me /

sometimes." The implication is unmistakable that the persona has been struck by the "bizarre" much more than his companion; she has been touched by the "imminence of bloom." Nevertheless, since the cereus cactus rarely opens its striking blossom, and then only in the season of darkness, the persona and his "dear" agree they "ought / to celebrate the blossom." The references to dancing and the painting of themselves have a joyous, primitive connotation of ritual observance. This atmosphere of primordial joy centers in the fact that they are honoring "archaic mysteries" reappearing before their modern sophisticated eyes. Choosing "The Night-Blooming Cereus" as the only poem he read at the White House in January of 1980, Hayden knew it expresses perfectly, beautifully, metaphorically, the awe and mystery he felt before the Bahai revelation:

> Lunar presence,
> foredoomed, already dying,
> it charged the room
> with plangency
>
> older than human
> cries, ancient as prayers
> invoking Osiris, Krishna,
> Tezcatlipoca.
>
> We spoke
> in whispers when
> we spoke
> at all . . .

"Foredoomed, already dying" emphasizes the cyclical nature of the flower and implies that it, too, shall atrophy as a "lunar presence," belonging to a heavenly realm elsewhere than here on this imperfect earth of muck. The unequivocal suggestion remains that the newly opened flower merits celebrating, is worthy of their "marvelling," their primordial human awe and adoration.

In *The Revolt of the Elites and the Betrayal of Democracy*, Christopher Lasch wrote, "Both left- and right-wing ideologies, in any case, are now so rigid that new ideas make little impression on their adherents." Trapped in the clichés of modernity, ideologues and intellectuals on all sides are convinced of their possession of the truth, often unflappable nihilism, or an enervated form of religion or polity, closed off to the currents of the modern human soul. Hayden said to me on more than one occasion, "Everything these academicians touch they ruin." As he suggested in a 1977 interview, Hayden understood his work addresses this modern crisis of belief and values:

> I believe in the essential oneness of all people and I believe in the basic unity of all religions. I don't believe that races are important; I think that people are important. I'm very suspicious of any form of ethnicity or nationalism; I think that these things are very crippling and are very divisive. These are all Bahai points of view, and my work grows out of this vision. I have the feeling that by holding on to these beliefs and giving them expression in my work, not always directly—most of the time not directly—at least I'm doing something to prepare, maybe for a new time, for a new world.

Elsewhere he speaks of "new concepts of what it is to be human"; "a new vision of our relationship to God, to one another"; "a new release of spiritual energy in the world"; "a new consciousness." Similarly, the Rhodes scholar and philosopher Alain Locke, a Bahai and the self-described midwife to the Harlem Renaissance, wrote in 1926, "Surely the cure for the ills of Western materialism is here, waiting some more psychological moment for its spread—for its destined mission of uniting in a common mood Western and Oriental minds. There is a New Light in the world: there must needs come a New Day." The Enlightenment brought much that is good into the modern world, much that we need not live without, as we move beyond modernism, but also much that has led to fragmentation, anomie, extreme individualism, and social violence and chaos.

Hayden understood he was preparing "for a new time, for a new world," built soundly on what is best in ancient and modern, Western and non-Western, human civilization. I recall what Czeslaw Milosz spoke softly at the end of *The Land of Ulro*: "Reader, be tolerant of me. And of yourself. And of the singular aspirations of our human race."

Hayden's example and work have helped me understand what I myself must write. I feel my debt to the man. More than anything else I miss him as a friend. I search for and recognize his voice, warmth, and wisdom in his poems and prose, and yet am still left alone, dissatisfied. Grief. Human grief for the times gone by, the things I should have said or done, reminding me of his own grieving words, "What did I know, what did I know / of love's austere and lonely offices?" Here in the darkness of another morning, alone in my study, strangely, so it seems, back in Michigan, even my suburban hometown of Rochester. Cervantes comes to mind, "To imagine that things in this life are always to remain as they are is to indulge in an idle dream."

I remember sitting in the morning on the *tatami* floor of my little house in central Japan, in Maebashi, with *shoji* doors, rain pattering on the roof, working on the manuscript of Hayden's *Collected Prose*. I think then of that autumn and early winter, as I walked out to his house, the yellow, golden, orange, and brown leaves blowing about, the red sunset glowing in the West through the window of the tiny bedroom he used as a study. When he showed me the final version of his "Homage to Paul Robeson," one of several poems he wrote or finished by mid-winter, I was especially struck by the last lines, telling him they were suffused with the same compassion of all his poems, a heartfelt observation that seemed to move him deeply:

> I speak him fair in death,
> remembering the power of his
> compassionate art. All else fades.

Isaac and Peter

Our faith well balanced by our doubt . . .
W. H. Auden

For two years I lived and taught English on the Colorado River Indian Tribes Reservation in Arizona, a hundred and seventy five miles from Phoenix in the Sonoran desert. Although I had been occasionally reading their writings for years, I found myself increasingly drawn to the work of Isaac Bashevis Singer and Walker Percy. Using my computer modem to access the database indexes on DIALOG and the library of the University of California at Berkeley, old systems outdated by the Internet, I read almost everything each writer had ever written or had published on him in literary magazines and journals and became in particular absorbed with Singer's book *The Penitent* (1973; 1983) and Percy's *The Thanatos Syndrome* (1987). Looking out of my study window across the creosote and fields of irrigated crops, I could see the desolate desert mountains of California and Arizona bordering the fifty mile long valley of the reservation on which I lived. I viewed America, Western civilization, and our many woes from a new perspective. The Hopi, Navajo, Mohave, and Chemuevi American Indians I knew represented in their own cultural way the complexities I found in the writings of Singer and Percy. Having lived in Japan for a year and a half, all the more devastating to me was the discovery, shortly after settling on the reservation, that my air conditioned brick ranch house was built exactly on the site of one of the largest internment camps for Japanese-Americans during World War II. Prepared by the convergence of so many strands of my experience, living in the scorching intensity of 115 degree summers, I found Singer and Percy spoke deeply to my soul.

And now here I am back in my hometown of Rochester, Michigan, one of the "best" white suburbs of Detroit when I was growing up, no longer primarily white, but enriched with people from all over the world. Here out of my study window I see the familiar suburban backyards, bushes, fences, and swimming pools, watch my South Asian Indian neighbors tend their vegetable garden, meditate again on the writings of Singer and Percy. I have often thought of these profound and insightful words on modern life from Singer's Nobel Lecture of 1978:

> The serious writer of our time . . . cannot but see that the power of religion, especially belief in revelation, is weaker today than it was in any other epoch in human history. More and more children grow up without faith in God, without belief in reward and punishment, in the immortality of the soul, and even in the validity of ethics. The genuine writer cannot ignore the fact that the family is losing its spiritual foundation. All the dismal prophecies of Oswald Spengler have become realities since the Second World War. No technological achievements can mitigate the disappointment of modern man, his loneliness, his feeling of inferiority, and his fear of war, revolution and terror. Not only has our generation lost faith in Providence, but also in man himself, in his institutions, and often in those who are nearest to him.

While his fiction ponders the experience of Jews in Eastern Europe and America, his criticism is just as true of Christians, as well as modern life in general, East or West, Japan or China, suburbia or reservation. Belief in revelation and the transcendence at the core of the Judeo-Christian religions, indeed all the great religions, all the spiritual paths, has atrophied, as every writer worth reading in the twentieth century has mourned or celebrated.

In *The Penitent* Singer probes the situation of the modern Jewish soul, cut off from the traditional Jewish past and assimilated into secular European and American culture. The most spiritually profound novel of the twentieth century, it presents a complex struggle between modern Jews and the ultra-orthodox extremists, who reject every vestige of modernity, and, within the author's own soul, between religious belief and doubt. In regard to the latter, Singer said once, "I find myself full of faith and full of doubt." Talking to an interviewer, Richard Burgin, referring to characters in one of his novels, he states,

Since there is no evidence attesting to what God is, I doubt all the time, as I told you. So I dramatize in these characters my own doubt. Actually, doubt is part of all religion. All religious thinkers were doubters. Even the Bible, although it is full of faith, is also full of skepticism. The Book of Job you can call a Book of Skepticism. . . . I believe in God, I also doubt. I have moments when I think maybe the atheist Feuerbach was right.

Dramatizing in *The Penitent* the human complexity of his own soul, Singer realizes and confronts the ineluctable fact that "doubt is part of all religion." He does not, it is to be noted, present a shallow, superficial, modern rejection of God and religion. Rather Singer gives his readers the rich tension crackling between the polarities of life, between the antinomies of his own modern soul. I am reminded of Robert Frost's own ambivalence. Singer, in his 1967 article "The Extreme Jews," unambiguously includes himself among the modern Jews.

The Penitent begins with the narrator visiting the Wailing Wall in Jerusalem in 1969. Someone comes out of "a crowd of Jews of all kinds" and introduces himself as Joseph Shapiro, a formerly devoted reader of his fiction who is now "a Jew like a Jew should be." The narrator calls him a *baal tshuvah*, "one who returns." It is clear the narrator does not share his form of religion, and it becomes increasingly so as the novel progresses. Nevertheless, Shapiro offers to tell him a story, "something unusual," and they agree to meet the next day at the narrator's hotel. This short introductory episode ends with the words "This is what Joseph Shapiro told me," making the next one hundred and sixty pages essentially Shapiro's story with only a few interspersed comments by the narrator. At the end, Singer appends an Author's Note that compliments the introductory piece and frames Shapiro's account, resonating with and undercutting the main story. The essence of the story resides in the tension created by this structure of the novel between an ultra-orthodox Jew who has returned to the extremely traditional ways of his grandfathers and a modern assimilated Jew, more moderate in his approach to religion and life. This structure allows Singer to say things through the persona of Shapiro that he himself truly believes, at least, to some extent, while rejecting Shapiro's extremism.

During the next two days in the author's hotel room, Shapiro tells him his life story, his early days in Poland and Russia, largely as a liberal progressive Zionist, and eventual immigration to New York where he becomes a successful businessman, all the time moving farther away from Jewish faith. The narrator demonstrates faith is the main issue when, early on the first day, he interrupts Shapiro for the only time, pointing out to him that knowing the "faults of modern man" is not enough to become what Shapiro calls "a full-fledged Jew": "For this you must have faith that everything stated in the holy books was given to Moses on Mount Sinai. Unfortunately, I don't have this faith." Acknowledging the tension of his own inner battle, the narrator discloses that he says "unfortunately" "Because I envy those that do." Even as he is repelled by Shapiro's extremism, the narrator envies him and reveals his own limitations as a modern Jew.

As Shapiro's own story in New York unfolds, he reveals that he too "didn't have this faith." Living a secular life of wealth and pleasure, on the very same night, he discovers his mistress and his wife are as unfaithful to him as he is to them and witnesses his mistress' worthless daughter beating her mother almost to death. Finally appalled and shocked by the modern world beyond endurance, Shapiro packs his suitcase and flees to "Jewishness, and not merely to some modern arbitrary Jewishness, but to the Jewishness of my grandfathers and great-grandfathers." Immediately "the question of all questions" arises: "Did I also possess their faith?" Full of moral fervor he lambasts and rails against modern Jews:

A Jew without God can easily be persuaded that Lenin, Trotsky, or Stalin will bring deliverance. Jews without God can believe that Karl Marx was the Messiah. Jews without faith not only clutch at straws but even at burned straws. Every few months they find a new idol, a new illusion, a new vogue, a new madness. They revere all kinds of murderers, whores, false prophets, clowns. They go wild over every little scribbler, every ham actor, every harlot.

To no small extent this denunciation of Jews constitutes Singer's own assessment of their spiritual plight. In an interview in *Encounter* in 1979 he said, "I'm a sceptic about making a better world. . . . People will remain people, and they have remained people under communism and all other kinds of isms." After finding and praying with "true Jews" in New York, Shapiro extends his sweeping denunciation of Jews to all of modern culture: "How perverse modern man is!" Shortly thereafter he decides to fly to Israel, abandoning, he thinks, Sodom entirely. At this point in the story, Singer undercuts Shapiro by involving him in a sordid affair with a young secularized Jewish woman on the airplane, groping and fumbling around under their shared blanket: "My journey had now become as meaningless as everything else about me." Again Singer shows him to be no better than those he denounces.

In Israel Shapiro quickly learns "We are a people like all other peoples. We feed our souls the same dung as they do." In words that reiterate faith is the issue, Shapiro observes, "The faith that had been ignited within me during the worst crisis of my life began to cool and grow extinguished." He decides to join the ultra-orthodox who reject the modern secular state of Israel and live in the Meah Shearim section of old Jerusalem:

> I must confess that at the time that I made this resolve, my faith wasn't yet that strong. I was still completely riddled with doubt and with what I might even call heresy. I went away from evil, you might say, not so much out of love for Mordecai as out of hate for Haman. I was filled with a raging disgust against the world and against the civilization of which I was a part.

Singer here has Shapiro speaking against himself, as it were, inescapably a member, a part of the very civilization he hates. His becoming a fanatic and fleeing to Jerusalem does not really change that fact, nor does his marrying an innocent young ultra-orthodox girl. "The Evil Spirit, or the beast within me," actually the voice of conscience and moderation, attempts to speak reason and caution him: "All this would be fine if you were a true believer, but actually, you are nothing more than a heretic afflicted with nostalgia." He observes, "The Evil Spirit harangued me: 'You're acting out a farce.'" Later, "the voice within me" shouts, "It's not for you! Not for you!" At one point Shapiro remarks to the narrator "how hard it is for a modern person to turn back to God; how deeply the doubt and despair are rooted within us." The other side of Singer's own soul speaks here building, probing, kneading the richly dialectical tension of his vision of the modern human being, while Shapiro ends his story, in contradistinction to the author's expressed doubts at the beginning, by saying, "I have accepted the Torah and its commentaries because I am sure that there is no better choice. This faith keeps growing in me all the time."

The famous author, visiting the Wailing Wall in Israel, has listened to all this autobiography largely without spoken comment. In his Author's Note at the end of the book, he addresses the reader directly mentioning an actual interview in *The New York Times* in which he himself had "voiced a severe protest against creation and the Creator." As in the Book of Job, the author asserts, "a belief in God and a protest against the laws of life are not contradictory. There is a great element of protest in all religion." To that extent, the story of Shapiro expresses Singer's own protest against modern life, against life, a protest many modern minds would prefer not to hear. But the very structural device of the framed story also undermines, calls into question, and qualifies Singer's own allegiance to Shapiro's fiery denunciation of modern life. Singer makes this fact clear when he states that he himself grew up "among extremists" like Shapiro, yet "I cannot agree with him that there is a final escape from the human dilemma." With humankind wracked on the horns, torn each way, Singer knows,

faith and doubt, despair and hope can dwell in our spirit simultaneously. Actually, a total solution would void the greatest gift that God has bestowed upon mankind—free choice.

A complex vision of the human heart must also recognize the resident antinomies. Anything less would constitute the banal vision of a child and negate the dynamic struggle that free will imposes on us. Singer's closing words undercut Shapiro once more and highlight the malaise of modern life: "The remedies that he recommends may not heal everybody's wounds, but the nature of the sickness will, I hope, be recognized." Far from Singer recommending a reversion to ultra-orthodoxy, he demonstrates how quixotic such an extreme attempt is while using the persona of Shapiro to voice the most scathingly eloquent moral condemnation of the "sickness" of modern secular life that American literature has to offer.

Walker Percy's perspective on modern life closely resembles Singer's indictment. In an essay "Why Are You a Catholic," published in 1990, the year he died, Percy presents his reader with a few "self-evident" axioms that I have often called to mind:

> The old modern age has ended. We live in a post-modern as well as a post-Christian age which as yet has no name. It is post-Christian in the sense that people no longer understand themselves, as they understood themselves for some fifteen hundred years, as ensouled creatures under God, born to trouble, and whose salvation depends upon the entrance of God into history as Jesus Christ. It is post-modern because the Age of Enlightenment with its vision of man as a rational creature, naturally good and part of the cosmos, which itself is understandable by natural science—this age has also ended. It ended with the catastrophes of the twentieth century.

Growing up Catholic in Rochester, living here now, I know these words are all too painfully true. No more risible idea exists in the suburbs than that of human beings as "ensouled creatures under God." It has become exceedingly blatant that "people no longer understand themselves" in this way, whether in the family, education, work, or play. Like Singer who remembers the Jewish past and wonders why and whereto, Percy, a Southerner, broods on modern civilization and thinks of two thousand years of Christianity. Percy strikes a deeper cord than Singer when he perceives the "old modern age" is gone, gone with the murdered millions, the victims of Hitler, Stalin, and Mao, part of the malignant, radical fruit of the Enlightenment.

Along with reading Walker Percy's *The Thanatos Syndrome* on the Colorado River Indian Tribes Reservation, I read St. Augustine's *City of God* and, as I looked across the shimmering heat of the desert, knew and felt the two respond to a similar crisis of civilization. In Louisiana, Dr. Thomas More, a psychiatrist, begins to notice possibly related symptoms in several patients, acquaintances, and loved ones. He begins to wonder if there might not be a syndrome and searches for the cause. Before long he discovers a group of social engineers who are lacing the drinking water with radioactive heavy sodium in order to manipulate the cerebral cortex of the population. As one of them claims, the neocortex is "the scourge and curse of life on this earth, the source of wars, insanities, perversions—in short, those very pathologies which are peculiar to Homo sapiens." Their good intentions allow the eradication of the problems of teenage pregnancy, abortion, crime, suicide, AIDS, the black underclass, drug abuse, rape, and murder, and lead to euthanasia of the weak and feeble. At times Dr. More is even tempted to consider the results as beneficent though he ultimately exposes and defeats the social engineers. As in Singer, the modern secular world Percy evokes has lost the religious, moral dimensions of the human past. Percy once said the main issue of *The Thanatos Syndrome* is "to what degree is the sacredness of the individual recognized," for modern man seeks answers to the dilemmas of life in a diabolical pseudo-science reminiscent of the eugenics of Germany under Hitler.

Percy especially makes explicit the parallel between Hitler and the local social engineers in "Father Smith's Confession," a section toward the end of the book. In a manner similar to Singer with Shapiro, Percy undercuts Smith by portraying him as mentally deranged while his observations on Weimar Germany, Hitler, and modern America resonate none the less. Dr. More visits Father

Smith, who is a modern day Simon Stylites living atop a forestry lookout tower searching for signs of fire. As he metaphorically says at an early meeting between them, where there is smoke there is fire, and Smith's experience as a young man visiting Nazi Germany in the early 1930s causes him to seek everywhere signs of modern society's conflagration. While in Germany, he witnessed the nationalistic romanticism of young Germans who dreamed of joining the SS and German military and the hubris of older Weimar professors of psychiatry who helped prepare the way for the extermination of the Jews. Full of concern and tender feeling for the sufferings of the weak and dying, they practiced euthanasia on a slippery slope leading to the gas chamber. At the climax of Father Smith's confession he reveals that he himself as a young man would have joined the young German soldiers had he not been an American, so attractive and seductive was the aura of Germany under Hitler. In a Footnote to his confession, he then recounts he returned to America and at the end of World War II became a captain in the US Army eventually fighting his way back to Germany. Inspecting then a famous German children's hospital associated with some of the psychiatrists he had known in the 1930s, he questions a nurse about the use of a particular room, sunny with a geranium plant on the windowsill. He learns, suggesting the banality of evil, that the room was used for the routine euthanasia of children. Akin to the evoking of historical experience and vision of Saul Bellow or Singer, modulating between Europe and America, Father Smith says, "That's all, Tom. End of Footnote." Dr. More and Father Smith "sit for a while in silence." Percy has Father Smith pointedly ask More, "Do you think we're different from the Germans?"

Early in the novel Dr. More alludes to his own loss of faith. When Father Smith cites the Jews as a sign of God, More replies, "the Jews I know are not religious. They either do not believe in God or, like me, they don't attach any significance beyond—" Father Smith interrupts him, leaving his statement hanging unfinished in the air. After the social engineers are put out of business, a ceremony is held to celebrate the reopening of a hospice for the care of the terminally ill. Father Smith, conducting Mass, in one of his crazy periods, offers a few words beforehand, implying modern violence and inhumanity are linked to the loss of faith:

> Don't you know where tenderness leads? Silence. To the gas chambers. Never in the history of the world have there been so many civilized tenderhearted souls as have lived in this century. Never in the history of the world have so many people been killed. . . . Listen to me, dear physicians, dear brothers, dear Qualitarians, abortionists, euthanasists!

Percy once stated in an interview in *The Paris Review* that the main target of *The Thanatos Syndrome* was "the widespread and ongoing devaluation of human life in the Western world—under various sentimental disguises: 'quality of life,' 'pointless suffering,' 'termination of life without meaning.'" Mentally breaking down in church, Father Smith aims at the target and nevertheless speaks, like Shapiro, words of truth, even as Percy undercuts him. Yet Percy has Dr. More walk to the Father and assist him in going on with the Mass, thereby dramatically affirming his sermon. Significantly, More, though a modern man, remembers only the "old Mass." Later, More relates that when Father Smith invites him at the hospice to help perform Mass, "I told him the truth: that since I no longer was sure what I believe, didn't think much about religion, participation in Mass would seem to be deceitful." Percy has Father Smith dialectically brush this objection aside: "You have been deprived of the faith. All of us have. It is part of the times."

Father Smith continues with a story of the Virgin Mary appearing to children in Yugoslavia, "as an ordinary-looking young red-cheeked Jewish girl," telling them,

> Do you know why this century has seen such terrible events happen? The Turks killing two million Armenians, the Holocaust, Hitler killing most of the Jews in Europe, Stalin killing fifteen million Ukrainians, nuclear destruction unleashed, the final war apparently inevitable? . . . Could it be a test like

Job's? Then one must not lose hope even though the final war seems inevitable as this terrible century draws to a close. Because almost everyone has lost hope. Christians speak of the end time. Jews of the hopelessness of the mounting Arab terror. Even unbelievers, atheists, humanists, TV anchormen have lost hope. . . . But you must not lose hope, she told the children.... Perhaps the world will end in fire and the Lord will come—it is not for us to say. But it is for us to say, she said, whether hope and faith will come back into the world.

Dialectically offered to the reader with irony and humor, Percy undercuts this passage with Dr. More's usual skepticism. Percy, though, seriously introduces this religious perspective into his narrative and allows it room to reverberate within the antinomies of his own story and soul. In a late interview on *The Thanatos Syndrome*, in *The Southern Review*, Percy acknowledges, "what I'm saying is that a good deal of the anxiety, the alienation, and the depression in the modern world is not due to any gene. It's due to something wrong with the modern world and something wrong with the way we live."

In contrast to the endemic anxiety, alienation, and nihilism, many Christians and Jews remember, as Singer and Percy remember, the Judeo-Christian religious and historical past that was instrumental to the evolution of Western principles of individual and civil order. Even as we continue to suffer from the excesses of modernism, we witness all around us, in the East as well as the West, the steadily dwindling end of modernism. The excesses of Nietzsche seem quaint compared to the nihilistic bacchanalia of the followers of Martin Heidegger, Michel Foucault, Paul de Man, and Jacques Derrida. To refute such excesses requires recovering, revivifying, restoring the lived reality of mankind's experience of the transcendent. We would do well to remember the words of Paul Tillich in 1958 in "The Lost Dimension of Religion":

In many cases the increase of church membership and interest in religious activities does not mean much more than the religious consecration of a state of things in which the religious dimension has been lost. It is the desire to participate in activities which are socially strongly approved and give internal and a certain amount of external security. This is not necessarily bad, but it certainly is not an answer to the religious question of our period.

This basic understanding of the spiritual state of modernity has been echoed by many brilliant and insightful Christians and Jews. Using the common theological terminology of "vertical" and "horizontal," Czeslaw Milosz remarked in *New Perspectives Quarterly* on the "horizontal" nature of both American fundamentalism and Polish Catholicism and wondered if "underneath there is an abyss." "After all," he warns, in a different issue of the same quarterly, "those ideas [of Western democracy] have had their foundation in religion . . . how long can they stay afloat if the bottom is taken out?" I remember George Mendenhall, my teacher at the University of Michigan, writing in his book on the Hebrew prophets, "The Tenth Generation is always faced with the alternatives of deification of force or the deification of ethic."

Throughout the centuries, humankind has experienced this situation many times. The Bible is one of the earliest documents to record and interpret this experience. Individual and social order must of necessity, by way of definition, be a moral order. And stable moral order can only be established on the basis of shared religious ethic or covenant. Whether in the history of the early Hebrews, fifth-century Greece, or the late Roman empire, to name only the most prominent examples of Western social and moral decline, the pattern and dynamics of vitiation and renewal read like current events, the background of Singer's and Percy's fiction. Our modern disruption, the crisis of the West and of the East, for well over two centuries now, has thrown down many hallowed ways and ancient institutions and dreamed of establishing many glittering utopian cities on top of the mass graves of the slaughtered millions. If a large part of the world is now beginning to awake, as from a nightmare, we must recognize our own individual, social, and spiritual woes are deeper than merely surface irregularities that can be ameliorated with a few conservative public-policy statements.

Eric Voegelin discusses in his study of the early writings of Marx how conscious Marx's decision was to dump the metaphysics of Hegel in favor of violent action. Nietzsche and Heidegger too dramatize the end of metaphysics and glorify the violent deed. The lust for power and the cruelty inherent in deconstruction and other radical theories show they are blood-line descendants of modern nihilistic philosophy. Allan Bloom insightfully documented how the problems of American higher education have a long lineage reaching back to the "advanced" thought of Nietzsche and other decadent thinkers. He also demonstrated how the same nihilism suffuses every level of our culture, popular as well as educated. Unlike Dostoevsky in *The Possessed*, Bloom fails to acknowledge adequately the religious dimension of this radicalization and ends with a flourish in the direction of the Great Books. Christopher Lasch, in *The Revolt of the Elites and the Betrayal of Democracy*, more perceptively observes, as Singer and Percy have in their fiction, the nature of the crisis: "Public life is thoroughly secularized." Further acknowledging the severity of public fragmentation, Lasch writes, "Both left- and right-wing ideologies, in any case, are now so rigid that new ideas make little impression on their adherents." Western society and the East must reclaim what Tillich and other theologians call the vertical and answer "the religious question of our period."

It is a question that baffles all nations and religious traditions. In Arizona, on the reservation, I observed the decline of the traditional way of life among the Hopi, Navajo, Mohave, and Chemuevi Indians. Most of their youth, like the rest of the youth of America, were more interested in the schlock of popular culture than in the old ways of their tribes. All the conflicts of the modern world were there. Looking out my study window, in this city that produced Madonna, I now see the same modern maladies in Rochester that I knew growing up here as a Catholic. I witnessed too in Japan and China the modern tidal wave of secularization sweeping everything before it. The modern experience of humankind is one, as God is one, as man is one, as the great religions are one. I remember the words of Baha'u'llah:

> The Revelation which, from time immemorial, hath been acclaimed as the Purpose and Promise of all the Prophets of God, and the most cherished Desire of His Messengers, hath now, by virtue of the pervasive Will of the Almighty and at His irresistible bidding, been revealed unto men. The advent of such a Revelation hath been heralded in all the sacred Scriptures.

Singer and Percy painstakingly document and brilliantly explore the modern straying from the path, from revelation, the nature of the "sickness." Singer once said, "I don't preach really, because if I would know how to go back to the old ways I would do it myself." After all that modern culture has been through, he had no delusions of a backward movement, while Percy once disclosed in an interview an attitude quite typical of many minds: "That's what attracted me, Christianity's rather insolent claim to be true, with the implication that other religions are more or less false." These ungenerous words fail to grasp the meaning of the modern experience of atrophy their author so marvelously evokes and suggest only an unimaginative reactionary return to a Day gone by. Part of the history of modern life for all cultures, Hellenistic in nature, involving now the entire globe, has been the chaotic spiritual quest or pilgrimage beyond such narrow notions to an appreciation of the truth and worth of other religious traditions, to a greater measure of knowledge of the Divine Being than He bestowed on humankind in past Dispensations. I recall Albert Camus's remark: "all of us, among the ruins, are preparing a renaissance beyond the limits of nihilism."

There is, too, a sense in which the bemoaning of modern culture, the loss of everything of value, has become a cliché. On the reservation and in Japan and China, I knew excellent human beings, nothing like the stereotype of the drunken or radical Indian or the racist caricature of the red or yellow heathen. I might add that one of the most intelligent *human* beings I have ever known was a black man. And I too have experienced the pain and humiliation of racist hatred and treatment from African-Americans, Japanese, American Indians, and Chinese. In real estate and elsewhere, I have witnessed African-Americans hating each other, ruthlessly taking advantage of South Asian Indians, Japanese despising Koreans and Chinese, some Mexican-Americans and Indians loathing each other with frightful ferocity, and so forth. On the reservation, I witnessed Indian and Mexican children beating up my seven-year-old son while chanting "Get the white kid! Get the white kid!" Liberal clichés leave out such complexities. Yet I can neither forget the awe I felt as a child before the icon of the Madonna, nor my experience of the truth represented by the Japanese and Chinese statues of Kannon or Kuan-yin, by the matchless temples of India, and by the Indian intaglios of the desert depicting animals and symbols of transcendence from long ago. In my hometown I delight in witnessing the change during the last thirty years. Now many African-Americans, Chinese, Japanese, South Asian Indians and others live, study, and work here enriching it with their God-given variety and beauty, their mosques, Sikh gurdwara, Buddhist and Indian temples. No utopia, but a hard, moral, modern spiritual struggle, full of rich, human tension and antinomies. I cling to the vision of Baha'u'llah, sullied as it is, the modern lotus blossom growing out of the muck: "Ye are the fruits of one tree, and the leaves of one branch."

The Victory of World Governance

The Middle Ages witnessed the periodic devastation of vast areas of territory for hundreds of years before the notion arose that social cohesion and order should take precedence over local ambitions, sovereignty, and religious belief. Thus the Magna Carta in 1215 and the first free European commune in Florence in 1266 marked significant steps toward formation of the nation-states that began to appear around 1500. Another sign of change was the feudal economy of the Middle Ages had been based on the bartering of a rural serfdom, while the Renaissance economy became increasingly based on the exchange of money in an urban society. So too the universal authority of the feudal church was irrevocably eroded by the rise of nation-states and by its own inability to keep pace with the intellectual and spiritual development of society. Slowly those qualities that distinguish the Renaissance from the Middle Ages acquired hegemony and transformed European society from one tied to the feudal estate or province to one determined by racial, linguistic, and national origin. By the time of Machiavelli, the complete detachment of power from transcendent moral authority had taken place and the beginning of modern totalitarian application of power to entire nations had begun. Unlike the emerging Machiavellian ethos, fledgling democracy drew both on the humanistic Greco-Roman and the Judeo-Christian traditions. Whereas Machiavelli had sought to extend the power of the state, the Founders of the American Union sought to limit it partly by affirming natural law in the interest of civil order and the individual. Steeped in the cosmopolitan heritage of Roman and European jurisprudence, especially British common law, the American Founders asserted the validity of basic human rights from a universal perspective. Accompanying if not leading to this split in the political realm was the rupture in the metaphysical universe. Regardless of the immense differences in ideology, I believe each tendency evolved as a response to the same crisis. As the old order continued to erode, the movements toward oppression and federation augmented and consolidated. The manifestation of the ontological rupture remains unresolved both in the political and individual, personal realms.

In *Crime and Punishment* in 1866 Dostoevsky confronts the severity of the rupture and its implications for the future. From 1840 onward, socialism was increasingly influential throughout much of Europe and even occasionally in America as at Brook Farm, depicted in Hawthorne's *Blithedale Romance.* In 1848 Karl Marx and Friedrich Engels published *The Communist Manifesto* at a time when national revolutions and workers' uprisings were beginning to occur throughout the European continent. Dostoevsky himself had been a member of the socialist, Fourier circle of Petrashevsky in the late forties and served a prison sentence in Siberia from 1849 to 1854. By 1866 Dostoevsky had come to regard socialism as the "new spirit of infidelity" that was further cutting the people off from the sacred traditions of the past by substituting "progress in the name of science and economic truth." The protagonist Raskolnikov, emulating his idol Napolean, oversteps all obstacles in his pursuit of power and murders an old pawnbroker in order to steal her money to finance his socialist schemes. He justifies the murder on the grounds that great benefit will eventually accrue to mankind from killing the "vile noxious insect." In an article foreshadowing his crime Raskolnikov argues that extraordinary men have the right to "step over a corpse and wade through blood," the right to destroy the prevailing order in favor of the future "New Jerusalem," the Marxist kingdom of freedom. This act of hubris at the core of the novel is explained at one point as a "turn away from God." Ultimately through the redeeming Christian love of Sonia, Raskolnikov replaces his socialist theories with the resurrection and reconciliation of a "new life." Despite the affirmative ending, Dostoevsky directly connects socialism with the loss of religious faith and adumbrates the devastation of the future. Repulsed by Dostoevsky's unequivocally religious understanding of his own work and of the events of his time, Western readers frequently reduce him, as they similarly reduce Murasaki Shikibu, author of the Japanese *Tale of Genji*, to merely an astute psychologist of human motivation—a reduction Dostoevsky himself would have certainly regarded as symptomatic of precisely the malaise against which he wrote.

Fourteen years later Dostoevsky achieved his most complete condemnation of socialism in *The Possessed*, which was published toward the end of the Franco-Prussian War of 1870 to '71. The years since *Crime and Punishment* had made it increasingly clear that socialism was an unprecedented threat to the order of civilization. Such events as the first attempted assassination of Czar Alexander II in 1866 and the purge by Nechaev of an insufficiently zealous revolutionary indicated the direction in which Russia was moving. The new barbarism was threatening the values upheld by the Slavophiles as well as the values of those persons in favor of Westernization. In the novel Dostoevsky succinctly formulates the situation as a choice between God-man and man-god. The socialists choose man-god and attempt to idolize Stavrogin, the most uncompromising nihilist of the book. Central to Dostoevsky's purpose is the chronicling of the progressive corruption of socialist ideas. Stepan Verkhovensky represents a liberal aesthete who exults over his own early involvement and fellow traveling with the radical cause in the 1840s and '50s. The next generation are all nihilists and anarchists who have debased Stepan's aesthetic and mildly socialist ideas. His son Peter Verkhovensky foments a socialist uprising and arranges the murder of a disaffected socialist. As one socialist confesses to the police, they were trying

> systematically to undermine the foundation of the existing order, to bring about the disintegration of the social structure and the collapse of all moral values, which would cause general demoralization and confusion. Then the broken, decaying society, sick and in full ferment, cynical and godless, but thirsting for some guiding idea and for self-preservation, could be taken over when the banner of revolution was raised....
>
> (tr. Andrew R. MacAndrew)

The Communist Manifesto had prefigured these strategies for revolution, as had Chernyshevski in his 1863 novel *What Is to Be*

Done? With overwhelming prescience, Dostoevsky foresaw the ontological rupture led from the "destruction of God" back to the "gorilla." That this debasement should proceed in the political as well as the philosophical realm only stood to reason.

Kirilov fully embodies the new barbarism by advocating the "total destruction in the name of the ultimate good" of "more than one hundred million heads . . . so that reason may be introduced in Europe." In this he merely conforms to socialist doctrine and therefore is declared by a fellow anarchist "ahead of everyone." Later Kirilov advances what to him is the heart of the matter: "If there's no God, then I'm God." Far from circumventing the problem, Kirilov connects the ethos of socialism with the determining loss of modern times. What Nietzsche was soon to discover, acknowledging Dostoevsky as his master, Kirilov perceives in his own deviant way: "If He doesn't exist, then all will be mine." Kirilov's decision to kill himself to affirm his unbelief, his refusal to "invent God," conforms faithfully to the logic of Marx, who had heavily imbibed the philosophy of Ludwig Feuerbach. That the mass of communists never imitated Kirilov can be explained only by their unmitigated pursuit of power. In "Modernity on Endless Trial," Leszek Kolakowski articulates exactly what concerns Dostoevsky in *The Possessed*: "A world that has forgotten God has forgotten the very distinction between good and evil, has made human life meaningless, and has sunk into nihilism." Kirilov chooses to affirm nihilism by what he imagines to be a grand gesture. In a manner very different from Dostoevsky, Tolstoy attempted to respond to this same crisis of the spirit, as in his book *The Kingdom of God Is Within You*. With the tell-tale cunning of the guilty, Soviet authorities, after their own wading through blood in 1917, never permitted the publication of a separate edition of *The Possessed*.

Despite enormous opposition, the late nineteenth century witnessed the continual spread of communism in Russia. The failure of the movement known as "going to the people" in the mid-seventies only confirmed the socialists in their use of violence, as in their finally successful assassination of Czar Alexander II in 1881. Unfortunately, radical tendencies, though widely held under control during the last decades of the nineteenth century, were exacerbated by reactionary policies and by endemic social injustices. As the twentieth century began, the reactionary rigidity at times provoked further unrest and anarchy. Meanwhile in Europe the imminent threat of socialism had been considerably defused by more enlightened social legislation that increasingly acknowledged the human rights of the masses. The peoples of Europe took for granted the continuity of civilization, and few persons foresaw the outbreak of World War I. The prevailing atmosphere was one of prosperity and optimistic abandonment to progress and to the immediacies of life. After all, it had been forty-four years, La Belle Epoque, since the Franco-Prussian War had convulsed Europe and welded together the separate saxon states into the German Empire. Although the demise of the Austro-Hungarian Empire had been prophesied for years, most persons were more than a little complacent, which was especially true of the common man. Even Thomas Mann and Franz Kafka were stunned by the outbreak of war and by the rapidity with which countries took sides, though the latter's writings had already expressed the angst produced by the pervasive ontological gloom. The European countries had been waging cold war for years and when open hostilities eventually came, the shock of the horror of modern warfare was so intense that it swept away, along with most of the surviving monarchies of the time, all vestiges of the nineteenth century belief in progress and the perfectibility of man. The very notion of unbridled nationalism was called into question as total war quickly produced more than ten million corpses and more than thirty million maimed soldiers and civilians. Walter Lippmann cut to the quick: "It was such a happy time up until 1914." Melville's verse on the outbreak of the Civil War reads like a prophecy of the twentieth century: "Horror the sodden valley fills."

During the Great War people in both Europe and the United States began to realize the extent of the barbarism that modern warfare constitutes. The Peace Conferences at the Hague in 1899 and 1907 had given impetus to the incipient notion that the threat of war and the maintenance of peace were the responsibilities of all nations, as had the many US initiatives and arbitration treaties of John Hay,

Elihu Root, President William Howard Taft, and William Jennings Bryan—the last of whom signed thirty Advancement of Peace Treaties prior to the war. After August 1914, within Great Britain, the Lord Bryce Group and the League of Nations Society, among others, such as the Fabian Society under Leonard Woolf, worked diligently to further the direction of the Peace Conferences by advocating the abandonment of the old method of secret diplomacy and alliances and by calling for some type of strengthened Concert of Powers, while, in the United States, the League to Enforce Peace had its beginning as early as January of 1915, with Taft at its head. Although such persons as Lord Robert Cecil, Norman Angell, Jan Christian Smuts, and Leon Bourgeois were instrumental in the development of the idea of the application of federalist principles to the community of nations, it was President Woodrow Wilson who fully perceived the necessity of world governance to champion "public right" over the "interests of particular nations." Like the ancient Greek Cleisthenes who realized Athens had to move forward from the chaos and oppression of the tyrants to democracy, Wilson understood it was essential to move forward from the chaos and upheavals of the nation states to democratic federalist principles on the international level. As the second Secretary-General of the United Nations Dag Hammarskjold in 1956 said, "Woodrow Wilson went to the heart of the matter." He had, as Stefan Zweig writes in *The World of Yesterday*, a "clear and simple plan." Wilson's experience as a historian of American history uniquely qualified him to recognize the imperative of federalism to stem the rising tide of barbarism. Surveying the ruins of the old monarchical world, he was the first statesman of stature to proclaim "There is a way of escape if only men will use it." Regardless of the postwar triumph of isolationism, the failure of the United States to enter the League of Nations, Woodrow Wilson succeeded in introducing into international affairs the highest federalist standards that had evolved out of Christianity, Roman law, and Greek democracy. At exactly the same time that Wilson was affirming these standards Lenin was undermining them in Russia. Though an attempt was made to assist the Whites against the Reds, the effort was actually half-hearted because the Western nations were eager to return to their domestic concerns. Few persons were sufficiently worried about the communist crevasse that was opening at the edge of Europe.

In *Doctor Zhivago*, written by the end of 1955 and only published in Russia in the '80s, Boris Pasternak takes account of the Bolshevik Revolution and of its implications from the events of 1905 to the early 1950s. Although Yuri Zhivago was "once filled with enthusiasm for revolution," the novel recounts his growing disaffecton with communism. At one point a young revolutionary he meets on a train reminds him of Dostoevsky's nihilists and of Peter Verkhovensky's "frivolity and shallowness." Everywhere Zhivago observes doctrinaire communism undermining the foundation of society and the well-spring of human affection. Lara, with whom he falls in love, sums up best their shared revulsion with the new regime: "All customs and traditions, all our way of life, everything to do with home and order, has crumbled into dust in the general upheaval and reorganization of society. The whole human way of life has been destroyed and ruined." Against this background of the devastation and aftermath of the October Revolution, Yuri and Lara endure and affirm the sanctity of individual life. Early in the novel Zhivago's Uncle Nikolai argues that "what has for centuries raised man above the beast is not the cudgel but an inward music." Later Lara's friend Sima defends "individuality and freedom" when she contends both have evolved out of Christianity and are equated with a life principle that flourishes free of ideology. Along these lines Zhivago refutes a revolutionary by insisting "I think that nothing can be gained by brute force. People must be drawn to good by goodness." Similarly Gordon defines Christianity as "the mystery of the individual." In place of Dostoevsky's God-man or man-god, Pasternak advances something approaching Life-god or Death-god, individual human freedom or mass communal oppression. What Zhivago calls the "madness" and "absurd nightmare" deprives him of a profession, a livelihood, his family and home, until there is "nothing personal left." According to his own diagnosis the strain of living a life of "constant systematic duplicity," in what Osip Mandelstam called the "Wolf-hound century," catches up with him and results in death by heart attack. Lara, "the representative of life and existence," is later arrested on a city street and sent off to the Gulag Archipelago. Their child ends up an uneducated orphan and laundry girl for soldiers in World War II. Thinking of the revolution that has victimized her and so many millions, Gordon remarks, "It has often happened in history that a lofty ideal has degenerated into crude materialism." Such understatement about the revolution and subsequent murder of millions of its own citizens can only grimly undercut the closing passage of the novel that seeks to draw sustenance from the "thaw" in political oppression during the fifties.

By the time the Soviet Union joined the League of Nations in 1934, what little influence the world organization had left was already waning. The twenties had been a period of relative success for the League since there were few significant challenges to peace. It had proven useful in settling or defusing minor conflicts and disagreements such as the Aaland Islands, Upper Silesia, and the status of Danzig. The Great Depression brought an end to international prosperity and initiated a decade-long decline in the effectiveness of the League, which the Kellogg-Briand Pact of 1928 could not prevent, despite its collection of sixty signatories committing on paper their countries, including Germany, Italy, and Japan, to repudiation of the use of force as an instrument of national policy and to peaceful settlement of disputes. With the Japanese seizure of Manchuria in 1931, the German withdrawal and rearmament, and the Italian subjugation of Ethiopia from 1935 to '36, there was little doubt that the efficacy of the League was a thing of the past and barbarism the in-coming wave of the future. Instead of attempting to revivify the League and its federalist principles, many nations after 1936 withdrew further into isolationism and thereby capitulated to the fascists. Nowhere was this more apparent than in Great Britain where Chamberlain shamelessly espoused accommodation and permitted Hitler's invasion of the Rhineland in 1936, his annexation of Austria in 1938, and his conquest of Czechoslovakia in 1939. Chamberlain's most cowardly act was surely his pandering to Hitler in September of 1938 at the conference of Munich. The despot who slept with a copy of

Machiavelli next to his bed and who invoked Nietzsche and Wagner was given exactly what he wanted in exchange for a few glib promises to leave the remainder of Europe alone. The collective will of Western civilization to resist the evil of power-hungry nihilists had atrophied and required Hitler's invasion of Poland in September of 1939 and the bombing of Pearl Harbor in December of 1941 to revive it. The League of Nations, as Wilson and others had emphasized, was only as strong as member-nations were willing to make it in the interest of "public right." Far from constituting a failure of the institution and its Covenant, the demise of its efficacy reflected the loss of commitment to defend the fundamental principles of civilization.

From February to May of 1938 Thomas Mann traveled across the United States lecturing on the threat of fascism and its radical departure from Western values. Revolted by the crude materialism and the aesthetic and moral barbarism of the fascist regimes, Mann excoriates what he identifies as his own German inclination to regard "life and intellect, art and politics as totally separate worlds" and laments the trampling of "the traditional values underlying Western culture." Because Mann recognized in *The Coming Victory of Democracy* "absolute force" or the will to power as the core of fascism, his denunciations are equally applicable to communism:

Democracy must understand this new thing in all of its thoroughly vicious novelty. Democracy's danger is the humane illusion, the virtuous belief that compromise with this new creature is possible, that it can be won over to the idea of peace and collective reconstruction by forbearance, friendliness, or amicable concessions. That is a dangerous mistake which is founded on the wholly different thought-process of the democratic and of the fascist mentality. Democracy and fascism live, so to speak, on different planets, or, to put it more accurately, they live in different epochs. The fascist interpretation of the world and of history is one of absolute force, wholly free of morality and reason and having no relation to them.

Mann's indictment concentrates on precisely the radical rupture that fascism posed for Western civilization. Fascism brought to the fore exactly those issues that Dostoevsky had observed in the nineteenth century. Aleksandr Solzhenitsyn, Leszek Kolakowski, and Czeslaw Milosz observed the same ontological rupture at the core of the thought-process of communism. The disjunction was irremediable and has led directly to the collapse of communism. As Ibn Khaldun observed in 1377, a regime that uses "forced labour" and robs people of their property destroys "all incentive to cultural enterprise" and ruins its own civilization. This correlation of spiritual with material collapse is attested by the official atheism of both Machiavellian regimes.

With the return of belligerent nationalism and militarism, few perceptive observers during the thirties failed to sense the approach of a day of doom. Unlike prior to World War I, many people now feared for the existence of civilization, while others deluded themselves with such fantasies as the New York World's Fair of the summer of 1939. Statesmen on both sides of the Atlantic stepped back and allowed barbarism to fill the void. Even before the commencement of concerted hostilities, some observers, instead of dismissing collective security, began to consider ways of strengthening it. Despite all the limitations of the League, it was a step toward rational maintenance of order and liberty for all peoples. In late 1939 the US State Department formed a committee on the desirable shape of the postwar world, the recommendations of which gradually moved toward some form of world organization. Franklin D. Roosevelt had accompanied the delegation of President Wilson to the Paris Peace Conference of 1919 and well understood the reasons for the creation of the League, as he made clear in his 1923 "Plan to Preserve World Peace." In his 1941 address on the State of the Union, President Roosevelt announced his Four Freedoms, which outlined his determination to defend the defining qualities of civilization. He also advocated the reduction of armaments, which had been part of the League Covenant, so that, as Roosevelt put it, "no nation will be in a position to commit an act of physical aggression against any neighbor." This articulation of collective security was reaffirmed by Roosevelt in August of 1941 in the Atlantic Charter, which both he and Churchill signed and which mentions "the establishment of a wider and permanent system of general security." They further stated that "all of the nations of the world, for realistic, as well as spiritual reasons must come to the abandonment of the use of force." Indubitably the realistic reasons included the atom bomb, about which Einstein had written Roosevelt as early as mid-1939.

Throughout World War II other significant steps were taken toward forming world organization such as the United Nations Declaration of January 1942, which was the first use of Roosevelt's term for the countries leagued against the forces of fascism; the UN conferences on Food and Agriculture and on Relief and Rehabilitation in 1943; the International Labor Organization and the Bretton Woods conference on the International Monetary Fund in 1944. All these and other efforts toward rational world governance and toward recognition that the world had become one unified economy in all spheres of life achieved fruition at Dumbarton Oaks in August to October of 1944. This meeting of British, Chinese, Soviet, and American representatives produced the first draft of recommendations that eventually evolved into the Charter of the United Nations. The thorniest barrier to world organization proved to be the method of voting in the Security Council. At Yalta in the Crimea in February of 1945 Roosevelt, Churchill, and Stalin finally agreed that all major powers would have the veto. The United States also insisted on having the veto, a fact impressed upon Carlos Romulo, the Philippine ambassador at the first United Nations Assembly in San Francisco in April to June of that year. After President Roosevelt's return from Yalta he addressed Congress on the first of March 1945 and presented the results of the long effort toward forming a universal organization:

For the second time, in the lives of most of us, this generation is face to face with the objective of preventing wars. To meet that objective, the nations of the world will either have a plan or they will not. The groundwork of a plan has now been furnished and has been submitted to humanity for discussion and decision. No plan is perfect. Whatever is adopted at San Francisco will doubtless have to be amended time and again over the years, just as our own Constitution has been. No one can say exactly how long any plan will last. Peace can endure only so long as humanity really insists upon it, and is willing to work for it, and sacrifice for it. Twenty-five years ago, American fighting men looked to the statesmen of the world to finish the work of peace for which they fought and suffered. We failed them. We failed them then. We cannot fail them again, and expect the world to survive. I think the Crimean Conference was a successful effort by the three leading nations to find a common ground for peace. It spells—and it ought to spell—the end of the system of unilateral action, exclusive alliances and spheres of influence, and balances of power and all the other expedients which have been tried for centuries and have always failed. We propose to substitute for all these, a universal organization in which all peace-loving nations will finally have a chance to join. I am confident that the Congress and the American people will accept the results of this conference as the beginnings of a permanent structure of peace upon which we can begin to build, under God, that better world in which our children and grandchildren—yours and mine, and the children and grandchildren of the whole world—must live, can live. . . .

The havoc of World War I had forced upon farsighted statesmen the only means of escape, and now the lesson had been repeated. Roosevelt's emphasis on the recurrence of the obligation of preventing war underscores the lesson that he and many statesmen drew from the immense devastation of World War II, from the slaughter of more than fifty million people. Isolationist elements in both the United States and Europe notwithstanding, the masses had also perceived to some degree the validity of the same lesson and longed for a cessation of war. Roosevelt's conception of world organization was more profound than Woodrow Wilson's ebullient optimism, which had led him to an unyielding position that kept the

United States from joining the League of Nations. Roosevelt did not intend to make that mistake. Roosevelt's conception was not a luminescent New Jerusalem descending from heaven already perfectly constructed for the habitation of humankind. He recognized from the vicissitudes of the League that the evolution of world federation was a tumultuous process dependent on the will of humanity to work and sacrifice for peace. At Yalta he had expressed the tough-minded realization, as he had on other occasions, that world organization would not yet secure peace but might at least last for about fifty years. From that perspective, he reported to Congress that the universal organization was "the beginnings of a permanent structure of peace."

Barely had Roosevelt returned from Yalta before the will to unity of the major powers began to falter. Stalin soon violated many of the agreements reached there, most flagrantly in regard to Poland. Churchill and Roosevelt himself had separately worked out exclusive alliances with Stalin on certain particulars, while Stalin had not even bothered to read before the meeting key documents from Roosevelt on world organization. With the death of Roosevelt in April of 1945, shortly after his return from Yalta, the responsibility of ending World War II and the future of the United Nations passed to Harry Truman. Even before the United Nations Charter was ratified in June of 1945 ominous signs were apparent throughout Eastern Europe, and, once the Soviet Union began to abuse the veto, in the United Nations as well. The shape of the future was set. In March of 1946 Churchill's speech "The Sinews of Peace" warned the free world of an iron curtain of barbarism descending upon Eastern Europe. In March of the following year President Truman praised the objectives of the United Nations and rightly committed the United States to helping "free people to maintain their free institutions and their national integrity against aggressive movements that seek to impose upon them totalitarian regimes." In little more than a couple of years the world had gone from a hopeful new beginning toward finding "a permanent structure" for peace to ominous alignments that, as Roosevelt told Congress, "have been tried for centuries and have always failed."

World War II brought the greatest affirmation of world organization the world had ever known and rendered impossible any full retreat into the traditional isolationism of the United States. With the Marshall plan simultaneously combatting economic ruin and, in effect, communism, the world economy soon took off and entered a long period of unprecedented prosperity. Poets and artists throughout the West continued to feel nauseated by the spiritual banality of modern society, which sank to further record depths of crude materialism after the war. Yet most writers actually embraced the general pattern of mass culture by withdrawing into their own solipsistic lives, supported only by the narcissistic anodynes of nihilism. No one, not even Sartre in *No Exit*, gave better expression to the virulent cynicism than Samuel Beckett. Sensing the ontological void at the core of world civilization, Beckett celebrated it with a vengeance, reveling in the nihilism that had become de facto public and private cultus. His play *Waiting for Godot* in 1952 concurs with and advances the perception of Henri Bergson and the modernist artists that "time has stopped," engulfing everything in a flood of relativity and synchronicity, in the blather of half a century. In *Endgame* in 1957 Beckett goes to the heart of the matter: "The Bastard! He doesn't exist!" The despair, alienation, and grim fortitude with which his personae greet the loss of all ideals constitutes an attempt at affirmation of the individual in the face of the devolution of everything for which Western civilization had once stood. His personae closely resemble Nietzsche's decadent anti-hero Zarathustra—minus the "gay wisdom." Such angst had as much to do with the ontological dislocation as with the new pressure of the fear of its ultimate expression through the atom bomb.

In *Herzog* in 1964 Saul Bellow connects the rupture that became evident during the Renaissance with the manifestation in the political realm of a brutal drive toward power and revolution. Moses Herzog, an intellectual in the middle of a nervous breakdown, desperately writes such letters as the following one to various historical and fictional persons in an attempt to understand the personal crisis of his divorce and the public decline of "post-Christian America":

In the seventeenth century the passionate search for absolute truth stopped so that mankind might transform the world. Something practical was done with thought. The mental became also the real. Relief from the pursuit of absolutes made life pleasant. Only a small class of fanatical intellectuals, professionals, still chased after these absolutes. But our revolutions, including nuclear terror, return the metaphysical dimension to us. All practical activity has reached this culmination: everything may go now, civilization, history, meaning, nature. Everything! Now to recall Mr. Kierkegaard's question. . . .

Herzog, "a specialist in spiritual self-awareness," seeks to comprehend the demise of "the passionate search for absolute truth" and its replacement with the crude materialism of modern times. In a manner reminiscent of Thomas Mann, Herzog perceives that barbarism is making the rupture explicit by revealing the bankruptcy of Western civilization. Because everything stands threatened, the "metaphysical dimension" returns. Kierkegaard's question, "the great earthquake" of his life, was whether or not the prosperity of his family was a sign of God's blessing or curse.

Despite the feeling that "everything may go now," Herzog denounces what he calls the wasteland outlook and declares he is "Very tired of the modern form of historicism which sees in this civilization the defeat of the best hopes of Western religion and thought." Bellow's ability to draw on the accumulated store of tradition allows him to oppose the dominant mode of despair and to affirm the quintessential values that distinguish civilization. With the world wars and mass killings in mind, Herzog chastises his friend Shapiro for his knee-jerk nihilism:

We mustn't forget how quickly the visions of genius become the canned goods of the intellectuals. The canned sauerkraut of Spengler's "Prussian Socialism," the commonplaces of the Wasteland outlook, the cheap mental stimulants of Alienation, the cant and rant of pipsqueaks about Inauthenticity and

Forlornness. I can't accept this foolish dreariness. The subject is too great, too deep for such weakness, cowardice—too deep, too great, Shapiro. It torments me to insanity that you should be so misled. A merely aesthetic critique of modern history! After the wars and mass killings! You are too intelligent for this. You inherited rich blood. Your father peddled apples.

What began as a legitimate criticism of the bourgeois banality of the nineteenth century has deteriorated into a mechanical mouthing of negation, as in the mimicking of Beckett and Robert Lowell. These reductions have been accomplished by a steady narrowing of "the whole life of mankind" to the alienated subjective consciousness. The disease has remained constant since Baumgarten— aetheticism—which Mann pointed out was responsible for Nietzsche's "glorification of barbarism." By repudiating "A merely aesthetic critique of modern history," Herzog proclaims, as Mann writes, "to go beyond this age means to step out of an aesthetic era into a moral and social one." The aesthetes who went home to listen to Bach and Beethoven after a hard day's work incinerating human beings at Auschwitz proved the everlasting inadequacy of aestheticism, of what Martin Heidegger in "The Age of the World View" approvingly called "the process by which art comes within the horizon of aesthetics." "We are," as Herzog reflects in regard to the Holocaust, "on a more brutal standard now, a new terminal standard, indifferent to persons." This inhuman indifference is exactly the same spirit of barbarism against which Zhivago attempts to affirm individual life. Herzog confronts this anti-human spirit because he continues to think and care about belief, continues "to believe in God."

In *Mr. Sammler's Planet* in 1969 Bellow again confronts the spirit of modern times, the lawlessness of Raskolnikovs. During the twenties and thirties Artur Sammler, a Jew, knows many Bloomsbury intellectuals and detects the unraveling of the social bonds of the West. Just before World War II his wife and he return to their native Poland, where they are shot and dumped into a mass grave. He alone survives and escapes to the West to live with relatives in New York, where he again detects the continuing collapse of civilization:

> Like many people who had seen the world collapse once, Mr. Sammler entertained the possibility it might collapse twice. He did not agree with refugee friends that this doom was inevitable, but liberal beliefs did not seem capable of self-defense, and you could smell decay. You could see the suicidal impulses of civilization pushing strongly. You wondered whether this Western culture could survive universal dissemination. . . . Or whether the worst enemies of civilization might not prove to be its petted intellectuals who attacked it at its weakest moments—attacked it in the name of proletarian revolution, in the name of reason, and in the name of irrationality, in the name of visceral depth, in the name of sex, in the name of perfect instantaneous freedom.

Noting as had Dostoevsky the inability of liberal ideas to defend themselves, Sammler brings the diagnosis up to date. The undermining of civilization by Marxism is particularly brought home to Sammler during a lecture he gives on his Bloomsbury days when a New Left radical shouts him down as an "Old Man" whose "balls are dry." On Sammler's way home a thief accosts him and exposes his penis to him as a totem of barbarous power. After such experience Sammler dryly remarks, "liberation into individuality has not been a great success" but has often resulted in license and exhibitions of decadence. Sammler shares Herzog's detestation of the wasteland outlook but concedes, as had many observers of the late Hapsburg monarchy, "it is in the air now that things are falling apart, and I am affected by it." Through a concerted effort of will, Sammler persists in affirming "human qualities" and thereby the standards of decency and civilization.

Collapse and decay are in the air, and everything is affected. Most of the sixty-odd years since World War II have witnessed an erosion of real commitment to the principles underlying the United Nations, while the fear of nuclear annihilation has not yet managed to weld the nations together. Despite the largely successful intervention of the United Nations in Korea, the Suez, the Congo, Cyprus, and, at times, the Middle East, the world community often drifted further from implementation of the UN Charter. Until the Gulf War in 1990 there was, as the Secretary-General of the UN in 1973 remarked, "an ominous drift back to nationalism." The world cannot now circumvent the fundamental issues which were involved in the formation of the League and UN or prudently move only halfway toward them. As Dag Hammarskjold stressed, the United Nations rose out of bitter experience—experience which can be repeated and which has been insufficiently understood. Similarly Secretary-General Javier Perez de Cuellar warned in May of 1986 at The University of Michigan against ignoring "the basic lesson driven home so brutally by two world wars: that international co-operation is a functional response to the complex interdependence of the modern world. To treat it as an optional matter is a deadly mistake." The reasons for the founding of the League of Nations and the United Nations have not disappeared but have become all the more compelling and urgent—as the Iraqi invasion of Kuwait, the chaos of Rwanda, and the disintegration of Yugoslavia have shown. In *The End of the Nation-State*, Jean-Marie Guéhenno in 1995 wrote, "Legitimacy demands the multilateral framework of the community of nations." Both organizations grew out of the cataclysm of total war that filled insightful statesmen with fear and trembling for the stability of civilization. Both world wars demonstrated that rabid nationalism is a cause of horror and not beneficent progress.

After World War II the West had to accept the maintenance of a volatile status quo: the postwar abandonment of Poland, Bulgaria, Rumania, Hungary, Czechoslovakia, Albania, Yugoslavia, East Germany, Latvia, Estonia, and Lithuania, the Berlin blockade of 1948, the building of the Berlin Wall in 1961, the Cuban missile crisis of 1962, the re-subjugation of numerous Marxist satellites, and the oppression of Afghanistan and Nicaragua. This very incomplete catalogue of offenses by the Movement of the Left to the family of nations represents a ruthless program of military aggression and brutalization of millions of human beings. It has been too often forgotten that Churchill in his 1946 "iron curtain" speech did more than lacerate what is now the former Soviet adventurism. He also invoked the sole hope of civilization in the face of all forms of tyranny and chaos by calling for the concerted implementation of Chapter VII of the UN Charter:

> A world organisation has already been erected for the prime purpose of preventing war. UNO, the successor of the League of Nations, with the decisive addition of the United States and all that that means, is already at work. We must make sure that its work is fruitful, that it is a reality and not a sham, that it is a force for action, and not merely a frothing of words, that it is a true temple of peace in which the shields of many nations can some day be hung up, and not merely a cockpit in a Tower of Babel. Before we cast away the solid assurances of national armaments for self-preservation we must be certain that our temple is built, not upon shifting sands or quagmires, but upon the rock. Anyone can see with his eyes open that our path will be difficult and also long, but if we persevere together as we did in the two world wars—though not, alas, in the interval between them—I cannot doubt that we shall achieve our common purpose in the end. . . . The United Nations Organisation must immediately begin to be equipped with an international armed force. In such a matter we can only go step by step, but we must begin now. I propose that each of the Powers and States should be invited to delegate a certain number of air squadrons to the service of the world organisation. These squadrons would be trained and prepared in their own countries, but would move around in rotation from one country to another. They would wear the uniform of their own countries but with different badges. They would not be required to act against their own nation, but in other respects they would be directed by the world organisation. This might be started on a modest scale and would grow as confidence grew. I wished to see this done after the first world war, and I devoutly trust it may be done forthwith.

Churchill's 1946 counsel to equip the United Nations with the international Force provided for in the Charter went unheeded. It is a great irony of history that Churchill, who had recognized the necessity of an international Force at the end of World War I and after an even more devastating war, lived to witness the means of escape again relegated to the sidelines of history. Yet no responsible statesman, as Churchill rightly understood, could finally "cast away the solid assurances of national armaments" when it was highly doubtful whether all member-nations shared the fundamentally democratic principles of the UN Charter.

President Roosevelt's Secretary of State Edward R. Stettinius attested that the President thoroughly realized the United Nations would not maintain peace forever but might result in a fairly stable balance of power that would buy time in which the Soviet Union might slowly evolve away from its harsher objectives, reminiscent to my mind of Alexander Hamilton's observation in *The Federalist Papers*: "I never expect to see a perfect work from imperfect man." Sixty-odd years later in the light of the collapse of communism in Eastern Europe and in the USSR that belief must be acknowledged as prescient and wise indeed. Brian Urquhart, former Under Secretary-General of the UN, significantly observes in his 1987 autobiography that "The Soviet bloc had never shown any real willingness to assist in developing an active and effective international system, and in the Secretariat we had long ago learned not to expect much help or support from the Soviets." The Soviet regime has been swept aside and through a conscious act of historical memory, the causes and upheavals that led the community of nations to world organization in the first place can lead to a revitalization of the UN. Such memory is exactly what motivated the heads of state at the UN Security Council summit meeting in January of 1992. They requested the new Secretary-General Boutros Boutros-Ghali to submit a plan to strengthen the United Nations "within the framework and provisions of the Charter." In July of 1992, Boutros-Ghali offered the member-nations of the Security Council his outstanding recommendations for post Cold War world security in *An Agenda for Peace*, with a *Supplement* in 1995 and his

Agenda for Democratization in 1996. Despite the tragic betrayals and deceptions Boutros-Ghali documents in his 1999 book *UNvanquished*, there can be no longer any reason to doubt that the United States and the Russians, indeed all of humankind, must continue to learn to cooperate under the UN Charter and the Universal Declaration of Human Rights, to learn, as Secretary-General Kofi Annan has emphasized, "The collective interest *is* the national interest." Recognizing that fact, Senator Alan Cranston wrote in *The Sovereignty Revolution*, "The looming task is evident."

The responsibility for succeeding or failing to grant the United Nations the commitment it requires "to protect future generations from the scourge of war" depends on the will of all the statesmen and peoples of the world. Roosevelt understood this fact when in 1944 he stated, "Peace, like war, can succeed only where there is a will to enforce it, and where there is available power to enforce it." He knew unilateral disarmament was a chimera. But the will and power to enforce peace has often escaped us and can still bring for a third time, even after the momentous changes in Eastern Europe, what the Charter describes as "untold sorrow to mankind." As an historian once remarked, "If one scrutinizes the tragic blood-stained history of humanity one must needs realize that the epoch-making changes have always involved incalculable agony and turmoil, both mental and physical, to weld together formerly antagonistic peoples and nations." The global havoc of World War I resulted in the first great affirmation of world unity, and the global havoc of World War II brought the nations together as never before. Roosevelt himself emphasized that Wilson's experience at Versailles Peace Conference of 1919, which both he and Churchill had attended, taught the futility of attempting to lay global foundations after the cessation of hostilities. Roosevelt therefore saw to it that the United Nations was established before the end of the common purpose given the nations by the tempest of total war. Only as the war worsened did the new structure for world organization evolve out of the debris of the League and out of the various conferences and forums of international consultation. Many observers have testified that the

United Nations now has much of the basic machinery in the Charter needed to become a truly representative and democratic system of world governance. A sense of realism requires the recognition that the United Nations itself is not up to the task, often has failed for lack of wisdom, political will, and the ability to act during a crisis, while the United States and other nations have been more interested in using it as a tool of their foreign policy, keeping it undeveloped and unsupported in numerous ways, justifiably at times because of the tendency to impractical radical views and political theories.

While the ontological fissure continues to manifest itself in the political and spiritual realms, the unequivocal development of civilization from the first elected assemblies of ancient Greece and Rome; from the British Magna Carta, Habeas Corpus, the Petition of Right of 1628, and the Bill of Rights of 1689; from the American Mayflower Compact, the Massachusetts "Body of Liberties," the New England Confederation, the Declaration of Independence, the Constitution, the Bill of Rights, and Lincoln's Gettysburg Address has been toward triumphant affirmation of individual human dignity and of universal authority consecrated to the oneness of humankind. In the secular realm nowhere have such values been affirmed more fully than in the Charter of the United Nations and in the Universal Declaration of Human Rights. Far from the risible conception of history advanced by Marx, this dynamic process of evolution from rockhard experience toward universal peace and human dignity has its roots in the most noble and trustworthy traditions of Western civilization—despite what is now clearly the spiritual failure of some aspects of capitalism and democratic liberalism. The further implementation of the UN Charter will signal the consummation of this epic process, heralded by seers and poets of all ages and nations, and will constitute another step toward the healing of the ontological rupture which shall gradually follow upon the resolution in the political realm of the Greek-like tragedy of the twentieth century, so reminiscent of that recounted by Thucydides.

In his speech on Puskin Dostoevsky argues "to become a true Russian . . . means only to become the brother of all men, to become, if you will, a universal man." Aleksandr Solzhenitsyn has also testified to what constitutes the core of a thousand years of Russian experience. In the long battle of history, Pasternak implies, though he remained sympathetic to an esoteric interpretation of the 1917 revolution, that universal man will overcome the vacuous pieties of Marxism. Unlike the foremost Russian writers whose dire experience has forced upon them the essential conflicts of human nature, most Western writers malinger in the shadows of the wasteland outlook, regurgitating Baudelaire, Eliot, and Beckett. Much can be learned from Thomas Mann who was perhaps seduced by the German Empire but later fled Hitler's barbarous consummation of the disease. In his 1947 lecture at the Library of Congress, "Nietzsche in the Light of Recent History," Mann correctly appreciates the implications of modern history for poets and artists, as well as the limits of "legal institutions":

What we really need is a new order, new relationships, the recasting of society to meet the global demands of the hour, certainly little can be done by conference decisions, technical measures, legal institutions. World government remains a rationalistic utopia. The main thing is a transformation of the spiritual climate, a new feeling for the difficulty and the nobility of being human, an all-pervasive fundamental disposition shared by everyone, and acknowledged by everyone within himself as the supreme judge. To the genesis and establishment of that disposition poets and artists, imperceptibly working through the depth and breadth of society, can make some contribution. But it is not something that can be taught and created; it must be experienced and suffered.

Such a "transformation of the spiritual climate" is all the more urgently needed by the global community given the "demands of the hour." Far from debasing artists into propagandists, Mann is calling for a fundamental reaffirmation of humane values. With all the tragic wisdom of his own intense mental agony engendered by the upheavals of the German Empire and the Third Reich, upheavals also crucial to Stefan Zweig, Mann acknowledges the establishment of the new disposition requires the experience of suffering to become a reality in the city of man. Poets and writers must dispose of the canned sauerkraut that has been sustaining us for so long, as no better than the imposed literary manacles of socialist realism. Rather, what Heinrich Böll called "a new realism" must renounce the formalistic sophistry of both East and West and seek to discover in the fundamental experience of humankind, not in abstraction, what it means to be alive at this most glorious juncture in human history.

Fundamental changes in the literary and political realms have always been contingent on the ontological universe. The universality of perspective itself now marks a step toward the resolution of the ontological conflict. The upheavals of our century are increasingly becoming explicit through international crisis and are thereby allowing and necessitating new modes of diplomatic and artistic endeavor. As vast changes in the outlook of the international community continue to manifest themselves, the human race remains on the path toward consummation of its highest hopes and visions. Though the hour might again become dark and threatening, with the world teetering on the edge of the Middle-East abyss, though the odor of decay lingers in the air, though many setbacks have been and will surely be experienced, the means of escape stands almost fully formed at the door and merely awaits complete and unqualified implementation to accomplish what all high-minded human beings throughout history have longed and hoped for. While the possibility of crisis from unexpected quarters continues to loom large, threatening the twenty-first century, while I cannot discern the exact steps, the direction of the international community is irrefutable, and there are clarifying tendencies that are struggling to grasp the opportunity of the hour and to establish what Tennyson called "the Federation of the world" on the quintessential values and traditions of civilization. Then shall the world become, as E. B. White once wrote, "A federation of free states, with its national units undisturbed and its peoples elevated to a new and greater sovereignty." Then shall the nations learn, as Jean Monnet wrote, "to live together under common rules and institutions freely arrived at." Then shall dawn that long awaited reconciliation of the tensions that first advanced themselves in the Renaissance and that have plagued civilization ever since. Then shall arise that glorious civilization animating the hopes of all peoples from the earliest days of recorded history.

Epopee

A good epic would grace our history.
Robert Frost

The disappearance of epic poetry and the rise of modern times go hand in hand. To look back over the last three hundred years is to observe the steady decline of the epic spirit and the ever-increasing substitution of subjective, personal modes of literary composition. The modern poems that strive for an epic effect—Wordsworth's *Prelude*, Whitman's *Song of Myself*, and Pound's *Cantos*—demonstrate the growing confusion both of Western civilization and of the function of epic poetry. Homer, Virgil, Dante, Spenser, Milton, and, to a lesser degree, Langland, all hold several fundamentally universal beliefs regarding the role of epopee. Far from wallowing in subjectivism, they affirm the locus of epopee is the public, historical domain, where the individual and society meet in common destiny, and they perceive, within the chaos, the hierarchical form that restores order and rationality. They recognize the antinomies of human experience and reconcile them, as much as possible, within their hierarchies. All the foremost epic poets of English and Western civilization unabashedly speak for the people, for the quintessential values and beliefs of the community. Without exception the metaphysical occupies a formidable position in their work by giving it profundity and by providing basic standards with which to portray the actions of their characters. All this has been lost in the would-be epics of the modern era.

In place of the expression of the values of the prevailing culture or the exposure of the discrepancy between ideals and reality, modern epopee substitutes an eccentric mixture of heteroclite material. W. H. Auden, in his essay "Yeats as an Example," identifies the malaise:

> Yeats, like us, was faced with the modern problem, i.e., of living in a society in which men are no longer supported by tradition without being aware of it, and in which, therefore, every individual who wishes to bring order and coherence into the

stream of sensations, emotions, and ideas entering his consciousness, from without and within, is forced to do deliberately for himself what in previous ages had been done for him by family, custom, church, and state, namely the choice of the principles and presuppositions in terms of which he can make sense of his experience.

I believe this excerpt is as applicable to East and South Asia as it is to Western civilization. I have seen at first hand that anomie is a worldwide phenomenon, as is the destruction and decline of all traditions and religions. Add the vast upheavals of communism, which swept away forever the pristine traditions of so many millions, and the magnitude of "the modern problem" begins to be discernible. Although Yeats was a lyric poet, he fully manifests the modern poet's creation of an ersatz to fill the void left by the loss of tradition. Wordsworth, Whitman, and Pound essentially grapple with the same problem and attempt to solve it by the study of their own minds. It is doubtful that "the choice" was ever as mechanical as Auden implies or that it was ever less conscious, less of a struggle, for epic poets. At the beginning of the twenty-first century, a reassessment of epopee must be made since it is the only literary form that is capacious enough to embrace thoroughly the disparate, violent, tragic experience that marks modern times. Epopee is the only form with which I can ever imagine getting close to supporting the weight of the vision of modern life that impinges on my consciousness.

Foremost among epic poets stands Dante who alone takes the fullest account of the entire range of human experience, from the anarchic and violent to the sublime and transcendent. What is important about Dante is not his language, his imagery, numerology, structure, or allegorical medium, though all these are distinguished by the hand of his genius. Rather what is important about the *Commedia* is what Dante is saying—that is, the content of his vision. Doubtlessly, were it stripped of the aesthetic, it would no longer be a poem, and, conversely, were the aesthetic somehow preserved, drained of its high import, neither would the *Commedia* any longer merit the distinction of epic poetry. All too often our century debases poetry into merely rhythmical language, or bland as the taste has become. But for Dante poetry is a form of epistemology, a distinct method of acquiring knowledge. Its method is different from the method of science, and only an age in confusion would want it otherwise. While modern poets divide to define poetry, Dante unites the aesthetic with both knowledge and moral understanding—that is, he locates the role of the epic poet in the creation of a whole, not a fragment. As he wrote in his letter to Can Grande, "*The purpose is to rescue those living in this life from a state of woe and to lead them into a state of blessedness.*" He would not settle for less than the entire range of human experience.

Part of that range is the historical experience of humankind. He refused to turn away from the long conflict between the two major powers of his day, the Holy Roman Empire and the Papacy. In the clash between the Ghibellines and the Guelfs, Dante perceived universal federalist principles battling for ascendancy. Much of his success may be owed to the triumph of the Guelfs in 1266, the year after Dante's birth, for out of that victory rose the first nascent democracy of the Christian era. His allegiance to Henry VII and his defense of the Holy Roman Empire in *De Monarchia* must be attributed to his desire for peace and order since Boniface VIII had unequivocally proven to Dante and his age that the church could not secure social stability. But, like Milton, Dante was lessoned by historical events that devastated his hope for imminent political order, a lesson that fills me with fear and misgivings. He and Milton both chose the long visionary way that apperceives man's greatest good in the conquering evolution of the soul. It is on this note that Dante opens the *Commedia*:

> Midway the journey of this life I was 'ware
> That I had strayed into a dark forest,
> And the right path appeared not anywhere.
> Ah, tongue cannot describe how it oppressed,
> This wood, so harsh, dismal and wild, that fear
> At thought of it strikes now into my breast.

So bitter it is, death is scarce bitterer.
But, for the good it was my hap to find,
I speak of the other things that I saw there.
I cannot well remember in my mind
How I came thither, so was I immersed
In sleep, when the true way I left behind.

(Binyon)

In the allegory of life as a journey, in the beautiful simplicity of the earthly pilgrimage of the soul, known to the common people of the thirteenth century through the *Commedia dell' Anima*, Dante found, as had the Persian poet Attar in *The Parliament of the Birds*, the vision that enabled him to make sense of his own experience and that of his age. He announces in these opening lines his intention of probing the antinomies, "the good it was my hap to find" as well as what is "harsh, dismal and wild," "the other things that I saw there." On this theme of pilgrimage he strikes every note of human abasement and exaltation, both in the "mind" of the individual and in the domain of society. Unlike the poets of modernism and postmodernism, he unabashedly affirms "the true way" to which all else is but "a dark forest."

Literature has been in that "dark forest" for so long that finding again "the right path" appears to many observers quixotic since every form of nihilism has been the gruel of our upbringing. Although, as Dante says of himself to Brunetto Latini in Hell, we may be "lost in a vale of gloom," we can turn "back therefrom" and find the star of our guide. This is not to gainsay the contradictory elements of human experience for Dante himself knew well the dark side of our being and its claims. He acknowledges such in his inscription above the gates of Hell:

THROUGH ME THE WAY IS TO THE CITY OF WOE:
THROUGH ME THE WAY INTO THE ETERNAL PAIN;
THROUGH ME THE WAY AMONG THE LOST BELOW.
RIGHTEOUSNESS DID MY MAKER ON HIGH CONSTRAIN,
ME DID DIVINE AUTHORITY UPREAR;

ME SUPREME WISDOM AND PRIMAL LOVE SUSTAIN.
BEFORE I WAS, NO THINGS CREATED WERE
SAVE THE ETERNAL, AND I ETERNAL ABIDE.
RELINQUISH ALL HOPE, YE WHO ENTER HERE.

This city of woe is inhabited by those "who have lost the good of the intellect." It is, in that sense, the abode of "ETERNAL PAIN," where "THE WAY" has become perverted and merely leads "AMONG THE LOST BELOW." Obviously Dante did not intend a specific geographical location but rather, as an image of evil, Hell "ETERNAL ABIDE[s]." So Dante comments to Mark Lombard, in the Purgatorio, "The world is utterly despoiled, in truth, / Of all virtue" and asks him to explain the origin of evil. Lombard proffers him the implied counsel of the gates of Hell: "if the world now strayeth blind, / In you the cause is; track and seek it there."

Dante's journey is the one way of all men from the abode of hopelessness to that of the hopeful acceptance of suffering in the Purgatorio. There Arnaut Daniel tells Dante,

> "I think on my past folly and see the stain,
> And view with joy the day I hope to know.
> I pray you by that Goodness which doth deign
> To guide you to the summit of this stair
> Bethink you in due season of my pain."
> Then he shrank back in the refining fire.

Dante's correlation of the moral, the aesthetic, and the epistemological elevates this passage above the usual linguistic play that characterizes the poetry of the modern period. Unlike Ezra Pound who told Yeats that in the *Cantos* there would "be no plot, no chronicle of events, no logic of discourse," which is reminiscent of Byron's "I have no plan—I had no plan," Dante never relinquishes his hierarchical vision of man's struggle for the summit of the stair. So he answers Judge Nino, "by this journey the other life I gain." Etienne Gilson's observation that "The difference between the Renaissance and the Middle Ages was not a difference by addition but by subtraction" contains an element of truth. No rational person would repudiate the vast technological and scientific benefits of the modern era. Yet, for all the advantages, modernity has also resulted in the loss of belief in "the other life" and has trivialized the meaning of this one. Dante provides the necessary perspective from which to view such anomie and confusion because he lived in a still largely unified time, though signs of stress were everywhere. Soon Petrarch was wisely to begin the movement away from the medieval world. Yet Dante's vision is uncommonly sane and healthy because he was unafflicted by "the modern problem."

In the longing that pervades the Purgatorio the eternal remedy resides. So Dante narrates, when, in the Paradiso, he and Beatrice ascend to the Heaven of the Moon: "The inborn thirst, which never is allayed, / For the God-moulded realm, bore us on high." Beatrice to Dante says, "Turn to God in thanks." Though Shakespeare and Chaucer know as wide a range of human nature as Dante, they know nothing of the burning thirst. Confined merely to the earthly realm of wit and deceit, they fail to strike the higher notes and thereby present, in a lopsided fashion, what it means to be a human being. Dante knows the hell and the glory. In the magnificent last canto of the Paradiso, after his long hard journey through the mansions of Hell, purgatory, and paradise, Dante says,

> And I, who to the goal was drawing nigh
> Of all my longings, now, as it behoved,
> Felt the ardour of them in contentment die.

Of such poetry Longinus writes, "our soul is uplifted by the true sublime." But it has been the fad of modernism not to uplift the human spirit but to subject it to every form of degradation. The aspiring epic poet has so much to learn from Dante precisely because he is free of the fads of nihilism and achieves a positive, not merely a negative, understanding of his experience and of his age.

In *Piers Plowman* William Langland also writes of the earthly pilgrimage of the soul but is temperamentally and stylistically more akin to John Bunyan. Unlike Dante who created a superbly organized structure, Langland never achieved one but spent more than twenty years putting his poem through three major drafts. After the persona Will has a vision in the Prologue of a plain full of people, which conveys the chaos of existence, he meets Holy Church to whom he says, "tell me one thing: How May I Save My Soul?" She responds that "Truth is the best" and proclaims "Truth" dwells in the "Holy Trinity." The first part of the poem then traces the dreamer's search for salvation through various episodes with the allegorical figures Lady Meed, Fraud, Reason, Conscience, and others. This search is eventually abandoned and replaced with his search for the allegorical Do-Well, Do-Better, and Do-Best. Langland is merely varying his treatment of Will's search, which, after sundry episodes, trails off and blends into an account of Christ's harrowing of Hell and his triumph over worldly powers. Although Langland's poem is that of a great poet, it suffers from his undisciplined use of the allegorical method, unleavened as his poem is by classical example.

Langland is at his best in his satire of the corrupted clergy, almost as searing as Rabelais. Unlike Dante who had the audacity to put such popes as Nicholas III and Boniface VIII in Hell, where they belong, Langland's satire avoids specific historical persons but may be all the stronger for its vehement denunciation of entire groups of charlatans. In the Prologue Will views on the plain "Troops of hermits" who are "on their way to Walsingham, with their wenches following after." Not far off are all four orders of friars "preaching to the people for what they could get" and freely interpreting the scriptures "to suit themselves and their patrons." Nearby is a pardoner who cozens "the ignorant folk" "with letters of indulgence thrust in their faces" and rakes "in their rings and jewellery with his roll of parchment." Parish priests stream past as they leave their indigent parishes and head for London where "without devotion" they can "traffic in Masses and chime their voices to the sweet jingle of silver." In a passage on charity Langland unleashes all his ire on the corrupted clergy and, as he sums up the darkly tragic conception of life that undergirds his satire, writes of "a great flaw in those who guard the Church": "the metal of their souls is foully debased by sin.

And this false alloy is found in clergy and laymen alike, for it seems that no man loves either God or his neighbours."

His allegory of the seven deadly sins is especially successful at conveying the squalor and humor of bawdy plebian life. In a passage on Gluttony Langland shows him on his way to confession when an alewife invites him in to try her brew. Without a moment's hesitation he forgets about confession and enters the pub. There he finds just about everyone in town from "Clarice, the whore of Cock Lane with the parish clerk" to "Tim the tinker with two of his apprentices." They all "give Glutton a good welcome and start him off with a pint of the best." After some light gambling, Glutton ends up drinking a gallon of ale and "so they sat shouting and singing until time for vespers." It is not long before he has

> pissed a couple of quarts, and blown such a blast on the round
> horn of his rump, that all who heard it had to hold their noses,
> and wished to God he would plug it with a bunch of gorse!

Barely able to stand or walk he stumbles on the threshold and falls flat on the floor. He repays Clement the cobbler, who tries to help him to his feet, by vomiting on him: It "smelt so foul that the hungriest hound in Hertfordshire would never have lapped it up." After his wife and daughter manage to carry him home to bed and he awakens two days later on Sunday night, his first incorrigible words are, "Who's had the tankard?" His wife scolds him and he repents: "I, Glutton, confess that I am guilty." The following confession of his dissipations is too glib to be sincere and one suspects it will not be long before he will be back in the pub. In such episodes as this one there is much in common between Langland and Chaucer, who both share the medieval delight in ribaldry. The latter, however, fails to achieve Langland's seriously sustained affirmation of the earthly pilgrimage.

And while Chaucer gives us some poignantly descriptive passages of the plight of the poor or, more often, of their buffoonery, Langland's poem absolutely melts with ruth:

> The poorest folk are our neighbours, if we look about us. . . .
> For whatever they save by spinning they spend on rent, or on
> milk and oatmeal to make gruel and fill the bellies of their
> children who clamour for food. And they themselves are often
> famished with hunger, and wretched with the miseries of
> winter—cold, sleepless nights, when they get up to rock the
> cradle cramped in a corner, and rise before dawn to card and
> comb the wool, to wash and scrub and mend, and wind yarn and
> peel rushes for their rushlights—The miseries of these women
> who dwell in hovels is too pitiful to read, or describe in verse.
> Yet there are many more who suffer like them.

The compassion that pervades this account of the miseries of the
medieval poor has no equal in all English poetry. When the poor are
admitted by other poets, or rather if, it is often in a highly stylized
manner or for the reprehensible motive of providing fodder for a
cruel joke. Langland's realism has no such low purpose but seeks to
set forth their plight in order to appeal to the rich, as Baha'u'llah
wrote, to hear "the midnight sighing of the poor." Thus he scorns the
"great theologians" who mouth "God's name" but shoo the hungry
away from their doors like dogs. Of the wealthy he writes, "For the
greater the wealth and riches they amass, and the more houses they
have to let, the less are they willing to give away!" Langland is in
earnest. For him poetry treats all of man's experience and does not
divide it into specious, academic categories. Yet for the last hundred
years or more, the scope of poetry has steadily been decreasing
despite the omnipresent claim that the subject matter of poetry has
been broadened. By taking in everything divorced from moral and
humane knowledge, poetry has in fact failed to accomplish much
beyond a veneer of aestheticism. Langland knows one of the highest
indications of human development is concern for the welfare of the
weakest and most vulnerable members of society. His achievement
is exemplary for he writes of them not through abstractions but
through such details as their spending their pittance "on milk and
oatmeal to make gruel and fill the bellies of their children who

clamour for food"—an observation that bespeaks, to allude to Robert Hayden, his own loving, close concern.

As evidenced in Langland's treatment of the poor, wound together with the theme of pilgrimage is the theme of love. In the closing book "The Coming of the Anti-Christ," which depicts the continuous battle between the church and the world, Will cries out to Nature to rescue him from his misery and from the threat of approaching Death. Nature advises him to "go into Unity" and "learn some occupation." To Will's query about what occupation, Nature replies, "Learn to love . . . and give up everything else." This counsel of love suffuses the entire poem and undergirds the pilgrimage itself. At one point Will derides learning only to be corrected by Imagination, who asserts "its root is the love of Christ." That the knowledge of God was the source of all wisdom and learning was a pervasive idea in the late middle ages, as throughout much of Christianity. Our age has largely lost this understanding and bungles along without any unifying conception of learning and life. Dante also finds unity in love, as Bernard says to him in the penultimate canto of the Paradiso: "And turn we to the Primal Love our eyes, / So that, still gazing toward Him, thou may'st pierce / Into His splendour, far as in thee lies." The late middle ages was still a time when men widely believed love permeated the universe and commemorated its beauty and truth in such public undertakings as Chartres Cathedral. As much as Dante, perhaps even more than he, Langland speaks for the reality of love primarily by intimating its frequent absence in society.

For Homer reality is the clash of men and arms in the battle for honor and glory, where he counsels unity of arms and action, not spirituality. Homer's realism focuses on the world of history, the world of the objective contention for power between warring nations. In the destruction of Troy, which was probably a liege of the Hittites, Homer contemplates, given the Greeks were loosely organized, the clash of two of the superpowers of his day. The modern excavation of the mound of Hissarlik has proven beyond any doubt the historical veracity of Homer's poem, which supremely attests to the link between the social milieu and the work of the epic poet. Achilles and Agamemnon's conflict becomes the cause of the needless slaughter of many Achaeans and is meant to instruct peevish, arrogant leaders to rein in their passions for the good of all. The poem would make little sense without this moral, which, to a civilized mentality, expresses the desperate condition of life in any age, identifies the force Simone Weil perceives "today as yesterday, at the very center of human history." Although Homer asserts the superiority of reason to passion, his reason is not that of Dante or Milton. It is rather the self-discipline of prudent rulers and strongmen in pursuit of their will to power.

While love undergirds *Piers Plowman*, the threat of passion undergirds *The Iliad*, where terror and powerful impulses break out everywhere into the slaughter of war, as in *Beowulf*. To such impulses Agamemnon ascribes his seizing the mistress Briseis, whom Achilles had won as a prize of war. This act infuriates Achilles and causes the conflict around which the entire poem is structured. After Achilles has announced his return to battle, Agamemnon tries to justify himself in Book XIX to the assembled Achaeans:

>   yet I am not responsible
> but Zeus is, and Destiny, and Erinys the mist-walking
> who in assembly caught my heart in the savage delusion
> on that day I myself stripped from him the prize of Achilleus.
> Yet what could I do? It is the god who accomplishes all
>   things.
> Delusion is the elder daughter of Zeus, the accursed
> who deludes all; her feet are delicate and they step not
> on the firm earth, but she walks the air above men's heads
> and leads them astray. She has entangled others before me.
> Yes, for once Zeus even was deluded.   (Lattimore)

"*Ate*," translated as "delusion," might be better rendered as "divine destruction," which follows reckless impulse and ambition. Agamemnon claims his actions were not of his choosing but thrust upon him by the gods to bring about the destruction of the

Achaeans. He makes no distinction between the various irrational impulses that drive him into blind destruction, pleads his helplessness, and reminds the assembly that even Zeus was once blinded or deluded by passion. This abdication of individual responsibility could never occur in a poem of the Christian era, which stresses the inescapable volition of each human being.

For all the sadness and determinism of Homer's world, he brilliantly suggests throughout the poem the world of peace that constitutes the background to all the deeds of terror. In such incidents as Hector's anticipation of Andromache's captivity, in the peaceful city on the shield of Achilles, and in Thetis's premonition that Achilles would have to choose between winning honor in war and living a peaceful, domestic life, Homer interjects a world diametrically opposed to the one of realistic battle and bloodshed. Near the end of the poem when Priam begs Achilles for the body of his slain son Hector, Homer ties together all such strands of repose:

"Honour then the gods, Achilleus, and take pity upon me remembering your father, yet I am still more pitiful; I have gone through what no other mortal on earth has gone through; I put my lips to the hands of the man who has killed my children."

So he spoke, and stirred in the other a passion of grieving for his own father. He took the old man's hand and pushed him gently away, and the two remembered, as Priam sat huddled at the feet of Achilleus and wept close for manslaughtering Hektor and Achilleus wept now for his own father, now again for Patroklos. The sound of their mourning moved in the house.

They both weep for the lost domestic peace that might have belonged to their loved ones and to themselves. But to win honor and glory requires the bitterness of war, which rules out such peace. The primitive scale of the Homeric values reveals itself precisely at such junctures in the poem. Achilles compassionately tries to offer Priam and himself solace by claiming "Such is the way the gods spin life for unfortunate mortals, / that we live in unhappiness but the gods themselves have no sorrows." Although this type of thing appealed to Thomas Hardy and at times to Shakespeare, it is a primitive conception of deity that justifies suffering as providing the gods with a spectacle or as emanating from their indifference. More poignant are the marvelous words of Zeus: "Of all creatures that breathe and creep on Mother Earth / There is none so miserable as man." Instead of man at the apex of creation, where the Judeo-Christian tradition usually places him, Homer has Zeus wisely relegate man to the level of a creeping beast, unredeemed by a hopeful dualism, as in *Gulliver's Travels*.

Aristotle aptly calls the structure of *The Iliad* "simple and fatal." He favorably uses "simple" to mean the brilliant sequential development of the plot, which Homer strengthens by weaving together two themes—the war at Troy and the conflict between Achilles and Agamemnon. By working with these themes Homer creates much more suspense and tension than he would have otherwise. In the first book he presents the background of the war and Achilles' angry withdrawal from it. The gods get involved in the siege of Troy, take sides throughout the poem, and give greater significance to the action by the interest they take in it. From Book I to Book IX the battle rages with various warriors distinguishing themselves in the slaughter, but, without Achilles, the Achaeans steadily lose ground and are driven back to their ships. Despite Agamemnon's attempt at making amends in Book IX, Achilles stays out of the fighting until his friend Patroclus is slain by Hector. He then renounces his recalcitrance in Book XIX and he and his men return to battle. Before long Achilles has slain Hector and Priam begs him for his son's corpse. Such is the outline of what Aristotle called Homer's "unified action." Unlike Homer's "simple" and "unified action," Ezra Pound spurned ancient example and once discussed his own method in an interview: "I picked out this and that thing that interested me, and then jumbled them into a bag." The result is Pound's study of his own desultory mind, strung out over fifty years.

The structure of *The Odyssey* is more complex than *The Iliad* but still retains a basic simplicity of design. The poem begins in the midst of things with Athene urging Telemachus to search for his father Odysseus. After requesting the suitors of his mother to return to their homes, Telemachus sets off for Sparta, where he learns Odysseus is on Calypso's island. In Book V the poem turns to Odysseus and his departure from Calypso. After various adventures he relates his past wanderings to the Phaeacians, who give him refuge, and then returns secretly home to Ithaca. The plot swings back to Telemachus, who is still in Sparta but hastens home and soon meets Odysseus. The last several books treat Odysseus' slaying of the suitors and his reunion with his wife Penelope. Virgil's and Milton's imitation of this structure attests to its ability to create suspense and tension. An epic poem demands an unusually effective design if it is to be successful and not devolve into a long narrative poem, such as the best narratives of Edwin Arlington Robinson and Robert Frost. Langland's poem barely succeeds because of his willingness to wander away from his theme into every byway of his imagination. This leads him into a vast morass of repetition and false starts that his various drafts never eradicate or harmonize. Nevertheless, Langland's fairly consistent reliance on the theme of the earthly pilgrimage manages to hold his deeply flawed masterpiece together. Pound learnt the lesson too late, as he admitted in a late interview: "My poems don't make any sense."

In both *The Iliad* and *The Odyssey* Homer demonstrates that "sense," hierarchically structured, holds together an epic poem. It is precisely the poet's ability to select his material and arrange "the structure of events," the plot, that Aristotle calls "the greatest thing of all." *The Odyssey* has proven to be the most influential of Homer's poems primarily because of its inimitable structuring of events. As in *Gilgamesh*, Odysseus' long journey home from the Trojan war is the universal journey of man through the vicissitudes of life. Odysseus demonstrates a hero can withstand any adversity that the combined forces of the gods and man can hurl at him and, in this way, prefigures the medieval religious wayfarer. In the pre-Christian Homeric world one must endure the will of the gods, who glorify and degrade mortal man. So Nausicaa emboldens and admonishes Odysseus when she says, "It is Zeus himself, the Olympian, who gives people good fortune, / to each single man, to the good and the bad, just as he wishes / and since he must have given you yours, you must endure it." Despite Homer's primitive conception of deity, "long-suffering great Odysseus" bears the burden of his fate and has none of the whimpering, subjective maladies of the work of Shelley, Coleridge, or Poe. Just how different modern poetry is from classical epic Poe reveals when he writes, "the day of these artistic anomalies is over"—as though his work were anything but an anomaly. How reminiscent of Callimachus' "A big book is a big pain." In place of the epic Poe erects a vague blend of "Beauty" and "Truth," the latter deprived of all intellectually respectable content. Following the general tendency of modern times, Baudelaire and the other sickly subjective symbolists embrace Poe's doctrine of art for art's sake, cast derision on epopee, and whine endlessly about their fate. Homer knows how a man should suffer.

The Aeneid recounts not merely the journey of an individual hero but also the destiny of a people. Virgil had at his back nearly one hundred years of unprecedented civil war and anarchy that he could not ignore. Somehow he had to take account of the steady decline of the republic and make sense of it. Despite all the intrigues of such dictators as Sulla, Pompey, Ceasar, and Antony, Virgil embraced the national vision of the destiny of eternal Rome and could not relinquish it to write such ahistorical narratives as those of the Alexandrian poets. He fully shared the war-weary sentiment of the late republic and evinces it throughout *The Aeneid*. John Dryden accurately elucidates what must have been Virgil's attitude toward the universal rule of Augustus:

I say that Virgil, having maturely weigh'd the condition of the times in which he liv'd . . . that this conqueror . . . was the very best of it; that the arts of peace flourish'd under him; that . . . he shar'd a great part of his authority with the senate . . . and . . . exercis'd more for the common good than for any delight he took in greatness . . . he concluded it to be the interest of his country to be so govern'd; to infuse an awful respect into the people towards such a prince....

The restoration of peace and the unparalleled prosperity of the empire by A.D. 14 attest Virgil correctly "weigh'd the condition of the times." As the patron of the arts Augustus restored the public domain to the forefront of artistic endeavor. This was as true in sculpture and architecture as in literature, where the epic again interpreted life and spoke for those who had no voice. Unlike Apollonius Rhodius' *Argonautica*, which ignores the war-torn world of his day, Virgil's *Aeneid*, from its inception, takes into account the civil strife that necessitated the unifying rule of Augustus. Virgil knew the imperium of Augustus to be in the best interest of his country, which he deeply loved, as well as in the best interest of the entire known world of the time. For the most part Virgil consciously chose, as the epic poet often must, "the principles and presuppositions" in terms of which he made sense of his own experience and that of Rome. That Augustus and Maecenas were attempting to revivify the public dedication to the ancestral virtues, traditions, and religion, as well as to the empire, did not compel Virgil into blind submission. He embraced such standards because he believed in them and not because some absurd deterministic principle was operating on him and his society.

It is unfair to call *The Aeneid* propaganda. Virgil does more than extol the imperium of Augustus, and, besides, such passages are rare and often embued with *lacremae rerum* or his sweet melancholy. He is concerned not with Augustus but with the destiny of a people. At the end of Book Six, Anchises, in the underworld, foretells the tumultuous history and bloody strife of the late republic and enunciates for Aeneas the timeless qualities of Rome:

> Let others better mold the running mass
> Of metals, and inform the breathing brass,
> And soften into flesh a marble face;
> Plead better at the bar; describe the skies,
> And when the stars descend, and when they rise.
> But, Rome, 't is thine alone, with awful sway,
> To rule mankind, and make the world obey,
> Disposing peace and war thy own majestic way;

> To tame the proud, the fetter'd slave to free:
> These are imperial arts, and worthy thee.
>
> (Dryden)

Other nations and peoples will surpass Rome in their casting of bronze and in their marble statues, in their rhetorical facility and astronomy, while Rome will excel in state-craft and "rule mankind." Contrary to their common reputation of blood-thirsty barbarians and unlike Homer's heroes, the Romans often negotiated for peace and preferred diplomacy to violent conquest. They upheld the rule of law and highly valued the ordered, domestic life. Such "imperial arts" were the qualities that Virgil esteemed and that led to Pax Romana, which lasted more than two hundred years. Far from supporting propaganda, Virgil's prescience almost overwhelmed him with the only possible remedy for his country. Hence he served his people and the world by inspiring "an awful respect" for the supreme institution, limited though it was by the times, that alone could restore and preserve the peace and social harmony he so loved.

The Aeneid is the story of the long historical process leading to Pax Romana. Virgil writes neither history nor poetry, in the latter's postmodern sense of solipsistic fantasy, as in James Merrill's *The Changing Light at Sandover*, which brings to mind such works as Pope's mock-epic *The Dunciad*, Cowper's "I sing the sofa," and Byron's "I want a hero." Virgil writes something vastly more serious and compelling—the epic meaning of history. So Aristotle writes, "Poetry is a more philosophical and serious business than history; for poetry speaks more of universals." But solipsism neglects the universal and wallows in the particular individual's mind. Robert Lowell's essay "Epics" suggests his recognition of the waning of the postmodern Alexandrian wallowing or at least an intimation of an eventual return to narrative and plot. He almost seems to foreshadow this development in early reviews of William Carlos Williams' *Paterson* and Robert Penn Warren's *Brother to Dragons*. The latter review reveals that Lowell, at the outset of his career, understood he was putting aside any ambition to truly major work. In "Epics," written shortly before he died in 1977, he acknowledges "great epics . . . must mean something . . . by their action," their "murky metaphysical historic significance," and their "sober intuition into the character of a nation." Lowell never achieved such a "sober intuition" but remained bound, like a would-be Prometheus, bringing the dark light of modern times, to the aesthetic of solipsism.

Although most of *The Aeneid* has no basis in fact, Virgil sufficiently connects with historical events to broaden the scope of the poem to the entire destiny of Rome. After the fall of Troy to the Achaeans, Aeneas leads the survivors toward Italy but is forced by a storm to take refuge at Carthage. There he meets Dido and relates to her the history of Troy and his own Odyssean wanderings. She falls in love with him and delays him until he resumes his mission and arrives in Sicily. There he holds funeral games for his father Anchises, who had died in the midst of their wanderings. During the games the women set fire to the ships in protest and it appears Aeneas may never fulfill his mission, but, miraculously, Jupiter saves most of them. Even after such an unambiguous intervention of divine assistance, Aeneas still despairs of accomplishing his task and Virgil comments,

> But doubtful thoughts the hero's heart divide;
> If he should still in Sicily reside,
> Forgetful of his fates, or tempt the main,
> In hope the promis'd Italy to gain.

Such thoughts have wracked Aeneas' mind since he left Troy and at this point he still doubts his destiny. His long affair with Dido was itself the result of his shirking his duty and required Mercury to convince him to resume his god-given mission. An old man, Nautes, who perceives the despair of Aeneas, admonishes him,

> O goddess-born, resign'd in ev'ry state,
> With patience bear, with prudence push your fate.
> By suff'ring well, our Fortune we subdue;
> Fly when she frowns, and, when she calls, pursue.

Anchises appears that night in a dream from the underworld and urges Aeneas to accept this admonition. From this time on Aeneas puts aside such misgivings and bears the fate that he never wanted to pursue. The founding of Rome becomes based on an act of self-abnegation and acceptance of the heavy burden of the will of the gods. His submission to his fate in Book Five acts as a turning point in the whole poem. From then on the only question is the best means for prosecuting his mission. Before long he lands in Italy, tries to negotiate prior to launching into battle, and, after sundry episodes, defeats his redoubtable opponent, Turnus. His victory assures the founding of the city and marks the foundation of the divinely ordained process leading to Pax Romana.

Virgil is everywhere a civilized poet. He reveres the rational mind and its bounteous fruits. Aeolus he would keep in check forever, as would Jupiter, were such forces not part and parcel of human nature. Aeneas is as different from Homer's warlike heroes as Virgil could make him. His *pietas*, his devotion to the gods, country, family, and friends, sets him off from the honor-hungry barbarians who long for domestic peace but slaughter others in order that they might be remembered in song. The Stoic virtues of social duty, acquisition of wisdom through tests and suffering, and subordination of passion to reason constitute an entirely different type of hero from the Homeric one. Added to these civilized virtues is the fact that Aeneas is merely the instrument for the transfer of civilization from the fallen eastern city of Troy, from the wreck of Greek culture, to the new civilization of eternal Rome. The social milieu, its meaning and purpose, its preservation and extension, absorb the attention of Virgil. So he selects his details and arranges his plot to illuminate the historical process he perceives culminating in his day and moving beyond.

Virgil derives his power from more than merely his attention to the public domain. Near the end of Book Six Aeneas asks his father in the underworld the meaning of some spirits he sees there. Anchises responds with a much broader answer:

Know, first, that heav'n, and earth's compacted frame,
And flowing waters, and the starry flame,
And both the radiant lights, one common soul
Inspires and feeds, and animates the whole.
This active mind, infus'd thro' all the space,
Unites and mingles with the mighty mass.
Hence men and beasts the breath of life obtain,
And birds of air, and monsters of the main.
Th' ethereal vigor is in all the same,
And every soul is fill'd with equal flame.

Virgil is entirely serious in his presentation of this "one common soul" or spirit, which he equates at times with Jupiter and more loosely with fate or the general will of the gods. It is the core of his belief and cannot be gainsaid as a merely primitive, Pythagorean accretion. Although occasionally it seems to be mixed up with eclectic detritus, Virgil's own serious pietas reveres the traditional Roman gods and asserts their influence on man's destiny, as well as the utter dependence of man on them. Far from a puerile anthropomorphism or pantheism, this spirit or mind that "animates the whole" with "ethereal vigor" is as close to the Judeo-Christian tradition of immanence and transcendence as one can get without revelation.

Edmund Spenser unabashedly acknowledges the Judeo-Christian tradition and affirms the truth of revelation in *The Faerie Queene*. For most of the romantic poets Spenser existed merely as an example of gorgeous imagery and language. They found in his sensuousness what they themselves could use and abandoned the rest of his formidable achievement. Keats, for instance, takes Spenser's beadsman and stanza and fails to learn anything of substance from him. For most poets thus far in this century Spenser barely exists. But Spenser is the first great master of English epic poetry, whom Milton rightly recognized as such. Content to write little poems about themselves, postmodern poets ignore the very master who has so much to teach. They have been perhaps infected by Yeats's essay on Spenser in which he has the temerity to claim, as though he himself were a paragon of piety, "He had no deep moral or religious life." It is precisely a deep moral and religious life that distinguishes Spenser's work from the folderol of such modern poets as Yeats. Spenser, Dante, and Milton allow their allegory the fullest scope for probing and evaluating the given world, while their belief in moral and religious truth surges with the waves of their matchless allegory. Often the allegory increases their awareness of the social world and aids them in penetrating its surface forms, as in their overwhelming sensitivity to the abuse of ecclesiastical authority and the sundry social dislocations it can produce. Their ire is directed not against Christianity but against its corruptions, as they understand them. Because modern poets have had no use for religion, they have had no use for most of the work of these epic poets. Dante, the only one widely admired in the modern era, has been of interest only after draining him of all content, as though poetry were not also a form of epistemology.

As a result of his deep belief in God, Spenser held poetry, especially epic poetry, to be a very serious matter indeed, which he suggests in "October" of *The Shepheardes Calender*. He was, however, writing at a time when the English language had yet to produce sufficient examples of excellence and therefore had to turn elsewhere for sustenance. He unfortunately found Ariosto, whose rambling procedure does so much to harm *The Faerie Queene*. Had Spenser followed the practice of Homer and Virgil, as Milton was to do and whose own practice stands as a criticism of Spenser, he would certainly have produced a much more coherent epic that would have found many more readers down through the centuries. Yet, as it is, Spenser's poem, after Milton, ranks as the greatest monument of English epic poetry. He is a master not only of the subtle interweaving of sensuous imagery and sound but also of incomparable allegory. In the first book of *The Faerie Queene* he achieves what no other English poet accomplishes: a superbly structured rendition of the medieval theme of the spiritual pilgrimage of the soul. For centuries readers have commented on Spenser's superlative attainment in this book and some have rightly called it a brief epic, which perhaps conforms to Aristotle's suggestion that the length of an epic be restricted to "one view." The other books of *The Faerie Queene* take place in an entirely natural world of value, where man is the measure of all things. It may be correct to suppose that Spenser, had he lived long enough, would have rounded out the theme of *The Faerie Queene* since the "Mutabilitie Cantos" seem to be preliminary steps in that direction. His high sense of thematic form would alone have necessitated such symmetry.

"The Legend of the Knight of the Red Crosse" opens its twelve cantos in the midst of things with the knight riding along accompanied by his lady. Spenser arrays him in the armor of Christian belief on which he bears a cross in "deare remembrance of his dying Lord." Una, his lady, represents the one true faith. They happen upon the cave of Error, where the knight commits the sin of pride but eventually slays the monster. Spenser then sets forth in one stanza the theme of spiritual pilgrimage:

> Then mounted he upon his Steede againe,
> And with the Lady backward sought to wend;
> That path he kept, which beaten was most plaine,
> Ne ever would to any by-way bend,
> But still did follow one unto the end,
> The which at last out of the wood them brought.
> So forward on his way (with God to frend)
> He passd forth, and new adventure sought;
> Long way he travelld, before he heard of ought.

The "path he kept" is the well-worn path of faith, which ultimately leads them "out of the woods"—essentially the same wood as Dante's. Spenser makes this connection at the very end of the book when the knight says, as he recounts his adventures to Una's parents, "unawares I strayed / Out of my way." True to the form of earthly pilgrimage, the knight forges "forward on his way" with God as a friend and guide. Unlike Aeneas, Spenser's knight relies on the God of historical revelation. This fact sets the book in a much more serious realm than Homer, Virgil, or the phantasmagorias of the romantics, such as Shelley's *Prometheus Unbound*.

Spenser's knight becomes separated from Una by the "great Enchanter," Archimago, but he still manages to slay Sansfoy, who is his antithesis and who is accompanied by a "Lady clad in scarlot red." Duessa, as she is called, beguiles him into pledging his fealty to her and leads him off to the House of Pride. Meanwhile, forsaken Una or truth seeks her lover and falls into the hands of a lecher, Sansloy. The tale shifts back to the knight in the House of Pride, where he is tempted by the Seven Deadly Sins and is challenged to a fight by Sansjoy. After he nearly slays Sansjoy, Duessa, the "Daughter of Deceit and Shame"—"I that do seem not I"—saves Sansjoy by carrying him off to Hell, while the knight comes to his senses and flees the House of Pride. Spenser shifts back to Una, who is saved from Sansloy by woodland creatures from whom she in turn escapes. Spenser, always carefully varying his plot from one canto to another in order to create suspense and tension, turns in the next one back to the knight who is defeated by the giant Orgoglio, irrational spiritual pride, and thrown in a dungeon. Una meets Prince Arthur, heavenly grace, and together they ride off with the intention of redeeming the Knight of Holiness from Orgoglio and the dungeon. Spenser then begins Canto VIII by unfolding much of the allegory in this opening stanza:

> Ay me, how many perils doe enfold
> The righteous man, to make him daily fall?
> Were not, that heavenly grace doth him uphold,
> And stedfast truth acquite him out of all.
> Her love is firme, her care continuall,
> So oft as he through his owne foolish pride,
> Or weaknesse is to sinfull bands made thrall:
> Else should this Redcrosse knight in bands have dyde,
> For whose deliverance she this Prince doth thither guide.

This theistic view of the world has increasingly come to be threatened during the modern era, especially since the advent of Freud and other advocates of irrationalism. Freud decries individual responsibility and supplants it with a gnosticism of the dream that destroys personal conscience with collective guilt. Of the divine nature of man, which Spenser presupposes in this stanza, Freud, in 1927 in *The Future of an Illusion*, writes, "The religions of mankind must be classed among the mass delusions." Freudianism, or some form of psychological ersatz, pervades the thinking of our century on the nature of man. For Spenser, man is defined by his struggle to attain salvation during his pilgrimage on earth, where man's foremost defender is the armor of "stedfast truth" and "heavenly grace." Spenser's belief is that when man relies solely on his "owne foolish pride," destruction will be his inevitable lot. Our century has become so habituated to every form of specious thinking imaginable that the purity of his testimony cannot avoid sounding preposterous to confused and deafened ears. Spenser's answer to the likes of Freud can be found later on in Canto VIII, when Arthur slays Orgoglio, defeats Ignaro, ignorance of spirituality, and strips Duessa of her false appearance so that the Redcrosse Knight and the people can see her sinful ugliness.

When the knight and Una resume their journey, they suddenly notice a knight fleeing something and galloping so fast toward them "That of himselfe he seemed to be afrayed." The Redcrosse Knight prods him, Sir Trevisan, to recount how he and a friend were accosted by "A man of hell, that cals himselfe Despair" and how "He pluckt from us all hope of due reliefe." His friend commits suicide and Trevisan flees in terror. The Redcrosse Knight, seduced by pride, dares to test the "subtle tongue" of Despair and insists Trevisan lead him back to his cave. When the knight finds the corpse of Trevisan's friend still lying in his own blood beside Despair, he boldly condemns Despair to death. In one of the most marvelous episodes in Spenser, Despair weaves a web of sophistry to beguile and ensnare the knight. He says of the dead man by his side,

> He there does now enjoy eternall rest
> And happie ease, which thou doest want and crave,
> And further from it daily wanderest:
> What if some litle paine the passage have,
> That makes fraile flesh to feare the bitter wave?

> Is not short paine well borne, that brings long ease,
> And layes the soule to sleepe in quiet grave?
> Sleepe after toyle, port after stormie seas,
> Ease after warre, death after life does greatly please.

In a torrent of such sophistry, which Milton must have known well, Despair's "subtle tongue" breaks down the knight's bold resistance and lures him toward killing himself. By recalling the knight's sins, especially with Duessa in the House of Pride, Despair's speech "in his conscience made a secret breach" and "all his manly powres it did disperse." Despair almost succeeds in driving him to suicide until Una intervenes and hurries him away while scolding him: "In heavenly mercies hast thou not a part? / Why shouldst thou then despaire, that chosen art? / Where justice growes, there grows eke greater grace." Although he is mesmerized by the dark light, she leads away the "fraile, feeble, fleshly wight."

Recognizing the Redcrosse Knight's weakness Una takes him to the House of Holiness to recover. There he is taught "repentance, and / the way to heavenly blisse." He further learns of grace, hope, mercy, patience, and, through the old man Contemplation, is granted a vision of the New Jerusalem. Contemplation urges him to "seeke this path, that I to thee presage, / which after all to heaven shall thee send." After thanking him who "taught the way that does to heaven bound," the knight returns to Una and they set out for her parents' kingdom, where the knight battles the dragon of sin for two days and slays him on the morning of the third. The faithful knight and Una return to her parents' castle and are triumphantly greeted by them and all the people. Spenser then acknowledges the antinomies, always mindful of their due, when Archimago delivers a letter shortly after the king has offered Una's hand in marriage to the knight. In the letter Duessa claims the knight is already pledged to her, but he foils her and Archimago in their perfidy, though it "continues and endures." Everyone joins in celebrating the couple's betrothal with music and merry-making until the end of the book when the knight resumes his journey, postponing their marriage until the Last Judgment. In the first book of *The Faerie Queene*, this brilliantly structured brief epic, Spenser unabashedly affirms the reality of the earthly pilgrimage and fully confronts the contradictory material of existence.

Partly by following Spenser's example, John Milton affirms and confronts similar realms of human experience. Yet his reputation has unjustly suffered a diminution during the last two centuries. The romantics, repulsed by his religious theme of the earthly pilgrimage of the soul, corrupted his poem by maliciously interpreting Satan as the hero, despite Milton's unequivocal condemnation of Satan and his equally lucid characterization of the repentant Adam as the true hero. T.S. Eliot and those who ape his opinions also find Milton the man and his religious beliefs repellent. The poets of the modern era deride Milton because, in general, they have lost and abandoned religious belief and turned to vague forms of idealism, as in Whitman's *Democratic Vistas*, and to the creation of idiosyncratic ersatzes, as in Poe's *Eureka*, while Joel Barlow's *Columbiad*, and other poets, fail by slavish imitation of Milton. John Keats's *Endymion* and the *Hyperion* poems fail as much because of their superficial content as their poor structure and execution. In Auden's analysis, "the modern problem" hamstrings the romantics as much as Yeats or Pound. Milton never suffered from such a malady and hence the envious detestation he has received from minor poets who are unquestionably his inferiors. Milton possesses a serious vision of history and humankind that could only achieve full expression in the most demanding form of poetry—the epic. But most poets of the last few hundred years have not found themselves entrusted with such a vision. Much to the contrary, they excel in every imaginable type of turpitude and triviality that the human mind is capable of producing. Like Yeats they have often thrown together every decadent principle or superstition that has ever happened along. This sorry state of affairs has become so common in postmodern poetry that anyone who would attempt to restore epopee to its glorious heights of noble seriousness and serenity would find ranked against him every academic hack and, as Milton phrased it, every "libidinous and ignorant" poetaster who has "scarce ever heard of that which is the main consistence of a true poem."

Milton knew the "consistence of a true poem," and both *Paradise Lost* and many passages scattered throughout his prose attest to it. In *The Reason of Church Government* he surveys the abilities of such masters as Homer, Virgil, Job, and Sophocles:

> These abilities, wheresoever they be found, are the inspired gift of God rarely bestowed, but yet to some (though most abuse) in every nation; and are of power beside the office of a pulpit, to inbreed and cherish in a great people the seeds of virtue and public civility, to allay the perturbations of the mind and set the affections in right tune, to celebrate in glorious and lofty hymns the throne and equipage of God's almightiness, and what he works and what he suffers to be wrought with high providence in his church, to sing the victorious agonies of martyrs and saints, the deeds and triumphs of just and pious nations doing valiantly through faith against the enemies of Christ, to deplore the general relapses of kingdoms and states from justice and God's true worship.

Along with the modern loss of belief in God has gone this high and serious belief in the office of the poet. It has been replaced by Allen Ginsberg stroking his dildo in his arse, Sylvia Plath sticking her head in an oven, and Ezra Pound denouncing the free world and supporting the fascists whose virulent antisemitism forms a crucial part of his *Cantos*. Equally banished from the modern conception of poetry is all respect for positive values, morals, and virtues. The story of twentieth-century literature is the abuse and misguided replacement of such healthy standards with the perversions of modernism and postmodernism. In brief, "the modern problem."

Above such decadence Milton towers as the Californian sequoias above the surrounding canopy of lesser trees. He sums up and surpasses most of the entire epic tradition of Western civilization, while there stands none to equal him in the English epic. Milton fully takes account of the examples of Homer and Virgil, knows and benefits from the work of Langland and Dante, and acknowledges Spenser as his primary teacher in English. Added to his command of the literary tradition is his thorough mastery of scripture. His uniting all these sundry strands in *Paradise Lost* gives the poem its scope and power. Far from constituting a hodge-podge of allusion and sensuous linguistic violence, *Paradise Lost* stands as one of the greatest monuments of the human spirit, one that is all the more inestimable for its vast difference from the modern age. For Milton God not was but is. And his belief informs the entire poem to a depth and purity that can stand only as a chastisement of the frivolous and unambitious age of solipsism. W. H. Auden's comments on the only book of the twentieth century that has the positive moral breadth of Milton comes to mind: "If, as I believe, a good story is one which can persuade us to face life neither with despair nor with false hopes, then *The Lord of the Rings* is a very good story indeed."

Milton knew that to survey universal history was tantamount to the Judeo-Christian conception of time and space. He could not cut off the flow of events with the deification of the Augustus of his age or merely recount the slaughter of a multitude and the fall of their civilization. He had to confront the metaphysical principles of twenty-five-hundred years of belief in the revelation of God's will to man as manifested in his Word and in the course of historical events. He accomplishes this largely through a few allusions to the state of contemporary England and Christianity and through his survey of biblical history. His primary method is to use the account of Adam and Eve as etiological material from every standpoint—religious, philosophical, theological, and historical. This procedure gives profundity to his poem as nothing else can for his claim is one of truth and the very meaning and nature of our being. To the proponents of relativism, who have been proliferating since the deistic and romantic periods, such a claim is preposterous. But throughout this century the fruits of relativism have been augmenting and exposing their shoddiness. The twisting of Einstein's theory of relativity, the spread of Freud's atheistic psychology, the devastation wreaked upon so much of the modern world by the delusions of communism, the hubris of science and its distortion of the nature of man, have all increasingly been revealing their spiritual nakedness and fundamental bankruptcy. To all such fallacies of relativism, Milton, more than any other English poet, is the elixir.

In the grand tradition of Homer, Milton begins *Paradise Lost* in the midst of things. Satan has already been thrown out of heaven and into the fiery lake of Hell. After considering the situation he swims to shore and gathers his fallen angels around him. He calls a council of all the fiends in Pandemonium, the newly built palace of Satan, where, following a debate, they determine to subvert by "covert guile" "the happy seat / Of some new Race call'd Man." Satan himself alone qualifies for the perfidious mission and passes through the gates of Sin and Death into the chaos separating Hell from heaven and earth. Milton then shifts the action to God in heaven, who relates to the Son of God the plan of Satan and how he will succeed in leading man astray. The Son of God freely offers himself as a ransom for man and God accepts his sacrifice to the adulation of all the denizens of heaven. Meanwhile Satan enters the new world and in Book IV tempts Eve in a dream to disobey God and eat the forbidden fruit. Eve recounts to Adam her dream in Book V, and, though he is alarmed, Adam fails to take it seriously enough. After they separate and go about their daily work of tending the Garden of Eden, God sends Raphael to Adam "to render man inexcusable" by admonishing obedience. Raphael then chronicles the history of Satan's revolt, his seduction of a third of the angels, and his construction of a rival city in the west of heaven. Only the seraph Abdiel denounces Satan's revolt and sophistry. Raphael's description of the heroism of Abdiel is one of the finest passages in *Paradise Lost*:

> Among the faithless, faithful only hee;
> Among innumerable false, unmov'd,
> Unshak'n, unseduc'd, unterrifi'd
> His Loyalty he kept, his Love, his Zeal;
> Nor number, nor example with him wrought
> To swerve from truth, or change his constant mind
> Though single. From amidst them forth he pass'd,

Long way through hostile scorn, which he sustain'd
Superior, nor of violence fear'd aught;
And with retorted scorn his back he turn'd
On those proud Tow'rs to swift destruction doom'd.

This passage demonstrates how very different Milton's conception
of the hero is from Homer or Virgil. Abdiel is not solely admired for
his military prowess or embodiment of Roman virtues but for his
steadfast cleaving to truth in the midst of universal opposition.
Abdiel becomes, as it were, an exemplar of what Milton calls "the
victorious agonies of martyrs and saints." He alone among the
angels of Satan's legions scorns "those proud Tow'rs" and returns
to God.

In Book VI the war in heaven ensues and the Son of God drives
the apostates into Hell. Raphael then recounts in Book VII God's
decision to create earth and man and ends his narration of history
with another admonition of obedience. In Book VIII Adam touches
on the clash between the Ptolemaic and Copernican conceptions of
the universe and then recalls what history he can since his own
creation. With a final warning against "Passion," Raphael ascends
back to heaven. The poem reaches its climax in both their fall and
regeneration in Books IX and X when Satan succeeds in tempting
Eve to eat the forbidden fruit, Eve persuades Adam to partake of it,
and God sends the Son to judge them. After much poignant
lamentation, Adam and Eve accept their guilt and pray for
forgiveness and mercy. In Book XI the Son intercedes for them with
God. Michael is sent down to lead them out of paradise and foretells
the history of mankind from Abel and Cain to the flood. The last
book, Book XII, carries Michael's account of future history forward
from Abraham to the coming of Christ. Michael also foretells the
corrupted state of the church from Christ until the "New Heav'n"
and "New Earth" are "reveal'd / In glory of the Father" and raised
"From the conflagrant mass, purg'd and refin'd." His chronicle of
history inspires new hope in Adam who attains "the sum of wisdom"
in one of the central passages to the understanding of the entire
poem:

Henceforth I learn, that to obey is best,
And love with fear the only God, to walk
As in his presence, ever to observe
His providence, and on him sole depend,
Merciful over all his works, with good
Still overcoming evil, and by small
Accomplishing great things, by things deem'd weak
Subverting worldly strong, and worldly wise
By simply meek; that suffering for Truth's sake
Is fortitude to highest victory,
And to the faithful Death the Gate of Life;
Taught this by his example whom I now
Acknowledge my Redeemer ever blest.

Unlike in the work of Jacques Derrida and his academic flies, the "presence" of God is a reality for Milton. Here in the abstract Milton gives us what throughout *Paradise Lost* he has been dramatizing—the "principles and presuppositions" to which Adam, representative man, must obediently submit, not merely in Eden, but for the fulfillment of his life during his journey on the earthly plane. In Satan, Milton presents the picture of the rebel, almost a type of the Renaissance hero Benvenuto Cellini, who through pride usurps power and whose fundamental actions and motives have their most appropriate modern analogue, as many have observed, in the archvillains Hitler, Mussolini, Lenin, Stalin, and Mao. Such men fully embody the will to power that the nihilist Nietzsche, as Thomas Mann put it, glorified. Such totalitarian dictators were the inevitable product of the romantic fascination with Satan, as though he were a hero and not an arrogant aspirant after power. Such cultural confusion reveals itself in Goethe's *Faust* as well as in Nietzsche's *Thus Spake Zarathustra*.

Such errors in judgment, such fundamental confusion of values, mark the modern era and set it off from the spiritually healthier times of Dante, Langland, Spenser, and Milton—healthier only in terms of possessing to a degree a unified spiritual vision that provided universal standards with which to confront the damnable deeds of their day. Far from the banal optimism of the modern era, as in Whitman, they know that the long hard way of man is through suffering and turmoil and that the assurance Michael gives Adam about future generations abides eternally: "Doubt not but that sin / Will reign among them." Despite Freud's "freeing" man from sin, the twentieth century proved to be the most sinful in history, precisely because the unique spiritual reality of each soul and its fundamental limitations were denied. The violent, arrogant, insidious deeds of the archvillains of modern political nihilism alone account for the suffering and deaths of hundreds of millions of people, while much of the so-called intelligentsia of the West and East defended or prepared the way for the slaughter. Whereas Virgil denounced war except as the last resort for establishing peace, modern poets often ignored the inhumanities and cruelties of the age—save for those like Pound whose totalitarianism abetted the brutalizing of millions of innocents and the early Auden who approved "the necessary murder."

Here at the beginning of the twenty-first century, when humankind still stands technologically capable of destroying much of the vast expanse of the globe and much, though not all, God willing, of its population, here when a more trustworthy political form has yet to be securely established to channel the will of the citizens of the international community, epopee must again take account of the social domain and man's earthly journey through these immense atrocities. For by faithfully treading the dark way of horror, by weighing the modern loss of belief, humankind may begin to regain the path, and, like Dante's persona, attain the highest summit of peace and glory, the visionary summit invoked from the dawn of the American experiment:

> But all subside in universal peace.—
> —Such days the world,
> And such AMERICA at last shall have
> When ages yet to come, have run their round,
> And future years of bliss alone remain.

Printed in the United States
82479LV00001B/1-87